THE

BIBLE

COMPANION

THE
BIBLE
COMPANION

A Handbook for Beginners

— RONALD D. WITHERUP, S.S. —

A Crossroad Book
The Crossroad Publishing Company
New York

Nihil Obstat: Rev. Michael L. Barré, S.S., S.T.L., Ph.D.
Imprimatur: Rev. Msgr. W. Francis Malooly, V.G., Archdiocese of Baltimore

The Crossroad Publishing Company
481 Eighth Avenue, New York, NY 10001

Copyright © 1998 by Ronald D. Witherup

Printed in the United States of America

Library of Congress Cataloging-in-Publication Data
Witherup, Ronald D., 1950-
    The Bible companion : a handbook for beginners / Ronald D. Witherup.
        p. cm.
    ISBN 0-8245-1746-6 (pbk.)
    1. Bible – Introductions.   I. Title.
BS475.2.W56   1998
220.6'1 – dc21   98-21653

    4   5   6   7   8   9   10   11   12   06   05   04   03

For Dr. Susan V. Lenkey
Art historian and amateur Bible enthusiast
In love and friendship
Ephesians 3:14–19

CONTENTS

Part II
INTRODUCING THE OLD TESTAMENT

Part III
INTRODUCING THE NEW TESTAMENT

PREFACE

The author of the Book of Ecclesiastes (Qoheleth) complains: "Of making many books there is no end, and much study is a weariness of the flesh" (12:12). While every author knows the truth of this observation, we might notice that it did not prevent Qoheleth from producing his own work of wisdom! Books on the Bible abound, but for true novices many introductions are either too much or too little to suit their interests. This book aims to claim the middle ground. It seeks to provide just enough basic information on the Bible to answer initial questions but not so much information that it might overwhelm or discourage someone on the verge of beginning Bible study. In essence, the book is an invitation to those unfamiliar or minimally familiar with the Bible's riches to pick the Bible up and read it — with a "companion" by your side.

Books are produced with the aid of many people and much hidden influence. In a nontechnical work of this nature I am not able to give full credit to all those biblical scholars over the years whose writings have influenced my own thought. They may well recognize their own influence in these pages. Additionally, in my twenty years of teaching biblical studies in various settings my students have contributed greatly to my fund of knowledge. Their questions often enticed me to explore new ways of explaining the Bible's treasures. I extend my sincere thanks to these two groups of people for their insight. Also, I would single out some colleagues who have been gracious in reading sections of the manuscript and offering advice about content or style or assistance with research, especially Michael L. Barré, S.S., of St. Mary's Seminary and University (Baltimore, Md.), Richard M. Gula, S.S., of the Franciscan School of Theology (Berkeley, Calif.), and Dr. Cecil White, librarian at St. Patrick Seminary (Menlo Park, Calif.). Their comments, suggestions, and assistance have always been helpful. A special word of thanks goes to the editors and staff of Crossroad Publishing Company, especially to Robert T. Heller, who invited me to write this book, to Dr. James LeGrys, who guided its production, and to John Eagleson for expert typesetting. Any mistakes, of course, remain my own responsibility ... but may be attributable in part to "a weariness of the flesh."

R. D. W.

Passion (Palm) Sunday, 1998

ABBREVIATIONS

ca.	circa, around
cf.	compare or refer to
ch.	chapter(s)
LXX	Septuagint
NAB	The New American Bible
NRSV	The New Revised Standard Version of the Bible
NT	New Testament
OT	Old Testament
REB	Revised English Bible
v./vv.	verse/verses

Part I

GETTING ACQUAINTED

INTRODUCTION

If you are like many people, the Bible is at once an old friend and a stranger. You recognize it easily, as you would an old friend, and trust it as a companion. You know that it contains a record of God's sacred word to humanity. You take comfort in knowing that you can pick it up at any time and find something in it of value. Possibly you even know some of the Bible's stories by heart. Who does not know the basic details of such potboilers as Adam and Eve, David and Goliath, David and Bathsheba, Samson and Delilah? You may also be familiar with the ten commandments, the stories of Abraham and Sarah, of Ruth and Esther, and in the New Testament the infancy and passion stories of Jesus, the good Samaritan, the woman at the well, and the conversion of St. Paul.

But general familiarity is not the intimate relation of old friends. The Bible for many people is like a stranger from a foreign land. To pick it up and begin to read it in depth is to enter a strange, bizarre world. Foreign names, places, and concepts abound in the Bible. Many people quickly lose heart when they attempt to read it. They abandon the attempt to become more intimately acquainted with the Bible when they begin to hit the long tedious sections that dot the literary terrain. This is even more the case if one starts from the beginning and tries to go to the end. The stories of Genesis and Exodus hold one's attention for a time, but along about Leviticus patience gives way to frustration. Just what are all those food laws about anyway?

I believe many people find themselves paralyzed when it comes to *reading* the Bible. I'll use a couple of analogies to illustrate. When I was a child learning to swim, the one aspect that frightened me for some reason was diving headlong into the pool. Try as I might, I could not quite master diving. Jumping into the pool was easy, but I had a phobia about plunging head first into the water. Only after several years of coaching from more experienced divers did I overcome my fear. Now, diving into a pool is an exhilarating experience. As an adult I experienced an initial fear about computers. Entering the electronic age was not a simple matter. Many people suffer from "computer phobia." Only after being coached by some friends who had mastered computers did I finally get my own. Now I can scarcely imagine living without it.

Similarly, most people need a companion to teach them to take the plunge into the Bible. The point is not simply to read *about* the Bible in a secondary way. Rather, it is to become comfortable with reading the Bible itself. This book is like a coach to help you achieve the goal: to take that refreshing plunge into the world of the Bible so that its riches can be tapped freely without hindrance or fear.

Unlike many modern appliances, the Bible does not always come with an owner's manual. This book is like such a manual for true beginners. If you find yourself with nothing more than general familiarity with the Bible, this book's for you. This book is for you also if you have ever attempted to read the Bible but gave up after a time, or if you just don't know how to get beyond a mere casual acquaintance with a book you'd rather befriend.

This is a handbook, a "how-to" book. No prior knowledge is needed. The only requirements are an open mind, a desire to learn, and a willingness to open that Bible that's been sitting on your shelf or your coffee table. This book will provide you with a general introduction to all kinds of areas that will help you begin basic Bible study on your own, including:

- how to choose a Bible
- how the Bible came to be
- the divisions of the Bible
- the world of the Bible
- the differences in Jewish, Protestant, and Catholic Bibles
- how to read and study the Bible
- how to pray with the Bible
- basic resources for further study

◆　◆　◆

Some initial explanations will help you orient yourself to your new companion. This book contains three sections. The first section is devoted to matters of a general introduction to the Bible and its world. Without bogging down in too much detail, the first several chapters will provide background to the outline and origin of the Bible, how to choose an appropriate translation, and basic biblical history. The second section will introduce each book of the Old Testament (OT), or Hebrew scriptures. Each chapter will contain the same four-part structure:

1. a "bird's-eye" *summary,* set in a box, for quick reference of the title, authorship, date, structure, and major themes of every book

2. a brief description of the *structure* and *content* of each book of the OT

3. comments on the *interpretation* of each book

4. an *exercise* with a suggested passage to read and ponder

The same procedure will follow in the third section, which is devoted to the books of the New Testament (NT). The appendixes include helpful charts that can be referenced quickly, a glossary of terms used in this book, and recommended resources for further study. Because most Bibles contain their own maps, no maps are included with this book. To follow references to places or geographical features, I recommend that you consult carefully any maps available in your own Bible. I have also not included a section on where to find themes or passages, since most Bibles come equipped with such a tool.

A word about the approach taken in this book will also be helpful. I am a Roman Catholic; my approach, however, is intended to be broadly ecumenical. My background as a biblical scholar undergirds my professional method, which is common to most biblical scholars regardless of faith. I will utilize insights from Jewish, Protestant, and Orthodox positions wherever appropriate. The book will retain the basic conventions of Christian terminology. For instance, the expression "Old Testament" will remain even though Jewish readers would refer to it as Tanak or the Hebrew Bible. Tanak is actually an acronym for the three parts of the Hebrew Bible, *Torah* (Law), *Nebi'im* (Prophets), and *Kethubim* (Writings).

Remember the basic goal of this book is to help you become more comfortable with reading the Bible. The emphasis is on acquiring basic familiarity with the contents of the Bible. An essential commitment on your part is to keep your Bible handy as you read through this handbook. You will gain greater confidence, for instance, if you read and reflect on the specific passages mentioned in the various chapters. The chosen passages in the exercises will provide a small taste of each book in the Bible. In fact, you will recognize that the Bible is not *a* book but a library of books. The origin of the word "Bible" from Greek (*ta biblia*) is "the books." It is a large and diverse library. That is why it is important to taste at least a morsel from each book. As you do, I believe your appetite for more will be whetted.

But enough of introductory matters. Let's take the plunge together by addressing some preliminary questions like: "What is the Bible?" "How does the Old Testament relate to the New Testament?" "How did the Bible come to be?" and "Which Bible should I choose?"

Chapter 1

THE BIBLE AND ITS ORIGIN

What Is the Bible?

In its simplest terms the Bible is God's Word in human words. It is a collection of books that spans thousands of years and gives testimony to the faith, history, and culture of a people whom God called to be in a special relationship. Because the Bible has such an extensive origin, it contains many different kinds of literature. Much of it is narrative, but it also contains poetry, prayers, parables, laws, sayings, proverbs, riddles, sermons, letters, prophetic oracles, history, mythology, and so on. Reading different sections of the Bible requires some attention to the *literary form* (genre) of these materials. Just as we would not read every section of a newspaper in the same manner, so also we should not read every type of biblical literature from the same perspective.

The Christian Bible contains two basic sections, an Old Testament and a New Testament. The word "testament" is another word for covenant. It indicates that the Bible records the covenants, or relationships, between God and human beings. The OT is the thicker half, while the NT is much thinner. The OT not only contains more books, but many of them are also longer than the books of the NT. The OT, of course, originated in Judaism, and the Hebrew scriptures, or Tanak, are the only sacred writings of the Jews. Christians, however, accept the NT as an outgrowth and fulfillment of the OT. Christians accept both sections as God's Word.

It is possible to study the Bible simply as an ancient history book or a literary masterpiece. These are valid and fruitful endeavors. Our approach, however, will be from a faith perspective. Most people want to read the Bible because it is an essential part of their faith. This is true among all believing Jews and Christians. The Bible contains sacred writings; thus they are called sacred scripture. These writings are inspired literature. Inspiration, however, is a troubling concept. To say *that* the Bible is inspired is an assertion of faith. To say *how* the writings are inspired is another matter. There are many different theories of inspiration. The most simplistic can be called the "dictation method." This explanation suggests that God directly whispered into the ears of the sacred authors telling them exactly what words to write. Modern biblical scholarship recognizes that this is a naive explanation of inspiration. The fact is that no single theory of inspiration has proven to have unanimous appeal. To discuss the options in detail would become overly technical. We can merely say that the Bible is inspired literature in a way that our Judeo-Christian tradition accords to no other writings. Thus we read the Bible to bolster our faith in God and to discern God's message to us.

How Does the Old Testament Relate to the New Testament?

The relationship between the OT and the NT is an age-old problem for Christians. Already in the early church Christians reflected upon it. One person, Marcion by name (ca. A.D. 130), was very influential. He concluded that the OT was obsolete for Christians because of the coming of Jesus Christ. He thought that the OT described a stern God of vindictiveness while the NT described a God of love. He even thought that only certain parts of the NT (Luke and Paul) were worthy to be used by Christians. Rather quickly the church decided that Marcion's rejection of the OT was heretical and totally unacceptable. Yet that did not resolve the problem of how the two main divisions of the Christian Bible were related.

Through the ages Christians have proposed different theories to relate the two testaments. One theory holds that the primary relationship is in the notion of prophecy and fulfillment. Hence, the OT is the section on God's prophecies, and the NT describes how those prophecies came to fulfillment in Jesus Christ. Another theory uses the notion of typology. According to this theory, the OT contains older prototypes of what eventually came into being in the NT. Thus, Adam was a kind of Christ, as in the letters of St. Paul (Rom 5:12–14). No theory by itself, unfortunately, does justice to the relationship between the OT and the NT. While aspects of these theories are appropriate and indeed are found in the NT itself, the danger is that we will try to force the OT into a preconceived Christian mold that does an injustice to it. It is unacceptable, for example, to think of the God of the OT as a vengeful God whereas the God of the NT is all loving. God is often portrayed in the OT as incredibly patient and understanding despite Israel's stubbornness and failings, and the NT contains many references to judgment and eternal punishment that must be placed into the total picture of its message. Nor can we understand the NT without the OT. Perhaps a beautiful image from the Middle Ages speaks to this issue. At the medieval cathedral of Chartres one finds a stunning stained-glass representation of the four evangelists seated on the shoulders of four OT prophetic figures. The evangelists can see farther precisely because they have built their observations on the foundation of those who preceded them. As Pope John Paul II has said, "To deprive Christ of his relationship with the Old Testament is to detach him from his roots and empty his mystery of every meaning" (April 7, 1997, address to the Pontifical Biblical Commission).

My recommendation, then, is not to stereotype either the NT or the OT. For Christians, both present God's Word in the form of human words. There is a back-and-forth flow between them that will remain somewhat mysterious, yet we will be able to appreciate both testaments uniquely for what they say about God and God's relationship with humanity.

How Did the Bible Come to Be?

Let me address the question of how the Bible came to be by first telling a story. Elie Wiesel, the great Jewish writer, tells a tale at the beginning of one of his novels, *The Gates of the Forest:*

> When the great Rabbi Israel Baal Shem-Tov saw misfortune threatening the Jews, it was his custom to go into a certain part of the forest to meditate. There he would light a fire, say a special prayer, and the miracle would be accomplished and the misfortune averted. Later, when his disciple, the celebrated Magid of Mezeritch, had occasion, for the same reason, to intercede with heaven, he would go to the same place in the forest and say, "Master of the Universe, listen! I do not know how to light the fire, but I am still able

to recite the prayer." And again the miracle would be accomplished. Still later, Rabbi Moshe-Leib of Sassov, in order to save his people once more, would go into the forest and say, "I do not know how to light the fire, I do not know the prayer, but I know the place and this must be sufficient." It was sufficient; and the miracle was accomplished. Then it fell to Rabbi Israel of Rizhin to overcome misfortune. Sitting in his armchair, his head in his hands, he spoke to God: "I cannot even find the place in the forest. All I can do is to tell the story, and this must be sufficient." And it was sufficient. God created man because he loves stories!

This beautiful story illustrates an important fact about the origin of the Bible. It did not fall from the sky, nor did God simply place it in people's minds. Rather, the Bible grew out of a long process of God's people recounting for generation after generation the stories of their experience of God and God's relationship with them. Most of the Bible originated in a three-part process:

- *Oral tradition:* People recounted stories orally of their experience of God and passed them to their children and grandchildren, who passed them on to their children and grandchildren, and so on by word of mouth.

- *Written tradition:* Eventually, especially when crises erupted that threatened to destroy the faith heritage of the chosen people, trained scribes wrote down the stories of faith to preserve them for all time.

- *Edited tradition:* Over time, scribes collected the various written traditions, grouped them together in different categories, and edited them to apply them to their own situation.

This threefold process became enshrined when official bodies of faith (Jewish and Christian in separate circumstances) later declared these collected works as sacred, inspired scriptures to be preserved unaltered for all time. This was the establishment of the *canon* of sacred scripture. Essential to this process is the recognition that the Bible is a record of stories of faith. Just as people today often narrate personal stories of their heritage, their relatives, and their life experience in order to pass them on to succeeding generations, so did ancient peoples preserve their stories of faith. The Bible originated in *oral* tradition, that is, faith testimony. The extensive process of moving from oral to written to edited traditions was not a uniform evolution. Nor is it easy to separate the three layers like peeling back the layers of an onion. Rather, all three levels are intertwined in our Bible. The levels often overlap so much that it is difficult to separate them, as is indicated by the following diagram.

ORIGINS OF THE BIBLE

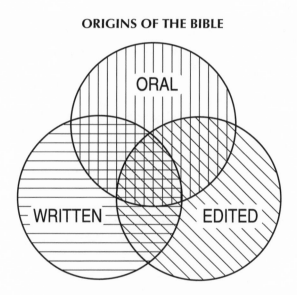

You can probably see that this process would inevitably produce varied results. Sometimes details of oral stories would get confused as they passed from hearer to hearer. As stories became more fixed in written and edited traditions, applications would vary, and the final form of the story might differ from the original. The point of the story, in fact, might dramatically change in this process. Yet from a faith perspective, the stories of the Bible exist for the purpose of religious messages. Literal accuracy is less necessary than assurance that God's Word is generally preserved in these sacred accounts. Many generations have found these sacred words life-giving, and that is why we still read the Bible today.

What Is the Canon?

As we have just noted, from a faith perspective the Bible applies to our lives *today*. This is why Jews and Christians continue to read their scriptures, use them for prayer and worship, and refer to them for ethical guidance. They provide inspiration, support, and challenge. More importantly, the Bible has given people a strong sense of identity, addressing questions like "Who are we?" "Where do we come from?" "What is life's meaning?" and "What is our destiny?"

The Bible basically provides a means to measure the quality and direction of our lives. Children provide an example. Many parents have in their homes a yardstick or other measuring rod so that children can stand up against it every so often and measure how much they have grown. Children love to see the evidence of how tall they have become, just how much they have grown from the last measurement. This is essentially the meaning of the "canon" of sacred scripture. It derives from the Greek *kanōn,* which means "reed, measure, standard, or norm." The canon provides a moral measure of how we stack up against God's expectations.

This concept is easy enough to understand. A difficulty quickly arises, however, if you compare *your* canon with your neighbor's. Have you ever noticed that Protestant editions of the Bible are shorter than Catholic ones? In fact, the Protestant canon contains only thirty-nine books in the OT. The Catholic canon has forty-six in the OT. Both contain the same twenty-seven books in the NT. The chart in appendix A (p. 233) outlines the differences between the various canons, or collections, of sacred scripture. But why do such differences exist?

The reasons are rooted in history. The Jews were the first in the Judeo-Christian tradition to develop a canon of sacred writings. The Hebrew Bible contains thirty-nine books. When this Bible was translated into Greek for Greek-speaking Jews around the third or second century B.C., other books were added, resulting in forty-six books. This edition is known as the Septuagint (often abbreviated with the Roman numeral LXX). Its name derives from the Greek word for seventy (rounded off) because tradition held that seventy-two different scribes (six from each tribe) worked for seventy-two days to produce the translation. Most of the writers of the NT used this edition rather than the Hebrew canon because they spoke and wrote Greek. In the fourth century A.D., when St. Jerome translated the Latin Vulgate edition of the Bible on which Catholic Bible translations were based for centuries, he used the Septuagint to supplement the Hebrew Bible. Thus, the Catholic canon was always longer.

The seven complete books (along with portions of other books and other materials listed on the following page) that were included in the Septuagint but not found in the Hebrew Bible include: Judith, Tobit, Baruch, Wisdom of Solomon, Sirach, and 1 and 2 Maccabees.

Protestants call these the *apocryphal* books of the OT (meaning "counterfeit or false" from the Greek word for "hidden"). Catholics refer to them as *deuterocanonical* (meaning a "second" canon). The Protestant Bible excludes these works (except as an appendix) primarily because of Martin Luther. When he translated the Bible into German in the sixteenth century, he worked from the Hebrew text of the OT rather than the Septuagint. Consequently, the Protestant canon was shorter. To this day, Protestants do not consider the OT apocrypha canonical scripture. Catholics, however, use them in worship services, and the Septuagint remains the basis for Greek Orthodox Bibles.

Does this difference in the canons really matter? The main importance of this difference is to recognize what may or may not be used in public worship. Even though Protestants do not use the OT apocrypha for prayer, they recognize that there can be value (historical and ethical) in such books. But they are not viewed as God's Word or accorded the status of canonical works.

Another matter is the practical result of differing canons. As you read the Bible you will need to know where to find the various books in it. Do not be afraid if you have trouble finding a particular book or if it does not exist in the same sequence as another person's Bible. Because the canonical traditions vary, Bible editions also vary in their placement of specific books, especially in the OT. Always look in the table of contents of your Bible to find exactly where it places specific books. Be patient, consult the list in appendix A (p. 233), and you will find what you are seeking in due time.

To further confuse matters, I must mention here two more categories of writings that you may find mentioned in Bible foot-

APOCRYPHAL AND DEUTEROCANONICAL BOOKS
OF THE OLD TESTAMENT

The following is a standard listing of the OT apocryphal and deuterocanonical books or parts of books. Typically, they are listed according to four categories. The texts themselves are available in several editions, such as the New Revised Standard Version.

1. Books and additions to books accepted in the Roman Catholic canon but not in the Protestant canon:
    Tobit
    Judith
    Additions to the Book of Esther
    Wisdom of Solomon
    Sirach (Ecclesiasticus)
    Baruch
    The Letter to Jeremiah (=ch. 6 of the Book of Baruch)
    Additions to the Book of Daniel
        The Prayer of Azariah and the Song of the Three Jews
            (=Dan 3:24-97)
        Susanna (=Dan 13:1-64)
        Bel and the Dragon (=Dan 14:1-42)
    1 and 2 Maccabees

2. Books in the Greek and Slavonic Bibles but not accepted in the Roman Catholic canon or the Protestant canon:
    1 Esdras
    Prayer of Manasseh
    Psalm 151
    3 Maccabees

3. Books in the Slavonic Bible and the Appendix to the Latin Vulgate:
    2 Esdras

4. Books in the Appendix to the Greek Bible:
    4 Maccabees

notes. A separate category of ancient writings related to the Bible is called the OT *pseudepigrapha*. Dozens of ancient books exist that never made it into the canon of the OT. Titles include 1 and 2 Enoch, the Odes of Solomon, the Sibylline Oracles, and the Testaments of the Twelve Patriarchs. They are called pseudepigrapha ("false writings") because they do not represent inspired, canonical literature accepted into the OT canon either for Jews or for

Christians. Other books exist that were never accepted into the NT canon. These are called the *NT apocrypha,* and they include apocryphal gospels such as the Gospel of Peter and the Infancy Gospel of Thomas. The churches have judged these books also to be noncanonical. You do not need to concern yourself about these materials because they are not properly part of the Bible. If you really want to read them, they are available in libraries in separate collections called *Old Testament Pseudepigrapha* and *New Testament Apocrypha,* but their usefulness is primarily for historical purposes.

What Is Biblical Fundamentalism?

The approach I take in this book is based upon the standard scientific methods of biblical study accepted by most Christian biblical scholars. There exists, however, an alternative approach that is popular in the Bible Belt region and other parts of the U.S. It is broadly labeled "biblical fundamentalism."

Biblical fundamentalism is an approach to the Bible that connects a doctrine of *inerrancy* with the doctrine of inspiration. The doctrine of inerrancy is the belief that because the Bible is God's Word, and God cannot be in error, then the Bible is literally true in all that it says, including matters pertaining to history and science. Fundamentalists, for example, take the seven-day creation story in Genesis literally and reject any scientific notion of evolution as contradictory to the biblical account. Most interpreters view this as a naive reading of scripture. The purpose of the Bible is not to recount scientific or historical truth but to offer moral and religious instruction.

Biblical fundamentalism is widely appealing because it offers easy answers to complex questions. It believes that there is a one-to-one correspondence between what the Bible says and what it means in our day, as if the Word were meant for our ears alone. Mainline Protestant denominations, along with Catholics, reject such a fundamentalist approach to the Bible. The Bible was written for our ancestors long before it was meant for us. The Bible's inerrancy pertains to religious truth, not scientific or historical data. This is not to say that the Bible contains no accurate information. Rather, the Bible can easily contain historical or scientific errors (the limitations of the human writers) without impinging on the religious message contained in it (God's Word). Because God's message applies to all times, and not simply to our own, the interpretation of any passage in a given era might be different from previous or later interpretations. The reader must be aware, then, that this book does not offer a fundamentalist approach to the Bible but one that views scientific method as compatible with the religious value of the sacred text.

Chapter 2

LEARNING TO USE
THE BIBLE

Which Bible Should I Choose?

Many people already have a Bible in their home. Sometimes the Bible is a family heirloom. Perhaps grandparents or great-grandparents had a family Bible that passed from generation to generation. Often people record in their Bibles important family events, especially the dates of weddings, funerals, baptisms, and the like. While these are family keepsakes, the particular translation of the Bible may not be suitable for contemporary Bible study and prayer. The reason for this judgment lies in the nature of language.

The Bible was written originally in Hebrew and Greek. Obviously, for most of us to access the Bible we must use translations. The King James Version of the Bible (Authorized Version) is the most common authoritative translation in use by many Protestants. The difficulty is that this sixteenth-century translation is woefully outdated. Not only do we no longer speak the style of English employed in this translation, but also biblical scholarship has advanced considerably in the knowledge of the ancient biblical languages to warrant new translations. Catholics also have an older translation of the Bible, the Douay-Rheims, based upon the Latin translation (the Vulgate) that at one time was the only official Catholic edition of the Bible. It, too, is out of date and the names of some of the OT books may be confusing. The chart in appendix B (p. 235) shows the differences in the names.

If you are relying upon one of these or another older Bible edition, I recommend that you purchase a newer edition. People frequently ask me, "Which is the best translation?" My response is to ask, "For what purpose?" There is no *best* edition as such. It depends on what use you want to make of the Bible. If you want a translation strictly for prayer and meditation, one translation may be better than another. The same applies to a study Bible. Every translation has its strengths and weaknesses. Rather than recommending a specific Bible, I will sketch briefly the most common editions currently available. You do not need to have an expensive edition. Bibles with gilded edges and suave leather covers are lovely as gifts but are not essential to Bible study. Most important is having a modern edition of the Bible that makes you comfortable. Entering a bookstore to buy a Bible can be a bewildering experience. There are so many Bibles to choose from! For this reason I will provide brief descriptions of some current editions of the Bible.

Modern Bible Translations

We are fortunate to live in a time when many reliable biblical translations are available. The most common are in the following list. Many are available in either Catholic or Protestant editions.

• *The Revised Standard Version* (Oxford University Press, 1962). This translation is based upon a revision of the standard King James version and is still a wonderful, very literal translation. It has also been republished in some new attractive editions. It remains a standard for good Bible study because of its fidelity to the original text, but it retains some antiquated expressions in English and makes no attempt to be inclusive in its language. This standard translation is found in many different editions, including various study Bibles.

• *The New Revised Standard Version* (Oxford University Press, 1989). This is wholly redone translation in line with the Revised Standard Version but with sensitivity to inclusive language for human beings. It retains traditional language for God. Although it is fairly literal in its translation, the English expressions have been updated to reflect current American cultural preferences. It comes in several different study editions, which include introductory essays, extensive footnotes, and brief commentary. This is the translation I will use when quoting from the Bible unless otherwise indicated.

• *The New International Version* (International Bible Society, 1984). This version is intended to be ecumenical and to appeal to a broad range of English-speaking people. The translation is considered somewhat more conservative than the NRSV. Its language is suitable for private study and for public reading.

• *The New American Bible with Revised New Testament and Psalms* (Confraternity of Christian Doctrine, 1991). This has become the standard American Catholic edition of the Bible. It is a revision of the New American Bible (1952–70) done with a sensitivity to accurate yet easily understood language that can be used in public worship. It is also sensitive to gender-inclusive language wherever references to human beings are concerned. Note that the OT section of this Bible is under current revision.

• *The New Jerusalem Bible* (Doubleday, 1985). A translation from the new French edition of this famous Bible, *La Sainte Bible* (1966), the text is the most poetic of the translations we are considering. Its poetic character lends itself to prayer. This Bible is also justifiably praised for its extensive footnotes, filled with informative background material.

• *The Revised English Bible* (Oxford University Press, 1989). This translation contains British English that some Americans may find unusual. Yet it is readable and reliable for study purposes.

• *Contemporary English Version* (American Bible Society, 1995). This is a totally new edition of *The Good News Bible* published by the American Bible Society. A major goal of this translation is sensitivity to the *hearers* of God's Word. It employs popular contemporary English that is more colloquial in nature.

You may notice that I do not include in the list the immensely popular *The Living Bible, The Reader's Digest Bible,* or *The New Testament and Psalms: An Inclusive Language Version. The Living Bible* (Tyndale, 1971) is not a translation but a paraphrase of the biblical text. Paraphrases are not reliable for Bible study. Although it is true to say that *every* translation is an interpretation, paraphrases contain too much editorial judgment about the meaning of a given passage to be of use. The danger of such works is that they try to clarify ambiguity where sometimes it exists in the biblical text. This is an admirable but misdirected goal. Sometimes the very ambiguity of the text is exactly what we need to reflect on. A successor to the Living Bible is the *New Living Translation* (Tyndale, 1996). A much better product, it is a translation and not a paraphrase, but it retains tendencies to make predetermined judgments about the meaning of the text.

The Reader's Digest Bible (Reader's Digest Association, 1982), on the other hand, is truly a short version of the Bible. It has clipped out all repetition in the Bible. Unfortunately, the result is a distortion of the text because repetition is a vital part of the message of some biblical stories or poetry. Again the aim is praiseworthy. The purpose is to entice people to pick up and read the Bible, something more attractive in a short version rather than a long one, with the hope that they would advance to further Bible study. But I do not recommend using such shortcuts. They can cheapen the Word of God.

The New Testament and Psalms: An Inclusive Language Version (Oxford University Press, 1995) is another matter. It is actually an adaptation of the New Revised Standard Version that employs radically gender-inclusive language. Critics have dubbed it the "PC Bible" (for political correctness). To illustrate, an admittedly difficult title used by Jesus such as "the son of man" becomes "child of the human one," and the Lord's Prayer begins with the awkward address, "Father-Mother." The result is a clumsy and offensive translation that shows how distorted modern sensitivities can sometimes be with regard to ancient texts.

Electronic Bibles

In this day and age I would be remiss not to mention the existence of many different types of Bibles and translations available as electronic media. So many choices exist that it would require an extensive section of this book just to list and evaluate them all. That is not my primary purpose, so I will leave it to others to evaluate these products. (The magazine *Biblical Archaeology Review* periodically has articles evaluating Bible media.) I will offer a few general observations.

First, if a program costs hundreds of dollars and contains Greek and Hebrew editions, it is probably beyond your needs. Avoid such technical programs until you are a very advanced student. One inexpensive and easily mastered program that I have found useful is called *Online Bible* (Larry Pierce, Ontario, Canada). For about fifty dollars this program contains all kinds of resources on one compact disc. Another popular, inexpensive, and user-friendly version is *QuickVerse* (Parsons Technology).

Other similarly inexpensive programs are available at your local computer software store.

Second, some of the translations mentioned above come in CD-ROM versions either as "stand-alones" or as part of a larger package. They are useful for researching Bible passages or for tracking themes by means of words or phrases. They are not as useful for simply reading and studying the Bible. For this purpose nothing can replace a printed edition of the Bible.

Finally, if you are computer literate and use the Internet, don't forget that you can access all kinds of resources at various sites on the World Wide Web. One site with a new English translation and lots of explanatory notes is the *Net Bible* (http://www.bible.org/netbible). Many Jews and Christians are interested in expanding the influence of God's Word. The Internet offers seemingly endless creative possibilities. I think St. Paul would have been envious of such a resource of evangelization!

How to Choose

Now which version is the best for you? I cannot say, for it depends on whether you want it primarily for prayer, for study, for Sunday school classes, to take to church to follow the sermon, or for other purposes. It may also depend upon your denomination and its preferences in translation. Any one of the above recommended versions would do. Like people, they come in different sizes and shapes. Some are hardback, some are paperback. Some are large with supplementary notes, cross-references, or comments, and others are pocket editions. They can be found in most bookstores. If you feel that you can handle a study Bible edition, it will be a bit thicker and heavier, but it will also contain lots of other information that you will find helpful to do more intensive Bible study. The most important point is that you have a modern Bible translation at hand while you read this book so that you can read the passages yourself and explore God's Word directly.

How to Read, Study, and Pray the Bible

Reading, studying, and praying the Bible are three different but interrelated tasks. I would like to give some practical advice on these topics.

Reading the Bible

I once had a relative who was fond of telling people how many times he had read the Bible from cover to cover. Another relative was heard to mumble on one occasion, "... and he still doesn't understand a word of it!"

How to *read* the Bible may be seem obvious. It is not. That is why I offer some tips.

• *Don't begin at the beginning or the end.* Begin, rather, with a book that is somewhat familiar and attractive to you. For Christians, the NT is a better place to start than the OT. Perhaps begin with Mark, the shortest Gospel, or with one of the letters of Paul. Do not go to the Book of Revelation. As attractive as this book is to many people, it is not the place to begin reading the Bible. It is a more complex and symbolic book than most of the NT. I recommend tackling it only after you have become more familiar with other parts of the Bible.

• *Read sections rather than sentences.* The Bible will make more sense if you pay attention to sections that are grouped together. In most translations editors have made decisions about how to divide and subdivide each book of the Bible into sections. Many translations also offer titles to sections. These are helpful hints about the topic covered in that section, but note that they represent editorial decisions to aid the reader. Such titles are not part of the Bible itself, and they may not characterize properly the content of a section.

• *Read aloud.* Silent reading to oneself is a relatively modern convention. In the ancient world reading aloud was standard. Acts 8:30, for example, shows the Ethiopian eunuch reading aloud from the Book of Isaiah. Philip overhears him and offers to help interpret the passage. If you are in a place where it won't disturb others, I recommend reading the Bible aloud. It involves another sense (hearing) that may aid in understanding the passage. Occasionally *hearing* the Word may also call your mind's attention to other similar passages or themes. Besides, the practice reminds us that much of the Bible originated in oral form. It was meant to be *heard*.

In order to use the Bible properly, one also needs to learn the conventions of referring to specific Bible passages. Each book of the Bible is divided into *chapters* and *verses*. Each book also has a shorthand abbreviation that allows quick reference (see appendix C, p. 236). Let's look at a few examples.

Acts 8:30 noted above refers to the eighth *chapter* and the thirtieth *verse* of the Book of the Acts of the Apostles. Ps 109:13 means Psalm (rather than chapter) 109, verse 13. But note that Phlm 8 refers to the Letter to Philemon verse 8. It is too small a book to contain any chapters. This is also true of the Letter of Jude and the Book of Obadiah in the OT. Exod 13:1–10 refers to chapter thirteen of the Book of Exodus, verses 1 through 10. A reference such as Matt 5:1–7:2 would refer to a passage extending from chapter 5, verse 1 to chapter 7, verse 2 of Matthew's Gospel. Appendix C is a chart of the most common abbreviations used for biblical books. Most Bibles list their particular abbreviation schema in the front of the book.

This system of chapter and verse is not found in biblical manuscripts (from Latin, meaning "hand written") themselves. Scribes wrote manuscripts in a continuous style without breaking the text into smaller divisions. A scholar from Paris, named Stephen Langton, invented the chapter enumeration system in the thirteenth century A.D. Another Parisian, Robert Estienne, added the versification system in the sixteenth century A.D. to subdivide the chapters and make reference easier. If you find a reference to specific chapters and verses that you can't seem to find in your Bible, it may be due to differences in editions. The divisions in the OT are unfortunately not as uniform as they might be. This is largely due to the difference between the Hebrew Bible and the Septuagint. Even the numbering of the psalms is different. Don't worry about such discrepancies. You will be able to find any reference easily once you become more familiar with the text.

Studying the Bible

Studying the Bible is not necessarily the same activity as reading or praying the Bible. Studying the Bible should always contain some sort of educational input. Whether it involves the services of a group leader, an outside expert, or a predesigned Bible program complete with instructions and media presentations, studying the Bible involves some work. It requires a desire to learn background and a willingness to read and reflect on additional material besides the biblical text itself. I assume that the readers of this book are interested in Bible study whether individually or in a group.

STUDY VERSIONS OF THE BIBLE

Some of the more popular study Bibles are:

- *The Catholic Study Bible,* D. Senior et al., eds. (New York: Oxford University Press, 1990). Uses the NAB translation.

- *The Oxford Study Bible* (New York: Oxford University Press, 1992). Uses the REB.

- *The HarperCollins Study Bible,* Wayne Meeks et al., eds. (New York: HarperCollins, 1993). Uses the NRSV.

- *The Cambridge Annotated Study Bible,* Howard Clark Kee, ed. (New York: Cambridge University Press, 1993). Uses the NRSV.

The advantage of a study Bible is that it provides much more information than a standard Bible edition. The disadvantage: a bit heavy to lug around.

This book consequently provides the essential introductory information you need for Bible study. I offer just a few more specific pointers about this activity.

• *Read the introductions.* If your Bible contains an introductory preface or is a study Bible with added introductory material, read it *prior* to reading the particular book of the Bible that interests you. It will supplement the brief introductions to each book of the Bible given in this book.

• *Read the footnotes.* If your Bible contains explanatory footnotes on specific passages, read them as you study the passage. The Bible often contains material that is very foreign to our world. Customs, terms, symbolic names, etc. often require explanation. They are not self-evident in interpretation. Many Bibles consequently contain footnotes. They are not just for scholars but also for ordinary readers. (Note that even fundamentalist Bibles, such as the Scofield Reference Bible, contain explanatory footnotes.)

• *Use the cross-references.* Most Bibles place references to other biblical passages in footnotes or in a sidebar on the page. These are called *cross-references.* Their purpose is to refer readers to other sections of the Bible where either similar themes are treated or where allusions or quotations are found. Often NT passages contain quotations or allusions to passages in the OT. These cross-references will give you further background information to help you understand the passage you are studying. It takes time to find these extra passages and read them, but your reward will be a richer understanding of the text.

• *Be flexible in your interpretation.* You do not need to be afraid of misinterpreting the Bible if you remember that *your* interpretation is not necessarily *the* interpretation. Your ideas about a given passage may be right or wrong. What is most important is that you remain open to learning more about it. Group Bible study is a great asset in this regard. It is even more effective if the leader of the group has either professional expertise in the Bible or carefully prepares material in advance to add a historical or scientific perspective. Sharing ideas about Bible passages is a wonderful way to study the Bible, especially when individuals remain open to further guidance about their views.

As you study the Bible you will learn more and more about a principle very basic to this enterprise: *The interpretation of a given passage does not contradict the literal sense of the passage but neither is it limited to that sense.* For example, when Isaiah speaks of a young woman (or in the Septuagint, "virgin") giving birth to Emmanuel (Isa 7:14), Christians see in this passage a prophecy about Jesus Christ (see Matt 1:23). The literal sense of the passage had more to do with an expectation in Isaiah's day (eighth century B.C.) than it did in the first century A.D., but this new and deeper sense does not contradict what the passage meant to Isaiah. To safeguard against reading into scripture what we want to hear, we must remember to pay attention to the literal sense of the words. We cannot force them to mean what they cannot mean literally. Yet the literal meaning of the words is not the only meaning. This principle is true for Jewish and Christian readers alike. It simply reminds us of our own limitations as biblical interpreters.

Often people want to know *where* in the Bible they can find a theme, a name, a story, and so on. This process is actually easier than most people think. There are certain tools that make finding specific passages in the Bible easy. These days, of course, one could use a computer Bible program that allows electronic word searches. But a more common method is simply to learn how to use a *concordance.* A concordance is an alphabetical listing of

words found in the Bible accompanied by all the references where
those words are found. If you wanted to find out, for example,
where a well-known figure like Nathan the prophet is found, or
an obscure person like Methuselah, you would look up the respective name to find the references. Or if you wanted to track all
occurrences of the image of "mountain" or the theme of "hope"
or the concept of "shepherd," you could also do the same. Many
Bible translations have separately published full concordances or
sometimes short concordances in an appendix. The key to success
is remembering that different translations use different words.
"Justice" (Hebrew: *zedaqah;* Greek *dikaiosynē*) might appear in
a given passage of one translation while another uses "righteousness." If you want to get serious about Bible study, an inexpensive
concordance would be a good investment.

Praying the Bible

People of faith want to go beyond reading or studying the Bible.
They also want to pray it. Using the Bible for prayer is, of course,
dependent upon one's denominational background. Some Christian churches use the Bible regularly in their worship services
by means of a *lectionary.* A lectionary is a book of readings ex-
cerpted from the Bible and placed in a liturgical cycle throughout
the church year. Catholics, Lutherans, Episcopalians, and others
use a common lectionary with slight variations in readings. Given
the broadest ecumenical approach possible, I offer only a few
basic guidelines on praying the Bible.

• *Invoke the Holy Spirit.* Every time you sit down to pray with
the Bible I suggest you begin with a brief prayer to call upon the
guidance of the Holy Spirit. From a Christian perspective, the
Holy Spirit is the true interpreter of scripture. By the power of
the Holy Spirit we have the ability to receive and discern God's
Word. Something as simple as "Come Holy Spirit, be my guide as
I try to understand this Word" reminds us that we need to surrender to God in order to understand the Word properly. Letting the
Holy Spirit be your guide puts your role in proper perspective.

• *Choose a passage to reflect on.* You may choose at random
by simply opening your Bible, or you may plan to read sections
of a given book in a continuous fashion. I recommend the latter course of action. Working through a whole book of the Bible
prayerfully is more effective than random interpretations. For

those whose churches use a lectionary, another method is to pray with the liturgical readings specified in the lectionary. Sometimes these are published a week in advance in parish bulletins. Praying with them through the week can prepare you to hear the Word more fruitfully when it is proclaimed and preached upon during the worship service. One should note that the structure of the lectionary is built on a three-year cycle. One year each is devoted to the Gospels of Matthew, Mark, and Luke. On Sundays the first reading is usually from an OT text and is tied to a theme of the Gospel for that day. The second reading is usually taken from a NT letter, the Acts of the Apostles, or the Book of Revelation and is thematically independent of the other two readings.

• *Read the passage once through fully.* Even when you are praying a passage, I suggest reading it in its entirety before going back over it more slowly. Getting the big picture first helps you understand each section of the passage better.

• *Read each section of the passage slowly.* The ancient Christian practice of *lectio divina* is a method of praying with scripture with time-tested results. The slow, meditative reading of biblical passages draws the reader to new levels of understanding the text. Sitting with a text, mulling over its words and phrases, and soaking in its images or themes truly brings one to a prayerful understanding. This need not be a long exercise, but it is important not to rush one's meditation. Let the words sink in, and you will feel yourself in God's presence in the Word.

• *Use your imagination.* Another way of prayerfully being present to the text is to imagine yourself in the text. Where are *you* in the text? If the passage is a narrative, are there characters with whom you identify? Do you see yourself in any of the actions? This is an exercise in meditation that does not lend itself to every biblical passage, but it is useful in many instances.

• *Reread the entire passage.* Once you have spent some reflective time on the sections of the passage, reread it in its entirety a second time. Although certain sections of the passage may have been more meaningful to you, I recommend putting the text back together as you end your prayer. It emphasizes the whole of the passage rather than just the parts.

• *Conclude with a prayer of thanksgiving.* A brief expression of thanks to God for the gift of the Word is a most appropriate way to conclude a prayer exercise with a biblical passage.

The more comfortable you become with the reflective and meditative use of scripture the more you will see ways to refine these recommendations. You may find that in reflecting on a given passage, a word or phrase jumps out at you that you finally concentrate on for the entire period of prayer. That is fine. It probably represents God speaking to you through the Word in ways most meaningful to you at that time. What is essential is that you see that praying the Bible and studying it are not opposed activities. The one activity leads to the other. In my experience, one's learning leads to prayerful reflection, which in turn leads to yearning for more understanding of the Word. Good Bible study will lead you to prayer with the Bible, and good prayer with the Bible will lead you to seek more knowledge about it.

Chapter 3

A BRIEF HISTORY
OF BIBLE TIMES

The Bible is a book of faith. It contains religious truths, and that is the primary reason that believers read the Bible. Yet it also contains history. As a book that originated thousands of years ago, it contains the testimony of a very broad historical period. Obtaining the "big picture" of that history will be helpful to place the various books in context. For want of a better universal name, I will sometimes refer to the land of Israel as "the Holy Land." It actually had different names throughout its history which could otherwise be confusing.

You might be asking yourself two questions: What are the sources for this biblical history? and, Why does this history matter anyway? Let's briefly tackle both questions.

Besides the Bible itself, there are ancient historical writings that help scholars reconstruct the history of Bible times. For example, the writings of the Greek historian Herodotus help to understand the Persian period, while the writings of the Jewish and Roman historian Josephus help to expand our knowledge of the NT period. Important modern archeological finds, such as the Dead Sea Scrolls or the Nag Hammadi documents, also assist such historical reconstructions. In other words, the Bible can be corroborated or nuanced by historical materials outside of it. All of this contributes to a more accurate picture of life in Bible times.

The second question is more irksome. People sometimes find history boring or pointless. Does what happened so long ago really matter? My answer is strongly affirmative. Skip this chapter at your own risk! I believe that pausing here to examine a telescoped view of biblical history can place the rest of this book in a more appropriate context. The Bible did not grow in a vacuum. It also did not descend from heaven on a golden platter. It grew out of the history of many people over an extended period of time. To take the time now to examine this background is to be like pioneers sending out advance scouts to reconnoiter the terrain before moving on (see Josh 2:1 for a biblical precedent). It can help prevent detours later on. You might even want to return to this chapter periodically to review the particular time period and place it more firmly in your mind as references are made to this history in the course of introducing individual books of the Bible.

Old Testament Times

The Bible begins with the Genesis story of creation, but that is not the beginning point of OT history. Some Christian fundamentalists interpret the Bible literally and attempt to date the creation of the world to a specific time. This approach unfortunately misunderstands the nature of the creation stories themselves. They are not a *history* of creation but a *theology* of it. Thus, the origin of the OT does not begin at creation itself but around the eighteenth century B.C., the time of the patriarch Abraham, whom Jews, Christians, and Muslims alike count as their oldest ancestor of faith. The chart below (p. 33) summarizes the significant dates for Old Testament times, but I will add an explanatory summary of Israel's history here.

The history of OT times begins with the patriarchs. Abraham, Isaac, and Jacob are the significant ancient ancestors that the Bible makes central to the story of how God chose a certain people, the Jews, to be in a special relationship called a covenant. The best scientific dating of the patriarchs leads to the nineteenth or eighteenth centuries B.C., a period archaeologists call the Middle Bronze Age. This was a time in the ancient Near East (now our "Middle East") when life was lived in nomadic or wandering tribes. People moved from place to place with their herds of animals in search of new pasture land. According to Genesis, this is the period when God (under the mysterious name Yahweh) called Abram (later named Abraham) to establish a special relationship. The origin of "the twelve tribes of Israel" is obscure, but the Bible says that they stemmed from the sons of Jacob, Abraham's grandson (also called Israel). The tribes became associated with different areas in what later became known as the land of Israel. The majority of the tribes were from the north, but two were from the south. There were disagreements and difficulties among them, but eventually they became loosely tied together, probably to provide better protection from other ancient peoples.

As time passed, nomadic tribes who made their living by shepherding began to give way to settled groups who learned how to support life by farming. Settled, urban life began and with it the need for more societal structure. The next period of OT history was the time of the "judges." The word "judge" may be misleading. The judges were less legal overseers than they were charismatic leaders who helped their growing peoples deal with complex issues that inevitably accompanied the movement from tribal to urban life. Eventually even these leaders became insufficient to rule, and the people of the twelve tribes sought to have a king like other nations. Saul reigned for a time as king, but David (ca. 950 B.C.) is the one who can rightly be credited as the great king. In Jewish tradition, never was there another king like David. He brilliantly made Jerusalem the capital, a town situated near the border between the northern and southern sections of the country. An analogy might be seen in Washington, D.C., which was made the capital of the United States partly because it straddled the north and south. David also was the first to desire to build a temple for Yahweh, the God of Israel. His son Solomon accomplished this feat. When they were a nomadic people, the portable "ark of the covenant" was sufficient to remind them of God's presence in their midst. Once they became an urban people, a more permanent location was needed, and the Temple became the focal point for Israelite religion from then on.

The time of King David and his famous son, Solomon, is traditionally considered the golden age. The tribes were no longer separate but united into a nation called Israel. Israel was like any other powerful nation. They had the signs of success: a king, a capital city with a splendid temple and other buildings, a strong army, and a prosperous economy. This was also the period when the written traditions of the Bible began. Prior to this time, oral tradition was the primary means of preserving the stories of faith in Yahweh. Once a bureaucracy was established under the kings, a written record became the norm. But the prophetic tradition also developed. Prophets arose to advise, warn, or reprimand the kings and to remind them of God's will. The golden period, unfortunately, did not last long.

Upon his death, Solomon's sons did not have the ability to keep
the nation together. Old enmities emerged that split the nation in
two. Israel became two separate kingdoms: Israel, the northern
kingdom, and Judah, the southern kingdom. Each had separate
rulers and even separate religious traditions. The period of the
divided kingdoms was a complicated time. It spanned several
hundred years, during which each of the kingdoms struggled for
survival in the midst of the rise and fall of various mighty empires, especially Assyria and Babylon. There were also squabbles
between the two kingdoms themselves and disagreements with
surrounding nations. In the end, the northern kingdom, Israel,
was conquered and destroyed by Assyria in 722 B.C. The southern kingdom, Judah, lasted about 135 years longer but perished
under Babylon in 587 B.C.

Thus began the period known as "the exile." When the Babylonians conquered Judah they also totally destroyed the city of
Jerusalem, razed Solomon's majestic Temple to the ground, and
hauled the people off to Babylon. This was a very sad period of
Israel's history. It began what is known as the "Diaspora" ("dispersion"), when the Jews became a people scattered all over the
earth. Yet paradoxically out of the experience of exile came the
OT itself. Scribes in exile began to collect the various oral and
written traditions of this people and to edit them in order to
preserve them for their descendants. At stake was the need to preserve their very identity as God's chosen people. In addition, the
synagogue probably emerged in this period. Without the Temple
the Jews had no center for worship. Consequently, the notion of
a community of prayer apart from the Temple developed, and the
synagogue (meaning "assembly") was born. This shift refocused
inevitably the religious traditions of the Jews away from sacrifices toward meditation on the written Word of God, the Torah.
In the ancient world the Jews became known as "the people of
the book."

In 538 B.C. Persia conquered Babylon. Cyrus, the king of Persia, was a benevolent ruler who gave the Jews permission to
return to Judah and rebuild their lives, including their Temple.
This action began the last major period of OT history, during
which the Jews were under the rule of one power after another.
When Alexander the Great conquered the entire area (333 B.C.),
he also brought the influence of Hellenistic culture. That influence

IMPORTANT DATES IN OT HISTORY

This chart gives an overview of important dates in OT history. All dates are B.C. (Before Christ). Sometimes you will find in modern books the reference B.C.E. ("before the common era") used in tandem with C.E. ("the common era"). This is an attempt to be sensitive ecumenically. I retain the traditional usage. Many dates are approximate, since there are inevitable differences of opinions among scholars about the actual dating of some events. The dates offered here are generally accepted by most scholars. The chart also gives the location of the OT book or sections of books where the events are described. The narrative summary in the text provides a convenient interpretation of the dates on the chart.

Date	Events/Period	OT Book Description	Origin of OT Books
ca. 2000– 1750 B.C.	Patriarchs	Gen 12–50	
ca. 1250	Exodus event	Exod	
1200–1020	Period of the Judges	Judg & Josh	
1020–922	United Israel Saul, David, Solomon "Golden Period"	1 & 2 Sam 1 Kgs 1 Chron	"J" parts of of Pentateuch
922–721	Divided Kingdom Israel & Judah	2 Kgs 2 Chron	"E" & "D" parts of Pentateuch
721–587	Judah Assyrian rule followed by Babylon	2 Kgs 2 Chron Jer 39–44, 52	
587–539	Babylonian exile	Ps 137	"P" parts of Pentateuch
539–333	Persian rule Restoration under Ezra & Nehemiah	Ezra Neh	
333–63 333–300 300–200 200–175 175–135 134–63	Hellenistic period Alexander the Great Ptolemies rule Seleucids rule Maccabean Revolt Hasmonean rule	1 & 2 Macc 1 & 2 Macc	Septuagint
63–4 37–4	Roman rule begins with Pompey Herod the Great		

THE ORIGIN OF THE OLD TESTAMENT

The origin of the writings in the OT can be summarized by three some-what overlapping processes: oral tradition, written tradition, and edited tradition. Historically, the span of these traditions was very extensive over time.

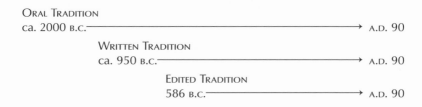

remained even throughout the NT period of history. It affected greatly the writing of some of the late materials of the OT as well as most NT books. Upon Alexander's death his successors fought over power and initiated a series of reigns, most notably that of the Ptolemies and the Seleucids. Jewish revolutionaries despised this foreign rule. This unrest led to the Maccabean revolt and the establishment of a Jewish rule under the Hasmoneans for about 130 years. This abruptly came to an end in 63 B.C. when the Romans conquered the area under the auspices of Caesar Augustus (Octavian) and his general, Pompey.

Somewhere around the second century B.C. the OT itself began to take on the three-part shape it now has in the Jewish canon: the Torah, the Prophets, and the Writings. These writings emerged primarily because they were a record of God's call to the people of Israel and their response. Also around this time scribes translated the Hebrew scriptures into the Greek translation called the Septuagint. This allowed the Jews of the Diaspora, who eventually lost command of their Hebrew and Aramaic languages when they adopted local languages, to have understandable scriptures.

This has been a very rapid review. It's like (I will confess) a "Reader's Digest" version of OT history, so it does not allow for much nuance. Nonetheless, I think it allows us to see that different writings arose at different times and under different circumstances. Through it all the Jews struggled to be faithful to God's covenant and to preserve their identity in the midst of terrible hardship and persecution. Their legacy, the OT, became "sacred scripture" for the writers of the NT, and thus provided the foundation for the Christian Bible.

Between the Testaments

From a historical perspective, there is a period of time *between* the OT and NT that contains some significance for the study of the Bible. This period is characterized by the "intertestamental literature." As Judaism developed between the time of Alexander the Great and the Roman empire, hope in the restoration of the Davidic monarchy diminished. Many Jews came to realize that the once glorious period of the Davidic kings in a united country was unrepeatable. Thus, they formulated a different kind of hope. Rather than expecting an anointed king in the immediate future, the hope for a messianic king of the distant future developed. They transformed the notion of a messiah, originally meaning merely an "anointed one," into a future expectation at the end of time. This is technically called an "eschatological" perspective (from Greek *eschaton,* meaning "end time").

The literature that evolved from this perspective is known as "apocalyptic" (from Greek *apokalypsis,* meaning "unveiling" or "revelation"). It speaks of God's revelation of what will happen when God is finally victorious over evil and establishes a kingdom of truth and justice. Both the OT and the NT contain examples of such apocalyptic literature (Book of Daniel, Book of Revelation), but the perspective is especially prevalent in the intertestamental literature that never made it into the canon.

Why did this perspective develop? The reasons are doubtless complex, but one view seems accurate. As the OT period drew to a close, the situation looked dire for the Jewish people. They were a defeated and dispersed people. Traditional leadership of prophets, priests, and kings was lacking (e.g., 1 Macc 9:27; Ps 74:9). A book such as Daniel could lament in the context of severe persecution:

In our day we have no ruler, or prophet, or leader,
  no burnt offering, or sacrifice, or oblation, or incense,
 no place to make an offering before you and to find mercy.
(Dan 3:38)

In such situations a literature of hope developed that transferred the expectation of salvation in the immediate future to salvation in a more indefinite and distant future. The OT itself ends on a note of expectation in the Book of Malachi, where the return of the prophet Elijah is foretold (Mal 4:5–6). The hope that God would once more act on Israel's behalf grew sharply. Messianic expectation appeared on the scene and prepared the way for the NT period. The intertestamental period, then, fleshes out more fully both the late OT period and the early NT period. While you do not have to read this literature to benefit from it, awareness of its existence shows that neither the OT nor the NT developed in a vacuum apart from the history that touched them both.

New Testament Times

The NT spans a much shorter time period than the OT, perhaps 120 years as compared with 1900 years. While the time span is shorter, the history is no less complex. The chart on the following page gives the major dates and events. I will again summarize the important aspects of this history in very brief fashion.

We can begin the period of NT history with the figure of Herod the Great. A half-Jew himself and a friend of Roman emperors, he was "king of the Jews" at the time of Jesus' birth (ca. 6–4 B.C.). Herod is important because he began a long line of "Herods" who are mentioned in the NT and because he built the Temple and many splendid buildings of Jerusalem that form the backdrop of the NT. Throughout the NT period Rome was the real power in the Holy Land, but local rulers like Herod and his descendants wielded much influence.

Virtually nothing is known about Jesus' life prior to his public ministry recorded in the Gospels. The period of time between Herod's death in 4 B.C. and Jesus' ministry was a relatively peaceful time in the Holy Land. Successive governors, or "procurators," ruled the Roman province called Palestine. The Romans allowed the Jews to maintain many of their religious practices, such as those at the Temple, but they also exacted considerable taxes from them.

At this time Judaism contained several diverse groups whose political and religious ideals varied greatly. The Sadducees were aristocratic leaders associated with the Temple in Jerusalem. They

IMPORTANT DATES IN NT HISTORY

Date	Event	NT Books
6–4 B.C.	Birth of Jesus (before the death of Herod the Great)	
4 B.C.–A.D. 34	Rule of Herod the Great's sons	
4 B.C.–A.D. 6	Archelaus	
4 B.C.–A.D. 39	Herod Antipas	
4 B.C.–A.D. 34	Philip the Tetrarch	
ca. A.D. 27–30	Jesus' public ministry, death, resurrection	
ca. A.D. 30–63	Paul's ministry	Paul's genuine letters (Rom, 1 Cor, 2 Cor, Gal, Phil, 1 Thess, Phlm)
A.D. 37–44	Herod Agrippa I	
A.D. 66–70	First Jewish Revolt	
A.D. 70	Siege and Fall of Jerusalem	
A.D. 70–100	Writing of most books of NT	Mark, Matt, Luke, John, Acts, Eph, Col, 2 Thess, 1 Tim, 2 Tim, Tit, Heb, James, 1 Pet, 1 John, 2 John, 3 John, Jude, Rev
A.D. 71–132	Roman rule under various emperors	2 Pet
A.D. 132–135	Second Jewish Revolt	

leaned toward compromise with the Romans to maintain the peace. Contrary to popular Christian understanding, the Pharisees were not "the bad guys" of the NT period. The Pharisees were a lay group of religious enthusiasts who tried to adapt the Law of Moses in such a way as to ease the burdens of the written Law. They permitted oral interpretation of the Law and eventually developed a tradition that would later be the foundation of modern Judaism. The Pharisees frequently opposed the Sadducees, especially in the latter's desire to placate the Romans.

Another group was the Essenes. They apparently were disgusted with the state of "official" religion in Jerusalem, so they fled to the desert near the Dead Sea to preserve authentic Judaism according to their own preference. The discovery of the Dead Sea Scrolls at Qumran in 1947 yielded an important source of information for their beliefs and way of life. Yet another group of Jewish radicals was called the Zealots. They opposed the Roman rule violently and were willing to cause civil unrest to achieve their ends. Most of the rebellious activity of these Zealots and other radical groups did not take place until post-NT times, around A.D. 135.

Jesus' public ministry took place around A.D. 27–30 and eventually led to his crucifixion, death, and resurrection under the Roman procurator Pontius Pilate. Shortly thereafter some apostles gained the courage to begin preaching about Jesus. Paul, formerly a zealous Jewish persecutor of those who followed Jesus, was converted. He became paradoxically the greatest evangelizer of the new faith, and his ministry spanned some thirty years before his martyrdom in the mid-60s. He wrote letters to many of the congregations he founded, and these became the basis for the NT canon. Christianity spread rapidly, especially among the lower classes of the Roman empire. The Christian preachers found greater success among Gentiles than among Jews, and Christianity slowly became a universal religion with broad appeal. The Roman government, however, perceived a threat in this new "pagan" religion and periodically initiated persecutions. Some of the later NT books (such as the Book of Revelation) reflect this intense experience.

The most significant catastrophic event in the NT period was the destruction of Jerusalem in A.D. 70. In A.D. 66 some radical Jews had begun a rebellion against the Romans. The Romans, in turn, sent an army to put down the revolt. They set siege to Jerusalem itself. Finally under the leadership of Titus, who later became emperor, the Romans were victorious. They burned the city and totally destroyed the Temple. For the second time in Jewish history all that the Jews held sacred in their holy city was annihilated. All that remains of the Temple of that period, often called the "Second Temple period," is the Wailing Wall (known

THE ORIGIN OF GOSPELS

Three distinct periods can be discerned in the origin of the Gospels. All three are found in the Gospels as we read them today, but they are often difficult to separate. We can roughly divide the first century into three time periods on the basis of this process:

A.D. 1–30	The time of the historical Jesus of Nazareth
A.D. 30–70	The time of the apostolic preaching
A.D. 70–100	The time of the evangelists

We must keep in mind that the process resulted from an interplay of three factors:

oral tradition ⟶ written tradition ⟶ edited tradition

to the Jews as "the Western Wall") in Jerusalem. Those who survived the destruction fled and ultimately tried to reconstruct their lives. Some Jewish leaders went to Yavneh (Jamnia) where they consolidated their scriptures and produced the final edition of the Hebrew scriptures. Some Christians fled to Pella where they did likewise, beginning to preserve the writings of the NT.

Thus concludes the "secular" history of the Holy Land in a thumbnail sketch down through the NT period.

Salvation History and the Bible

The Bible obviously contains a lot of history. Yet the Bible does not merely recount history; rather, it provides a "faith perspective" on it — what we might call "religious" or "theological" history. Most people are familiar with the expression "salvation history" to describe this perspective. Indeed, the structure of the Bible has been largely determined by the desire to express this salvation history. A short summary of the Bible's perspective of salvation history will be helpful as we prepare to outline its contents in more detail.

One way to summarize salvation history is to see it as a repeated cycle. It can be diagramed as follows:

Creation → Sin → Warnings and Threats → Punishment →
Repentance and Forgiveness → Re-creation

The Bible's view of salvation history begins with God's generous and loving act of creating all that exists. Existence is consequently not an accident of nature or the result of violent forces, but a free act of God. The best of God's creation is the human person, embodied in male and female, who both reflect God's own being. This original man and woman (Adam and Eve) are the origin of all the human species. They are given a beautiful garden in which to live. Only one thing is commanded of them: don't eat of the tree of "the knowledge of good and evil" (Gen 2:16–17). The name of this tree, of course, reveals that it is God's special tree because only God can fully know what is good and evil. The designation reflects a typical Hebrew expression of listing opposites to encompass everything about a topic. But you know the story. Adam and Eve ignore God's command. They sin. Suffering and death enter the world. They are punished with expulsion from the garden. After other violations of God's command, God finally wipes out the world in a huge flood. But God begins all over again with the human race, having preserved one faithful servant, Noah.

The pattern is thus established. The Bible goes on to record many different stories of such struggles, failures, and renewals. Along the way, certain key concepts emerge as essential to this salvation history. For example, God's intentions are expressed by the offering of a *covenant* over and over again to a chosen people, the Jews. The Bible explains the mystery of the choice of this people as purely an act of love (Deut 7:6–8). This divine election is not merely privilege. It is also commitment. They are to be instruments of bringing others to the God of all creation (Isa 2:2–3).

Creation itself may be seen as the first covenant, but others followed. They are usually accompanied by a specific symbol that represents the agreement between God and the individuals involved. Noah's covenant was sealed with the rainbow in the sky (Gen 9:16–17). Abraham's covenant was symbolized by circumcision (Gen 17:9–12). Moses' covenant contained the tablets of the commandments (Exod 20:1–17). And David's covenant included the promise of endless royal descendants (2 Sam 7:16), a promise the Christian Bible associates with Jesus Christ. In each instance, the covenant is violated by people. They sin, and God threatens and punishes. But a few good souls always remain with whom

God can begin again. And so the pattern continues...until the NT era.

With the coming of Jesus Christ, Christians believe that God has changed the pattern. The NT perspective on salvation history is that in Jesus Christ God has acted definitively with a "new covenant" that can never end (Heb 8:6–13). Now, because Jesus' obedience to God's will was perfect, there can be no other covenants. There is no longer need for the pattern to continue in exactly the same fashion. Instead, salvation has been assured in the person of Jesus Christ. But those who believe in him are expected to live out that salvation by lives that reflect it. The NT thus does not envision a laid back view of salvation history as if God has done it all, with the result that we human beings need do nothing else. On the contrary, because God has acted so definitely on our behalf by the gift of an only Son to the world, we are challenged to live out the stipulations of this new covenant (wholehearted love of God and neighbor). Sin still enters the picture. We fail often in our own commitment, but forgiveness and reconciliation remain in a community of faith (disciples) that is called both to support and challenge one another. God established a new community of faith, the church. It is to carry out the mission of spreading good news (the gospel) to the world (Matt 28:18–20).

This view of salvation history obviously comes from a faith perspective. I issue one note of caution: not every book of the Bible expresses this perspective! There are some discordant voices that take a differing view. For example, some of the OT wisdom literature (Job, Qoheleth) is more skeptical with regard to such a salvation-historical perspective. It reflects a more "humanistic" or secular outlook. Yet the dominant biblical perspective is from this vantage point of salvation history. The "chosen people" believed that God was reaching out to them in a special way. So they recorded their experience, implanting their faith perspective in their remembered tales. This view presumably matches our own. From our faith perspective, we believers read the Bible because we can see ourselves in it. In recounting these stories of faith, we encounter the God of eternity who reaches out from the pages of the Bible to touch our lives and lead us forward. This faith perspective need not blind us to analyzing the details of the Bible with scientific precision. Yet the *study* of the Bible also does not preclude our faith enrichment from these words. The most important caution to keep in mind is this: the factual history of the people of the Bible is deeply intertwined with this salvation history. The one influences the other. Both are of value in our own day, for both can teach us a lot about God and about ourselves.

Part II

INTRODUCING
THE OLD TESTAMENT

Chapter 4

GENERAL ORIENTATION
TO THE OLD TESTAMENT

The OT is a composite book made up of smaller collections of books that eventually formed the canon. Several different ways exist to subdivide the OT. The Jews traditionally thought of their Hebrew Bible (the Christian OT) as having three sections:

- Torah (Law)
- Nebi'im (Prophets)
- Kethubim (Writings)

This threefold division appears even in the NT in which one passage speaks of "the law of Moses, the prophets, and the psalms" (Luke 24:44). In this division the historical books (like Samuel and Kings) are understood as part of the prophetic collection. They were called "the former prophets" as distinct from "the latter prophets" whose names are attached to specific prophetic books.

Christians, however, developed a different system of understanding the divisions of the OT. Reflecting a more messianic outlook, Christians divided it into four sections:

- Pentateuch (Law)
- Historical Books
- Prophets
- Writings

The word "Pentateuch" comes from the Greek word for "five" because the Law consists of the first five books of the OT: Genesis, Exodus, Leviticus, Numbers, and Deuteronomy.

In both systems the final category of "Writings" is a catch-all category. Books that represent a diversity of styles are grouped into a rather loose collection. Also similar in both systems is the preeminence given to the Law. The first five books of the OT were always held in greater esteem because they contained God's revealed Law. In Jewish thought the study of the Torah is one of the highest forms of prayer imaginable. It is the beginning of understanding God's will.

We are not able to reproduce in our time what the environment out of which the OT grew was like. We can, however, note some important distinctions about the OT world that make us alert to patterns we will encounter as we read the OT. I will point out seven major influences that form the backdrop for OT texts.

1. *A belief in multiple divine beings.* Most modern people have come to accept *monotheism* — the belief in one God — as the norm of religion. In OT times, however, pagan religions readily accepted a multiplicity of gods. Even the religion of Israel, Judaism, in its early forms tended to think of their God, Yahweh, as the only true and effective God, but not necessarily the only God. Their God resided in heaven and was assisted in the duties of ruling the universe by "divine beings" who were not gods themselves but were also not of the human realm. Various kinds of angels, in particular, served as messengers of Yahweh. Our modern scientific mindset sometimes has difficulties accepting these ideas. They should not be dismissed out of hand; we need to recognize them as part of the cultural and religious environment of the OT.

2. *A three-layered universe.* The *cosmology* (understanding of the cosmos or universe) of the OT is also different from our own. People in OT times envisioned a universe that contained three distinct layers: heaven was up above and the realm of the gods; earth was below it, the realm of human beings; and the underworld (Sheol, or "shadows") was underneath the earth, the realm of the dead. The earth was flat and stood on pillars that held it up. Rain, snow, hail, and lightning fell from the heavens through flood gates. The sun rode around the sky from east to west in a chariot. There was, of course, no recognition that the earth was round and circled the sun or that precipitation in whatever form could be explained by the laws of physics. All was simply created and ruled by God.

3. *Honor and shame, purity and impurity.* A major factor in OT life was the dual belief that all life was dominated by states of honor or shame, purity or impurity. Life involved avoiding those realities that would place one in a negative state in relation to everyone else. Contact with bodily fluids such as blood or semen or with a dead body rendered one impure. An impure person would then have to perform prescribed rituals of cleansing in order to regain the pure state. Because life was lived in a more communal dimension than modern society, honor was also vital. If a person committed a crime, it brought shame to the family, the clan, and the tribe. Many modern cultures today retain this strong sense of honor and shame, such as those in parts of Africa and Asia. Certain immigrant groups, such as Hispanics and Vietnamese, may function in this manner, but American and other Western societies have lost this sensitivity. In the OT world, however, maintaining honor and purity was essential and is reflected in many laws in the Torah.

4. *Illness caused by sin and demons.* Most ancient peoples thought that illness came from either the individual's sin or the sin of his or her parents. A quick reading of Job 22:2–9 and John 9:2 illustrates this belief. Possession by demons was also thought to cause illness. The proper cure, therefore, was often an exorcism of the demon or repentance of the sin involved. They had no understanding of germs or viruses. Virtually any skin blemish came under the category of "leprosy" and rendered a person unclean. This very mechanical understanding of disease naturally led to the development of rituals that we now consider bizarre. This was simply the state of affairs at the time. The point is not to be critical of such attitudes but to recognize them when they appear in the biblical texts.

5. *Pleasing the gods.* Ancient pagan religions evolved a very practical approach to life's problems. Life was difficult. Humans were limited in their powers and were at the mercy of the gods. Procedures were needed to maintain a good relationship with the gods so that they would not work against you. Appeasing the gods by sacrifices was essential. Various rituals developed to meet the needs of society. For example, if one wanted fertile crops, engaging in sexual relations with cultic prostitutes at religious shrines would ensure such fertility. The religion of Israel naturally shunned many of these practices. Yet the OT bears witness

to the struggles of God's people through the centuries in trying to overcome such primitive religious behavior. Don't be surprised to find them narrated in the Bible!

6. *Society's structures.* The OT world was highly structured. Kings ruled over ordinary people. Identity was not bound up in oneself but in one's family, clan, tribe, and finally the nation. It was a patriarchal world in which men and women had diverse and almost mutually exclusive roles. Men were superior to women and thus had rights and duties not permitted to women. Women's place was in the home; men participated in war, politics, and religion. Many of these structures were adapted from foreign cultures. Even the notions of law and the covenant came from secular society, but OT religion adapted them to the religious situation. Such structures, even though they are found in the Bible, are not necessarily divine institutions. Yet we need to be aware of them in order to understand properly the Bible in its own context.

7. *The land.* Modern urban life has dulled our senses to the significance of the earth, but this was not the case in the OT world. God's very promise of a fertile land of "milk and honey" became a vital part of Jewish identity. The land itself is harsh. Much of it is desert, but with irrigation its mild climate, roughly similar to that of California with its dry and wet seasons, allows for an abundance of crops. The structure of the land consists of three main areas: the coastal plain, the hill country (called the "shephalah"), and the mountainous regions. A tiny country, Israel always found itself caught in the middle. It is situated in an area called "the fertile crescent" in which two axes of power vied continually for control. The one was Egypt, the other Mesopotamia. Both areas produced numerous successive empires that exercised control over Israel at different periods in its history. The significance of water rights and control of grazing lands and arable land for crops involved Israel in frequent disputes with other tribal peoples of the region. A sad legacy of this situation is the contemporary struggle between modern Israel and its Arab neighbors over control of the land. The Bible's frequent mention of the land and related topics, however, looms large in the reading of the OT.

These seven are not the only influences in the OT, but they are rather far-reaching. They basically tell us that the world of the

OT was very different from our own. Not everything in the OT is immediately self-evident or easy to understand. Nor does every passage automatically apply to our modern cultural way of life. Despite this situation, we should have no fear about reading the OT on its own terms. In the midst of its curious customs stands God's Word from which we can discern eternal truths that can guide us in our own environment. The peoples of the OT were in some ways exactly like human beings everywhere. Many human experiences and situations are ageless. With this overview we are now ready to take the plunge into the OT itself.

Chapter 5

THE LAW

Genesis	Leviticus
Exodus	Numbers
Deuteronomy	

The first major division of books in the Bible is the Torah. Christians call this section the "Law" or "Pentateuch." Because this section is comprised of five books (Gen, Exod, Lev, Num, Deut), the Greek word *pentateuchos* (the same root as Pentagon, from the Greek word for "five") is often used to describe it. No matter what title it is given, it is clearly the preeminent section of the OT. In the Jewish tradition God's Torah was the most important part of the canon. The very identity of the Jews was bound up with the Torah because it told them who they were in God's eyes and how to live as God's chosen people.

What Is Law?

Many people may consider law to be the most boring part of the Bible. Remember my warning about running into all those strange laws in the Book of Leviticus. That is why it is important to understand what the Bible envisions by the expression *torah*. The Hebrew word *torah* essentially means "instruction." Law in the Bible is a broader concept than in our culture. Law included commandments (that is, apodictic, or categorically defined, dos and don'ts), covenantal stipulations, regulations for all kinds of liturgical celebrations, and ethical instructions governing everything from tribal etiquette to sexual behavior.

Of course, not every book in the Pentateuch consists of actual laws or regulations. Genesis, Exodus, and Numbers contain mostly stories or narratives. These stretch from the creation of the world, through the lives of the patriarchs, to the exodus event and the entry into the promised land. The time frame of the Pentateuch, then, stretches from creation to about 1200 B.C. Quite a spread! Intertwined with this material are various collections of laws. Taken together, these five books are considered the quintessential expression of God's will for human beings. In the Jewish tradition, the prayerful study of the Torah is associated with the highest form of prayer. The longest psalm in the Bible, Psalm 119, is devoted to this theme. Strictly observant Jews study the various legal materials in the Torah rigorously. They attempt to fulfill them in literal fashion. Christians, however, read the laws in a broader fashion as an expression of God's will at different times in history. No matter which approach is taken, everyone can appreciate the magnificent stories that the Pentateuch contains.

Origins of the Law

Modern biblical scholarship has discerned different strands of tradition that provided the origins of the Torah. Most of the five books that comprise the Law stems from four different traditions spanning the period from about the tenth century to the fifth century B.C. Scholars have given these traditions the following names: Yahwist, Elohist, Deuteronomist, and Priestly traditions. Collectively they are known as "the documentary hypothesis," a reminder that the theory is a scholarly hypothesis about the origins of the Pentateuch over an extended period of time. Scholars often attempt to delineate in the Pentateuch each strand of the tradition, but this is a futile task. Over time the different traditions have become blended and are difficult to separate. Nonetheless, this hypothesis remains the best explanation for how the Torah took shape. Non-experts would find it impossible to discern these strands, but recognizing that they exist can alert us to the complexity of the biblical tradition.

THE DOCUMENTARY HYPOTHESIS

Since the nineteenth century A.D. scholars have generally accepted the hypothesis that the Pentateuch originated orally based upon different Jewish traditions from different time periods. The final written traditions retained vestiges of these early traditions, and these help to explain why different versions of the same biblical stories exist. The hypothesis posits four main sources for the origins of the Torah:

J: the Yahwist (tenth century B.C.), based upon the divine name Yahweh (Hebrew: YHWH)

E: the Elohist (ninth century B.C.), based upon the divine name Elohim

D: the Deuteronomist (seventh century B.C.), based upon the Book of Deuteronomy and its perspective

P: the Priestly tradition (sixth–fifth centuries B.C.), based upon the post-exilic priestly outlook

Genesis

This book may be the best known of the books of the OT. Who does not know the stories of creation, the great flood and Noah's ark, the tower of Babel, and the sacrifice of Isaac? Indeed, there are so may *good* stories in this one book, one might be tempted to linger a long time here and never move on.

The author of this book is unknown. Tradition attributed it and the entire Torah (Pentateuch) to Moses, but scholars have shown that this understanding is not factual. More important is that this book sets the stage for the entire Bible. It begins at the beginning. You can't go further back in time than the beginning of the universe. But Genesis covers this primeval history in short order and then moves on to the stories of Israel's most ancient and sacred ancestors — the patriarchs and their families.

Like most of the Pentateuch, Genesis originated in ancient, oral stories that recorded some of Israel's most cherished beliefs. The strands of these traditions span centuries, but the book most likely began in the tenth century B.C. and received its final form around the sixth century B.C.

TITLE: The Book of Genesis (Hebrew: *Bereshith,* meaning "in the
   beginning")

AUTHOR: Unknown, but probably multiple authors over centuries

DATE: Tenth–sixth centuries B.C.

STRUCTURE:
   1:1–11:32   Primeval History
   12:1–50:26   Stories of the Patriarchs

THEMES: Creation, sin and repentance, covenant, God's faithfulness

Structure and Content

Genesis conveniently divides into two major parts. The first part
(ch. 1–11) contains the primeval history of the world. At first
glance, these stories seem to require a literal interpretation. Many
Christians in recent history, in fact, have read them in this fashion. Thus they consider it essential to hold that God created the
world literally in seven days, just as Genesis 1 describes. Such an
understanding distorts the primary purpose of these texts. Rather,
they constitute a *religious mythology* whose primary purpose is to
describe in story fashion deep theological truths about primeval
themes like human life, death, sexuality, love, faithfulness, and so
on. The use of the word "mythology" should not frighten us. It
does not mean untruth but deeply profound truth couched in the
form of stories. In this way Genesis introduces the story of Israel
by situating it in the larger context of the creation of the entire
world. Once this primeval "history" is set forth, Genesis unveils
the story of how Israel came to be as a people.

   The second part of the book (ch. 12–50) is the patriarchal "history." Beginning with Abraham and his call by God to leave his
homeland and place his full trust in God, the stories of the patriarchs unfold in all their richness. These stories contain more
truths basic to Israel's faith. Examples: God can make the in-
fertile fertile (Sarah); faith often demands a test (Abraham and
Isaac); scoundrels can also be vehicles for God's will (Jacob and
Esau); injustice can be righted (Joseph). Many of these stories also
explain the origins of names and customs. Some of these details
have been lost over time and can appear very strange to us, yet

the patriarchal stories of Genesis provide the background for the later history of Israel described in other OT books.

Interpretation

The book of Genesis provides some of the most enjoyable stories in the Bible. These stories have inspired artists, singers, cinematographers, and others with an endless wealth of material to draw on for their trade. Can you visualize in some fashion famous images of creation, Adam and Eve, Noah's ark, the tower of Babel, or Jacob's ladder? Children, in particular, delight in these stories. Many children's Bibles contain retellings of these stories accompanied by illustrations.

Genesis is essentially a collection of stories of God and stories of faith. We should not misinterpret the word "story" in this context. It implies that we must not take every detail literally. But it does not preclude that some information in Genesis could well come from ancient historical events, the details of which have been long forgotten and now cannot be recovered. One will gain the full benefit of reading Genesis simply by looking for the religious meaning of the stories rather than trying to explain them logically. Genesis intentionally begins the Bible, for it establishes the pattern of God's relationship with humankind that plays itself out time and again.

Exercise

Read Gen 1:1–2:3. This is the first story of creation. It poetically describes how God created the universe in the span of a week. It is not meant to be a scientific account. After reading the story, sit back, close your eyes, and use your imagination to conjure up how the story can be visualized. What do you see? Can you describe a feeling that the telling of the story gives you?

Exodus

This book derives its title from the Greek term *exodos,* which means a journey or leaving. The Hebrew title is a shortened form of the first words of the book, "and these are the names of the sons of Israel who came to Egypt. . . . " This is essentially a book

---

Title: The Book of Exodus (Hebrew: *Shemoth,* meaning "names")

Author: Unknown

Date: Ca. tenth–seventh centuries B.C.

Structure:

1:1–22	Israel oppressed in Egypt
2:1–7:7	Moses
7:8–12:32	Struggle with Pharaoh
12:33–15:21	Departure from Egypt
15:22–18:27	Wilderness experience
19:1–40:38	Mountain experience

Themes: Covenant, God's Law, liberation, Passover, Moses and Aaron

---

of liberation. Its story has become a virtual paradigm for the victory God grants to those who are oppressed.

Like all the books of the Pentateuch, Exodus originated over a very long period of time, stretching from the tenth to the seventh centuries B.C. It describes events that took place around 1250 B.C. Many scribes had a hand in producing the book over time. Moses is the central figure of the book and its inspiration, but he is not its author. The stories of the ten plagues, the exodus event, the ten commandments, and the making of the covenant have inspired generations of believers and nonbelievers alike.

Structure and Content

Exodus contains six large sections of material. The first (1:1–22) is an introduction that sets the context for the rest of the story. The Israelites are in Egypt and under the oppression of a wicked ruler, the pharaoh Ramases II. They need someone to help them rally together and gain their freedom. The second section (2:1–7:7) describes the leader whom God chooses: Moses. His very life is a miracle, for his quick-thinking mother saves him from Pharaoh's slaughter of male Israelite children, and he grows up to be bold. The next section (7:8–12:32) narrates the many struggles between Moses and Pharaoh. These climax with the ten plagues God sends to Egypt. The final plague, the death of the Egyptians' firstborn males, is too much to endure, so Pharaoh lets the Israelites go but regrets it almost immediately.

GOD'S MYSTERIOUS NAME

What is God's name? Exodus 3:14 responds to this question mysteriously: "I AM WHO I AM." In Hebrew this is rendered by the ineffable word YHWH, called the tetragrammaton (Greek for "four letters"). Because God's name was sacred, Jews substituted the honorific title *adonai* (Lord) for God's proper name. The best rendering of YHWH in English is probably "Yahweh." Some have mistakenly appropriated the name "Jehovah" for the tetragrammaton. The Torah also contains another name for God, *El* or *Elohim*. This is an ancient Canaanite expression for God adopted by the Jews who created the "E" tradition of the Pentateuch.

With the departure from Egypt the next section (12:33–15:21) concentrates on the rituals of Passover. God instructs the Israelites about how they will avoid the angel of death as he "passes over" the land to slay the Egyptians' firstborn. After the exodus event itself is described (ch. 14), the wilderness experience begins (15:22–18:27). The Israelites grumble about all the hardships they must endure in order to achieve freedom. How they long to be back in Egypt where at least they had three square meals a day! God, however, miraculously provides manna, quail, and water in the desert for their nourishment. The final section (19:1–40:38) tells of the many different events that occurred while Israel was encamped around the Lord's mountain, which is called by two names, either Sinai or Horeb. The key event is the making (literally, "cutting") of the covenant between God and the Israelites (24:3–8). God agrees to be their God, and they agree to be God's people. The agreement entails obedience to God's commandments, especially the "ten words" that we know as the ten commandments (20:1–17). Most of the remaining material contains details about rituals, laws, and regulations that are supposed to govern the Israelites' lives.

Interpretation

The word "exodus" has become symbolic for movement from oppression to freedom. The inspiration of this book is wide-ranging. It symbolically represents the perennial underdog who defeats an evil foe against incredible odds. Moses and his siblings — Aaron, his brother, and Miriam, his sister — are shown to be flawed heroes who nonetheless are victorious in their ultimate goal: freedom for their people. But the major thrust of the book is God's initiative in acting on Israel's behalf. Exodus paints a striking portrait of God as simultaneously deeply moved by suffering but also strict and demanding. God's initiative of making a covenant with Moses is the most important act. In the exodus event itself, God's fidelity is already proven. But God's people must also do their part. Covenants have stipulations and sanctions. Israel's periodic failure to live up to their part of the bargain is what causes the dynamic of sin, punishment, forgiveness, and reconciliation to go on and on in the rest of the Bible. Exodus is truly a paradigmatic book. Its themes are repeated many times in the biblical tradition.

Exercise

Read Exod 3:1–6. This is the story of God's call to Moses to lead the Israelites out of Egypt. Why do you think God appeared in the form of a burning bush? Why would Moses be frightened? Is Moses' reaction what you would expect of a vigorous leader?

Leviticus

Many Christians find Leviticus tedious to read even though it is the shortest book in the Pentateuch. Some see this book more as a collection of antiquated Jewish laws than a contemporary Word of God for today. This impression, however, is mistaken. Although even some Jews today find some of the legal sections of Leviticus to be outmoded, the general direction of the text to promote holiness among God's people remains an appropriate universal message for all time.

The Greek name of the book (*leuitikon*) alludes to the priestly tribe of Levi. Little of the book is actually devoted to the Levites, the priests, but the concerns seen in Leviticus clearly derive from priestly interests. The book is essentially a mixture of narrative and legal prescriptions concerning the cultic practices of Israel. Many required festivals and celebrations are also described in Leviticus (see appendix D, p. 238). In all of these regulations Israel could judge its successes and failures according to God's exacting standards of behavior. Law became a tool by which Israel could judge its conformity to God's call to holiness. That is the primary purpose of Leviticus.

TITLE: The Book of Leviticus (Hebrew: *Wayyiqra'*, meaning "and he called")

AUTHOR: Unknown, but from the priestly (P) tradition of Israel

DATE: Ca. sixth century B.C.

STRUCTURE:
1:1–7:38	Sacrifices
8:1–10:20	Consecration ceremony
11:1–16:34	Laws of purity and impurity
17:1–26:46	Holiness Code
27:1–34	Rules on offerings

THEMES: Holiness, ritual purity, conformity to God's Law

Structure and Content

The entire book is structured as a series of regulations God gave to Moses at the tent of meeting (1:1). The first part (1:1–7:38) describes the various kinds of offerings that are to be made to God. OT religion was filled with cultic rituals of sacrifices and offerings. Different offerings fulfilled different functions, which Leviticus organizes and preserves. The second section (8:1–10:20) contains the description of the consecration or ordination of Aaron and his sons as priests. Accompanied by ritual bathing, being clothed with special vestments and liturgical tools, and anointed with oil, Aaron and his sons are seen as "priests," those entrusted with the duties of cult and sacrifice.

The third section (11:1–16:34) spells out the many regulations to maintain purity in the community. The ancients were particularly concerned about physical blemishes and bodily fluids. The regulations in this section provide advice on how to avoid pollution from these "unclean" elements so that one could remain ritually pure. The Holiness Code (17:1–26:46) is the heart of the book. Holiness means being set apart. Holiness was an essential quality of God that God imparted to Israel as part of their unique identity. This section describes the many aspects of Jewish life that reinforce their holiness, such as religious celebrations and feasts. The book concludes with final instructions on how to handle offerings (27:1–34).

Interpretation

The various subcollections of legal materials date from different time periods. Some of the rules may have originated as a result of experience. For example, the prohibition against eating pork may have resulted from severe cases of illness caused from undercooked pork. Other rules, such as the jubilee year, may have been an extravagant and generous means of equalizing society once disparities became too great between rich and poor. In any case, all the regulations are seen as God's command in order to keep the people ritually clean. Being clean and unclean, pure and impure, are important alternatives in Leviticus. Once one makes oneself impure by certain actions, then that person must follow special stipulations in order to regain a right relationship to the people and to God. This is a duty to maintain honor and integrity.

The key to Leviticus is holiness. God is the only true holy one, but God's people are holy by association with their God. "You shall be holy, for I the LORD your God am holy" (19:2; 20:26). This concept also underlies the notion of the holocaust offering so prominent in Leviticus. A holocaust offering is an offering that is fully burnt and offered in its entirety to God. Only when people continually can separate themselves from the material goods of this world and offer sacrifice to God without holding anything back can they maintain holiness. God's holiness is evidence that God is entirely *other.* God is not like us; God is ultimately mystery, totally separate from us. Yet God desires to share that holiness with those called to be a cherished possession. Whether we understand in detail the purpose of every minute law or regulation in this book, the goal is to draw us closer to the God who gave us life.

Exercise

Read Lev 19:1–4. Does this passage sound similar to any other part of the OT? (Hint: Read Exod 20:1–12 and you will recognize the form of this legal material.) Why would such basic instructions appear in different books in slightly different forms? Do you find these rules applicable today?

Numbers

The Greek name of this book (*arithmoi,* from which we derive "arithmetic") refers to the census of the Israelites to determine the members of each tribe. This book focuses on the time of Israel's wanderings in the desert after the liberation from Egypt in the thirteenth and twelfth centuries B.C. The desert symbolizes the place of testing. It is where Israel's faith was sorely tested by harsh conditions that made them long for the "good ol' days" when they were slaves in Egypt.

This book does contain a lot of numbers. One thing to remember is that in Hebrew numbers are often symbolic. They are not always meant to be taken literally. An example is the number forty. The forty years of wandering, like the forty days and nights of rain in the Noah story in Genesis, symbolize a long, long time. The symbol recurs in many stories (Noah, Moses, Elijah, Jesus). The symbolism of some numbers may have been lost over time, but the main point is not to get bogged down in trying to interpret too narrowly every numerical detail. In the case of people, for instance, the exaggerated ages of some OT figures (Moses, Aaron, Methuselah) is meant to convey the extent of their wisdom.

Structure and Content

Numbers can be partitioned in three large sections. The first section (1:1–10:10) describes preparations of the Israelites for the journey from Sinai to the promised land. God instructs Moses to take a census of the people, partly to gather young men for an army. Various rituals and regulations are described as well.

The second major division (10:11–21:35) recounts the many incidents that occurred during the desert journey from Sinai to Moab. The Israelites' faith is sorely tested by their difficult journey. They threaten rebellion, and Moses, Aaron, and Miriam have their hands full trying to keep them in line. The deaths of Miriam and Aaron occur (20:1, 28), and God tells Moses that he will not see the promised land (20:12).

The final section (22:1–36:13) narrates events that take place while the Israelites camp on the plains of Moab. God reveals that Joshua will be the successor to Moses (27:12–14). Preliminary victories take place that show that the Israelites, with God's

TITLE: The Book of Numbers (Hebrew: *Bemidbar,* meaning "in the wilderness")

AUTHOR: Unknown, but traditionally attributed to Moses

DATE: Ca. tenth–sixth centuries B.C.

STRUCTURE:

1:1–10:10	Preparations for departure from Sinai
10:11–21:35	Journey from Sinai to Moab
22:1–36:13	Preparations for the conquest

THEMES: Testing of faith, trials on the journey, trials and tribulations of leadership

blessing and strength, will be able to conquer Canaan and take possession of the promised land.

Interpretation

Fortunately, Numbers doesn't live up to its name. Only a small part of the book is devoted to the census. More influential is the notion of the journey and its accompanying trials and tribulations. God's chosen people show themselves to be rather ungrateful at times. They grumble against God's appointed leaders, Moses and Aaron, and they complain about the harsh circumstances on their journey. The desert becomes an image of testing and trial.

Exercise

Read Num 6:22–27. This famous blessing is a formula easily memorized and beautiful to impart to friends and family. Try using it at home on special occasions. What do you think the blessing means?

Deuteronomy

Deuteronomy comes from the Greek word for "second law." It is an apt description of the book because Deuteronomy adds to the legal material of the OT, especially that contained in Exodus. The Hebrew title is a shortened form of the first words of the book, "and these are the words that Moses spoke...."

TITLE: The Book of Deuteronomy (Hebrew: *Debarim*, meaning "words")

AUTHOR: Unknown, but attributed to Moses

DATE: Ca. eighth century B.C.

STRUCTURE:

1:1–4:43	Events on the plains of Moab and Moses' first address
4:44–28:68	Moses' second address and the ten commandments
29:1–30:20	Moses' third address
31:1–34:12	Moses' successor, Joshua, and the death of Moses

THEMES: Divine election, Law and justice, covenant, God's faithfulness, choose life

The entire book purports to record Moses' last set of instructions to the Israelites before entering the promised land. Like the other books of the Pentateuch, Deuteronomy does not stem from Moses alone but from numerous others over an extended period of time. The book achieved its final form probably around the eighth century B.C., and many scholars believe that this may have been the book that was found in the Temple at the time of King Josiah (see 2 Kgs 22:1–13). It caused a much-needed reform to take place in Judah as regards the religious practices of the Jews at the time.

Structure and Content

The book takes place entirely on the plains of Moab as Israel is perched near the promised land yet not entering into it. The main divisions of this book are determined by the large collections of Moses' instructions to the Israelites. The first section (1:1–4:43) recounts the defeat of certain pagan kings as Israel skirts around the promised land. Then Moses gives his first speech in which he urges Israel's obedience to God. The second address (4:44–28:68) is the longest. It contains another version of the ten commandments (cf. Deut 5:1–21 and Exod 20:1–21) that begins with the most sacred prayer of Judaism, the Shema Israel (6:4–9). A striking aspect of the legal material is the alternation of blessings and curses. All life is defined by these opposites. This is a typical stance of the Book of Deuteronomy. Reality is defined in firm choices that are direct opposites; little room is left for the gray areas.

The third address of Moses is much shorter (29:1–30:20). It describes the renewal of the covenant at Moab, urges the Israelites' fidelity to it, promises God's fidelity, and concludes with the exhortation that Israel choose the path of life over death. The final section of the book (31:1–34:12) describes how Moses, at age 120, decided he needed a successor to lead the Israelites: Joshua son of Nun. Moses then recites a lengthy prayer, gives a final blessing to the Israelites, and dies on Mount Nebo. Deuteronomy concludes with a testimony that has guided the traditional assessment of Moses: "Never since has there arisen a prophet in Israel like Moses, whom the LORD knew face to face" (34:10).

Interpretation

Deuteronomy has been a very influential book. We would misunderstand it, however, if we conceived of it only as bland legal material. On the contrary, the book is a heartfelt plea for right living in the eyes of God. The NT frequently quotes from or alludes to this book, and Jesus is remembered as having quoted the sacred Jewish prayer, the Shema (Mark 12:29–30), as a summary of the most important commandments God seeks: love of God and love of neighbor. It is not difficult to believe that Deuteronomy may have been the book that incited a reform. From beginning to end, Deuteronomy is filled with strong and vivid exhortation. Israel's periodic weaknesses and failures are recounted, but God's fidelity is what shines through the darkness.

Deuteronomy also contains many passages that beg for lengthy reflection. One example is the magnificent reflection on why God chose the Jews for the chosen people (7:7–8). It had nothing to do with size or ability or strength. The only reason was love. God simply "set his heart on you and chose you" (7:7). The mystery of divine election is that simple and yet that profound, and Deuteronomy explains it in the most eloquent terms available. If the dualistic nature of the book sometimes causes us concern, we should remember the power of choice in life and that love often requires difficult choices to be made.

Exercise

Read Deut 30:11–20. This passage describes a choice that God gives all people in their lives. Have you made such a choice? How would you describe a choice for "life" as compared with a choice for "death." Give examples from your own life. How might they compare to the choices God asked Israel to make?

Chapter 6

THE HISTORICAL BOOKS

Joshua	Ezra
Judges	Nehemiah
Ruth	Tobit
1 and 2 Samuel	Judith
1 and 2 Kings	Esther
1 and 2 Chronicles	1 and 2 Maccabees

The "historical books" section of the OT is actually a Christian designation. In the Jewish tradition most of these books are listed with the prophets. They are called "the former prophets" to distinguish them from the "latter prophets," that is, the books of Israel's classical prophetic tradition (Isaiah–Malachi). Christians consider these "historical books" because they deal mostly with various times of Israel's history and with some of the heroes of those eras. They cover the settling of the promised land, the period of the judges, the time of the kings of both the united kingdom and the divided kingdoms, and even later times of occupation by foreign powers.

Sections of the historical books may have been intended to be read together. Some scholars label one section, extending from 2 Samuel 9 to 1 Kings 2, "the succession narrative." The story unfolds as a type of royal court history, a record of David's kingship. It is also possible that four historical books (1 and 2 Chronicles, Ezra, Nehemiah) were intended to be read together as a record of the postexilic period. Ultimately, such smaller divisions are overshadowed by the larger unit.

What Is History?

Designating these books "historical" does not mean that they contain history as we modern people define it. We tend to think of history as a set of verifiable, objective facts. For instance, when we celebrate American history on a day such as the Fourth of July, we retell the story of the American Revolution or we remember the writing of the "Star-Spangled Banner" during the War of 1812. We think of history as a linear reality. One event follows another. That is the general way in which these historical books have been organized, but they were not composed in such a fashion. Rather, like the rest of the Bible, these books recount historical events from a "theological" perspective. The concern was not to preserve merely the objective facts, but to provide an interpretation of how God acted in the life of the chosen people.

Even the history of the kings is presented with a theological interpretation. Individually they are evaluated according to criteria established in the eighth and seventh centuries B.C. by anonymous authors known collectively by scholars as "the Deuteronomistic historian." Thus, the Books of Joshua, Judges, Samuel, and Kings are thought to have been composed together as a "history." Readers can easily perceive a unique and common perspective in these books. Kings are evaluated in a rather simplistic fashion according to clearly enunciated positions. Either they conformed to God's Law as expressed in the Book of Deuteronomy or they did not. Sometimes this perspective required the distortion of what we would consider the *facts*. This is not falsification but rather interpretation. The later authors of the Books of Chronicles retold much of this same history but from *their* perspective. The result is sometimes a different reading of "what really happened."

Scholars continually attempt to reconstruct the historical reality that underlies many of these stories. This does not minimize their value, nor does it resolve conflicting evidence. It simply means we must be vigilant when we attempt to reconstruct "historical" realities from these books. They can still be read with the security that they faithfully record God's Word in the context of Israel's history.

Joshua

Joshua, the first of the "historical books" of the OT, picks up where the Pentateuch leaves off. It records the history of how Israel took possession of the land God had promised to their ancestors, the patriarchs. The figure of Joshua, Moses' assistant and successor, dominates the book from beginning to end. He is portrayed as a great military leader who consistently obeys God's directives as he tries to lead the people to their destiny.

The book originated in written form probably during the seventh or the sixth century B.C. as a part of the larger unified history that scholars call the Deuteronomistic History (the books from Deuteronomy through 2 Kings).

Structure and Content

Joshua contains three large blocks of material. The first block (1:1–12:24) records the many military battles in which Israel engaged those who were already entrenched in the promised land. Beginning with the all-important hill country (shephalah), God provides the Israelites victory over the Amorites, the Canaanites, and all those other "ites" (see 12:8) as Joshua leads the people on one military campaign after another. There is even a victory list of the thirty-one conquered kings (12:9–24.) Some of the stories are told in detail, like the famous battle of Jericho (6:1–21).

The second block (13:1–22:34) narrates the distribution of the land among the twelve tribes of Israel. Each tribe was allotted a distinct portion of the land. An interesting feature is the designation of certain cities of refuge (ch. 20) where those who had unintentionally killed someone could take refuge from an avenger.

The final block of material (23:1–24:33) contains Joshua's farewell address, the covenant renewal ceremony at Shechem, and the story of Joshua's death at 110 years of age.

Interpretation

If there is one aspect of OT religion that offends modern tastes, it is probably the idea that God sanctions war. Not only that, but God seems to demand the slaughter of whole peoples who stand in the way of the chosen people. We must remember that OT religion had a concept of "holy war" that was a natural part

---

TITLE: The Book of Joshua

AUTHOR: Unknown

DATE: Ca. seventh–sixth centuries B.C.

STRUCTURE:

    1:1–12:24   Conquest of the promised Land
    13:1–22:34   Distribution of the land
    23:1–24:33   Covenant renewal and the death of Joshua

THEMES: Promised land, God's protection and fidelity, covenant renewal

---

of their culture. In those ancient times survival was a key reality. Subsistence living necessitated taking extreme measures to protect one's family, tribe, clan, and nation.

Joshua is a record of the covenant between Yahweh and the Israelites. In this sacred agreement God functioned as divine protector. Israel had to be obedient to God's directives. Joshua's greatest challenge was keeping Israel focused on what God intended. Sacred warfare was not a matter of gaining personal booty but protecting Israelite society. The most important point of the book is that God remained faithful to the promise. God provided victory at the most crucial times. The people, in turn, had to keep renewing their pledge to be faithful to God. Hence, we should read Joshua not merely in light of our modern moral sensitivities but as a record of God's faithfulness.

Exercise

Read Josh 5:13–15. Do you notice any similarities to the story of God's appearance to Moses (Exod 3:1–6)? What differences do you see? What do you think the passage means in its context right before the story of Jericho's collapse? Has God ever provided you a "victory"?

Judges

Judges takes its name from the male and female heroes who succeeded Joshua in the leadership of the tribes of Israel. A "judge"

TITLE: The Book of Judges

AUTHOR: Unknown

DATE: Ca. seventh–sixth centuries B.C.

STRUCTURE:
      1:1–3:6   Settlement of the land and Israel's
                                 disobedience
      3:7–16:31   Stories of the judges
      17:1–21:25   Other tales

THEMES: Fidelity and infidelity in life, charismatic leadership in Israel

was not so much a court authority as a charismatic political and military leader endowed with wise judgment. As part of the larger Deuteronomistic History, Judges spans the time from the death of Joshua to the period immediately before the monarchy, roughly 1100–1000 B.C. The first part of the book repeats in different fashion some material found in the Book of Joshua, for example, the death of Joshua (2:6–10).

Since scholars attribute the book to the unknown author of the Deuteronomistic History, it can be dated around the seventh or the sixth century B.C.

Structure and Content

Judges can be divided into three large sections. The first section (1:1–3:6) repeats some of the material from Joshua and places the settlement of the promised land into that context. The text emphasizes that the people of Israel were often unfaithful to God despite God's fidelity to them. Hence the need for charismatic leaders: "Then the LORD raised up judges, who delivered them out of the power of those who plundered them" (2:16).

The second section (3:7–16:31) narrates the deeds of the judges themselves. Some are little known (Othniel, Ehud, Shamgar) and others are much more famous (Deborah, Gideon, Jephthah, Samson). In each case, these heroes saved particular tribes of Israelites from disaster by calling the people back to Yahweh and by acting wisely on their behalf. The stories of Deborah (ch. 4–5) and Samson and Delilah (ch. 16) probably are the most familiar in the book.

The final section of Judges (17:1–21:25) collects together other disparate stories of Israel, including the migration of the tribe of Dan and the civil war that erupted between the tribe of Benjamin and the other tribes.

Interpretation

Judges provides testimony that the formation of twelve different tribes into a unified nation was not an easy task. The process did not proceed smoothly. There arose inevitable disputes and jealousies, and there was always the problem of a stubborn, unruly people. A constant temptation, and one that always would haunt Israel, was the temptation to idolatry, "forgetting the LORD their God and worshiping the Baals and Asherahs" (3:7). The Book of Judges illustrates a pattern that fits perfectly within the larger cycle of sin–punishment–salvation that permeates the OT. Israel's infidelities bring punishment; punishment forces Israel's appeal to God for help; God raises up a savior to lead the people. Thus judge after judge rules over Israel as it struggled to become a nation. The book concludes with an open-ended observation that entices the reader to the next level of political leadership: "In those days there was no king in Israel; all the people did what was right in their own eyes" (21:25).

Exercise

Read Judg 16:1–31. This passage is rather long compared to many of the exercises I have proposed, but the story is intriguing and easy to read. It is the story of Samson and Delilah. How do you feel at the end of the story? Is Samson a perfect hero for Israel? How does this passage speak to you of leadership and its necessary qualities?

Ruth

The Book of Ruth is actually more like a short story. It has two primary functions: (1) to indicate the universality of God's salvation, and (2) to set up the ancestral lineage of King David, Israel's greatest ruler. It fits neatly between Judges and 1 Samuel, almost like a connecting link in a chain.

TITLE: The Book of Ruth

AUTHOR: Unknown

DATE: Ca. tenth–eighth centuries B.C.

STRUCTURE:
1:1–22	Ruth and Naomi
2:1–4:22	Ruth and Boaz

THEMES: Universal nature of salvation, love, God's work in history

Although the author is not known, scholars generally believe the book was composed sometime during the tenth to the eighth centuries B.C.

Structure and Content

Ruth can be structured around the main characters in the story. The first part (1:1–22) focuses on Ruth and Naomi. Ruth is the Moabite daughter-in-law of Naomi, an Israelite widow who returns to Bethlehem after the death of her husband and two sons in Moab. Although she is a foreigner, Ruth insists on accompanying her mother-in-law Naomi and abandoning her own country to continue to serve Naomi. Once in Israel, Naomi plays matchmaker for Ruth. She arranges an encounter with Boaz, a wealthy relative of Naomi. The second part of the book (2:1–4:22) narrates how Boaz falls in love with Ruth, leading to their marriage. Boaz commends Ruth's tender care of Naomi and defends her status in front of the elders of Israel. They bear a son, Obed, who becomes the father of Jesse, the father of King David. The lineage of the Davidic monarchy is thereby established.

Interpretation

Ruth is a romantic tale. Ruth's sentiment expressed to Naomi, who tries to persuade her to remain in Moab, has become a staple in marriage ceremonies:

> Where you go, I will go;
>   where you lodge, I will lodge;
> your people shall be my people,
>   and your God, my God.

> Where you die, I will die —
> there will I be buried. (1:16–17)

The most prominent theme in the book, however, is not love. It is about the expansive nature of God's salvation. It stretches out to foreigners and strangers; it is more inclusive than exclusive. Given the tight tribal society that was typical in biblical times, this universalistic tendency is quite startling. In the NT Matthew has picked up on the significance of Ruth as a foreigner who nonetheless played a significant role in Israel's history. She is one of only five women recorded in the genealogy of Jesus' Davidic lineage (Matt 1:5), who possess either foreign background or tainted reputations. They provide a certain paradoxical proof that God truly can write straight with crooked lines.

Exercise

Read Ruth 2:8–12. Boaz speaks highly of Ruth's many sacrifices in life, especially as a stranger in a foreign land. Does this passage indicate how foreigners should be treated? Have you ever experienced being an outsider? What did it feel like? What do you think God's attitude toward outsiders is?

THE FESTIVAL SCROLLS

Ruth is one of the five books of the Hebrew Bible used by the Jews on particular feasts. They are called the *Megilloth,* or "festival scrolls." The five books and corresponding feasts are listed below. See appendix D (p. 238) for brief explanations of the feasts.

Book of the Bible	*Feast*
Ruth	Pentecost
Song of Songs	Passover
Ecclesiastes	Tabernacles
Lamentations	Ninth of Ab
Esther	Purim

---

1 Samuel

First and Second Samuel should be read together. They originally were a unified book but became separate books when the Hebrew Bible was translated into Greek. I will treat them separately to conform to the structure of the Christian canon. The two books of Kings, which we will treat separately, are also part of this royal history.

Three figures dominate 1 Samuel — the prophet Samuel, King Saul, and King David. Many of the stories may have originated separately, but the Deuteronomistic History has joined them into a unified tale of royal intrigue. The book probably achieved its final written form around the sixth century B.C.

Structure and Content

We can see three main sections in this book. The first section (1:1–7:17) introduces Samuel the prophet. The son of Elkanah and Hanna, Samuel was miraculously conceived and given by his parents to the Lord's work. After his call and anointing as a prophet, Samuel oversaw the establishment of Israel's first two kings, Saul and David. Samuel warns the people sternly about the dangers of establishing a kingship so that they could be "like other nations" (8:6). But they ignored the advice God gave through Samuel.

The second section (8:1–15:35) describes the early, hesitant activities of Israel's monarchy. Samuel anoints Saul as the first king (10:1) but later expresses regret (15:11) because Saul refuses to abide by the absolute demands of God not to spare Israel's enemies. The stage is thus set for a younger, bolder leader, who will go on to become Israel's preeminent king.

The final section (16:1–31:13) narrates the ascendancy of David to the throne. This young, unexpected upstart, a handsome shepherd with musical talent, is chosen to lead Israel. His confrontation with Goliath and subsequent defeat of the dreaded Philistines is the stuff of movies (ch. 17). The book also narrates David's friendship with Saul's son Jonathan and the jealousy that Saul felt over being rejected as king and replaced by a youth. This section contains many stories about the rivalry between Saul and David. The transfer of power climaxes tragically in a battle with the Philistines that concludes in the death of Saul and his sons at Mount Gilboa near the entrance to the Jezreel Valley.

TITLE: The First Book of Samuel

AUTHOR: Unknown

DATE: Ca. sixth century B.C.

STRUCTURE:
1:1–7:17	The story of Samuel
8:1–15:35	The rise of the monarchy in Israel
16:1–31:13	The rise of King David

THEMES: Prophecy and kingship, divine election, pros and cons of monarchy, Saul and David

Interpretation

The human dimensions of this royal intrigue do not overshadow the divine message contained therein. After the period of the judges, Israel needed a different kind of centralized leadership. Kingship was a natural social development. But Israel always saw God's hand at work in this process. God simultaneously fostered the development of another institution in Israel — prophecy. The kings may have been the political leaders after the judges, but the prophets retained the charismatic tendencies of the judges. The kings had to contend regularly with the words of the prophets. They were God's mouthpiece, sometimes cajoling, sometimes comforting, and sometimes challenging the kings to fulfill their obligations with God's expectations uppermost in their intentions. The stories contained in this book are fascinating on a human level as a record of ancient history. How much more do we value them for the assurance that God remains present to God's people even in the midst of these human foibles.

Exercise

Read 1 Sam 18:12–16. Describe how this little scene combines both human and divine elements. Do you see any resemblance to situations you may have experienced or heard about?

2 Samuel

Second Samuel immediately picks up from 1 Samuel with David's mourning over the death of Saul and his sons. David and the prophet Nathan are primary figures in this book, but there is a host of other characters who play innumerable roles in the establishment of the monarchy in Israel. David dominates the book, and despite its name Samuel never appears in the story. The time period spans approximately 1000–962 B.C.

Since it was connected to 1 Samuel and was originally part of Deuteronomistic History, it also achieved its present form around the sixth century B.C.

Structure and Content

The first part (1:1–12:31) of 2 Samuel begins with a continuation of the rise of David as king. His anointing as king does not take place until ch. 5. He brilliantly chooses Jerusalem, ideally situated near the border between the north and the south, as a capital for his united kingdom. The covenant God chooses to make with David (ch. 7) is important, for it established the Davidic royal line from which would spring messianic hopes at a much later period. The story of David's reign is not all positive, however. His infamous adultery/murder escapade with Bathsheba and her husband is not swept under the rug but hung out for all to see (11:1–12:15). David may have been Israel's ideal king, but like so many great leaders, he was terribly flawed.

The second section (13:1–20:26) is devoted to the rebellion of Absalom, one of David's sons, and the subsequent civil war. Like his father, Absalom was a deeply flawed individual. Handsome, ambitious, conniving, and impatient, Absalom attempts a coup against his father and is killed in the process. David's mournful remembrance of his son is one of the most poignant parts of the book (19:1–8).

The final section (21:1–24:25) contains diverse stories that center on an evaluation of David's words and deeds. In keeping with David's reputation as a talented minstrel, 2 Samuel records some of his "songs" for posterity (ch. 22). A listing of some of David's most important military leaders is also recorded (ch. 23), as well as other events during David's reign.

TITLE: The Second Book of Samuel

AUTHOR: Unknown

DATE: Ca. sixth century B.C.

STRUCTURE:
        1:1–12:31   The reign of King David and the Davidic
                                covenant
        13:1–20:26   Absalom's rebellion and civil war
        21:1–24:25   David's words and deeds

THEMES: Prophecy and kingship, the Davidic covenant, human
    weakness and God's strength

Interpretation

One might label 2 Samuel as "the promise and peril of royalty."
The book bears equal testimony to the greatness of royal leaders
and their folly. The British monarchy has no patent on intrigue!
One story after another spells out court intrigue, betrayals, adultery, murder, ambition, pride, arrogance, rebellion, and all the
wonderful imperfections we associate with human weakness. So
why is it so prominent in this history?

The point, of course, is that kingship brought with it many lia-
bilities. Bureaucracy and social structure have limitations. Yet we
yearn for them mightily and, indeed, need them to make human
existence proceed smoothly. In the midst of these natural social
developments, 2 Samuel sees God's hand at work. While it is
sometimes difficult to discern, God's will is being accomplished all
the while our human sinfulness may obscure it. In the telling and
retelling of these royal stories Israel reminded itself of their very
human roots. It also called to mind how God would permit such
human folly somehow to serve a larger mysterious divine plan.
At least we can be sympathetic to our distant ancestors. They suffered from the same temptations and weaknesses we do in our
day. And despite that God's will could still be accomplished.

Exercise

Read 2 Sam 12:1–6. In this passage the prophet Nathan con-
fronts King David with his adulterous affair with Bathsheba.
What is your reaction to the story? How does Nathan's "para-

ble" function in the story? Can you point out instances in your life where yourself or others have been condemned by your or their own words?

1 Kings

Like 1 and 2 Samuel, 1 and 2 Kings originally belonged together as one book. They became separated in the Greek translation. In fact, all four books from 1 Samuel to 2 Kings received the names "Kings" because they narrated the royal history of Israel. In the Christian canon they receive separate treatment.

First Kings resumes the story of David from 2 Samuel in David's advanced age. It describes the accession of Solomon to the throne and the subsequent splitting of Israel into two king-doms after Solomon's death. It then records the deeds of many of Israel's and Judah's kings. This period of time covers roughly 960 to 850 B.C. Since this book is also part of the larger Deuterono-mistic History, scholars date it to around the sixth century B.C. The book itself, however, shows that earlier collections of ma-terials may have been used. It mentions the "Book of the Acts of Solomon" (11:41) and the "Annals of the Kings of Israel" (14:19).

Structure and Content

We find two large divisions in 1 Kings. The first (1:1–11:43) de-scribes David's death, how Solomon succeeded his father David as king, and the remarkable achievements of Solomon's forty-year reign. Solomon gained a reputation for wisdom. Some of the sto-ries illustrate this wisdom, as in the case of the two women who claimed the same child as their own (3:16–28) and the queen of Sheba's visit to Jerusalem (ch. 10). The other major feature of Solomon's reign was the building of a magnificent temple for Yahweh, the God of Israel (ch. 6). His father David had always desired such a temple but in light of Nathan's oracle (2 Sam 7) did not accomplish its construction. His son did so in splendid fashion, but Solomon's human errors are also noted (ch. 11). In these, the son did not stray far from the father's footsteps.

The second division (12:1–22:53) begins with the reign of Re-hoboam, Solomon's son. Things quickly degenerate, as he was

---

TITLE: The First Book of Kings

AUTHOR: Unknown

DATE: Ca. sixth century B.C.

STRUCTURE:
1:1–11:43	The reign of King Solomon
12:1–22:53	The divided monarchy

THEMES: Kingship and prophecy, the Temple, the wisdom of
Solomon, the intertwining of political and religious realities

---

unable to hold the kingdom together. The northern tribes appointed Jeroboam as king, while Rehoboam remained king of
Judah. Jeroboam had been an able assistant of Solomon's who
had earned his disfavor and was exiled to Egypt for a time.
The rest of the book recounts the activities of the many kings
of both kingdoms and pronounces judgment upon them according to their deeds. The kings, however, are not the only topic.
Prophets appear regularly in the narrative. Most important of
these is Elijah the Tishbite, who makes his appearance in ch. 17.
Elijah is the main character in four cycles of stories that show
how prophets provide an independent check on secular leaders in
order to promote God's plan. (See the chart on the facing page.)

Interpretation

It is easy to get lost in the historical books. Readers can find
it difficult to keep track of who's who, let alone discern where
traces of God's presence are to be found. To maintain your balance I suggest keeping the big picture in the back of your mind.
The story of the kings is about how social and political realities
have religious dimensions. The kings are all evaluated according
to the standards of good and evil. The author, interestingly, judges
all the kings of the northern kingdom of Israel to be evil, while
only two (Hezekiah and Josiah) of the southern kingdom of Judah are judged to be good. In this contest, prophets definitely
have the advantage. How difficult it is for political leaders to
maintain their moral compass in a raging sea of diverse social influences. Prophets help kings to maintain their moral direction or
quickly point out where they have gone astray. In this history nei-

THE ELIJAH CYCLE

A cycle of four stories in the Books of Kings presents the powerful image of Elijah and his successor, Elisha, as precursors of the classical prophets.

Story #1:   1 Kgs 16:29–19:18. Elijah's miracles and the wicked
            Queen Jezebel

Story #2:   1 Kgs 21:1–29. Naboth's vineyard

Story #3:   2 Kgs 1:2–17. Elijah and King Ahaziah

Story #4:   1 Kgs 19:19–21; 2 Kgs 2:1–18. Elijah and his successor
            Elisha

These stories influenced later Jewish expectation of a messiah, especially with Elijah's miraculous ascendancy to heaven in a fiery chariot (2 Kgs 2:11; cf. Mal 4:5). They also greatly influenced the NT record of Jesus' miracles.

ther political kingdom really wins because both head toward their ultimate destruction by stronger powers. But narrating the history helps subsequent generations maintain their moral direction in life.

Exercise

Read 1 Kgs 17:17–24. Does this story sound familiar? Luke's Gospel makes reference to it (Luke 4:26) and Jesus performs a similar miracle (Luke 7:11–17). Why would Elijah act favorably to a non-Jew? Describe instances where God's grace has surprised you in relation to where it was found or to whom it was directed.

2 Kings

Second Kings is a direct continuation of the story of the divided kingdom. The span of time described extends from about 850 to 587 B.C. The origin of this book is the same as 1 Kings.

Structure and Content

There are two large sections to this book. The first (1:1–17:41) narrates the rest of the history of the divided monarchy. Just as

TITLE: The Second Book of Kings

AUTHOR: Unknown

DATE: Ca. sixth century B.C.

STRUCTURE:
1:1–17:41	The divided kingdom and the collapse of the northern kingdom of Israel
18:1–25:30	The kings and the fall of the southern kingdom of Judah

THEMES: Kingship and prophecy, idolatry and rebellion against God and its consequences, the intertwining of political and religious realities

the prophet Elijah figured prominently in 1 Kings, so his successor Elisha is the major prophetic voice of 2 Kings. After Elijah's ascent to heaven in a fiery chariot, Elisha picks up the mantle of his mentor (ch. 2). This section also follows in tandem the history of the royal leaders in both kingdoms. The climax of this section is reached with the collapse of the northern kingdom of Israel (16:5–6). The Assyrians captured it in 722 B.C. and carted off many Israelites to slavery in Assyria. This left only the southern kingdom, the tribe of Judah.

The second section (18:1–25:30) describes the kings of Judah and the events that led to the destruction of Jerusalem by the Babylonians. Two kings, Hezekiah and Josiah, are rated positively by the author. He portrays Hezekiah in pious tones as one who consulted the prophets (Isaiah, son of Amoz) and followed the Lord's bidding (ch. 19–20). Josiah, on the other hand, initiated a reform of the idolatrous practices that had crept into Judah's religious practices (ch. 23). The rest of the kings are evaluated negatively as having gone their own way.

Interpretation

Second Kings has a perspective harmonious with 1 Kings. The kings and the prophets are viewed together. Each has a distinctive role to play, and each is charged with God's commands, albeit from a different angle. The kings were to foster authentic religion in the midst of Israelite life by relying only on God to direct their decisions. The prophets were to ensure that God's Word was not overlooked in this process. The history, unfortunately, records that the kings often failed in their duties. They frequently sought out dangerous alliances that ended in disaster. The judgment of 2 Kings on the reason for the destruction of the northern kingdom is simple: "This occurred because the people of Israel had sinned against the LORD..." (17:7). The trauma of the southern kingdom's destruction some 135 years later was another blow to the Jews' understanding of their relationship with God. The Books of Kings stand as sentries to all believers: beware of your politics — it may impact your religion negatively!

Exercise
Read 2 Kgs 23:1–3. This passage describes a ritual renewal of the covenant initiated by King Josiah upon the discovery of another book of the Torah (the Book of Deuteronomy?) in the Temple. Do you have a covenant with God? Can you think of ways to renew that covenant?

1 *Chronicles*

In the Hebrew Bible the two books of Chronicles exist as one and are called by the collective title "The Acts of the Days," meaning the annals of Israel's history. As with the Books of Samuel and Kings the Greek Bible separated them into two books. They were called "the things left out," implying that they supplemented the Books of Kings. The Chronicles, however, are a very different retelling of Israel's history from Adam to the end of the monarchy. Such a sweeping overview was thought necessary after the destruction of Jerusalem because that particular disaster demanded explanation. How could God abandon the chosen people? How could God turn on the promise made to David that he and his ancestors would rule forever (2 Sam 7:12–13)?

The response to these questions was to create a work that retold that history with a certain theological twist. The Chronicles are part of a larger unified work that includes Ezra and Nehemiah. The author of these books is probably not a single individual but a group of scribes writing in the fourth century B.C. They reviewed the history of their people as they knew it and searched diligently for a way to explain what had happened.

Title: The First Book of Chronicles (Hebrew: *Divre hayammim,* meaning "the acts of the days")

Author: Unknown, but called the Chronicler

Date: Ca. fourth century B.C.

Structure:

1:1–9:44	Genealogies of Israel's ancestry from Adam to Saul
10:1–29:30	The reign of King David

Themes: The work of priests and Levites, sacredness of Judah, sin and its consequences, the challenge of leadership

Much of the material repeats almost verbatim parts of other OT books, especially the books of Samuel and Kings. But the perspective is always distinctive.

Structure and Content

Two major sections comprise the book. The first (1:1–9:44) consists mainly of genealogies from Adam to King Saul with occasional narratives breaking the rhythm of the lengthy lists. The second section (10:1–29:30) begins with the death of Saul and his sons and the anointing of David as King over Israel. Already in the judgment about Saul's tragic death one can perceive the perspective of Chronicles: "So Saul died for his unfaithfulness; he was unfaithful to the LORD in that he did not keep the command of the LORD ... " (10:13). Judgments are made about kings either favorably or unfavorably based on their faithfulness to the God of Israel. The rest of the book is devoted to David's exploits, concluding with Solomon's rise to the throne. One easily discerns that the evaluation of David is very positive.

Interpretation

The perspective of Chronicles is similar to but an expansion of that of the Deuteronomistic Historian. Kings are judged on the scales of fidelity and infidelity to God. We see the expansion of this approach in the application of the criteria to all of Israel's history. This pattern thus provides a response to the predicament faced by the Jewish people after the collapse of both kingdoms: Why had God acted so drastically? Because the leaders had often failed to maintain the terms of the covenant with God. The positive evaluation of David and his son Solomon is based upon their establishment of worship in Jerusalem and the building of the Temple. When reading Chronicles we must keep this perspective in mind. The approach may be somewhat simplistic in terms of the historical evidence. The religious perspective, on the other hand, provides a convenient yardstick with which to measure success.

Exercise

Read 1 Chron 29:10–19. This is David's prayer of praise to God near the end of his life. Describe the sentiments contained in this prayer. Ideally, if you could compose a prayer for the end of your life, what might its content be?

2 Chronicles

What I said in the introduction to 1 Chronicles applies equally to this book. Second Chronicles picks up with Solomon's accession to the royal throne and recounts the entire history of the divided kingdom down to the Babylonian exile and the restoration by Cyrus, king of Persia. The period covered, then, extends from around 960 to 539 B.C. The conclusion of the book, which describes Cyrus's decree of freedom to the exiles, leads immediately to the Book of Ezra.

Structure and Content

This book is basically divided into two large sections. The first (1:1–9:31) summarizes Solomon's reign as king. The Temple is the main focus, but Solomon's wisdom is also emphasized. The second and larger section (10:1–36:23) records the history of the kings after Solomon. Second Chronicles gives attention to both kingdoms of the divided monarchy. Negative events are not glossed over. Indeed, they are emphasized because they illustrate the infidelity of the leaders. Only the attempted reforms of Kings Hezekiah, Manasseh, and Josiah are rated positively. The book concludes with the freedom proclaimed by the Persian king Cyrus when he allowed the Jewish people to return to Jerusalem and rebuild their city, their Temple, and their lives.

TITLE: The Second Book of Chronicles (Hebrew: "the acts of the
    days")

AUTHOR: Unknown, but called the Chronicler

DATE: Ca. fourth century B.C.

STRUCTURE:
    1:1–9:31   The reign of Solomon
    10:1–36:23   History of the divided kingdom to the
                      Babylonian exile

THEMES: King Solomon's achievements, the Temple, fidelity and
    infidelity to God, the exile and its cause

Interpretation

The perspective is the same as in 1 Chronicles. Rulers are judged
according to the basic standard of fidelity and infidelity to God's
commands. Interestingly, Chronicles evaluates Manasseh positively whereas Kings views him with unqualified contempt (cf.
2 Chron 33:18–20 and 2 Kgs 21:17–18). Chronicles acknowledges his sin of idolatry but claims that God forgave him. Biblical
authors obviously could differ in their perspectives. The key to
understanding Chronicles can be found in the explanation for
the exile:

> The LORD, the God of their ancestors, sent persistently to
> them by his messengers, because he had compassion on his
> people and on his dwelling place; but they kept mocking
> the messengers of God, despising his words, and scoffing at
> his prophets, until the wrath of the LORD against his people
> became so great that there was no remedy. (36:15–16)

This passage basically summarizes the main point of the Books of
Chronicles. God is patient, but not forever. As can be seen in the
history of our ancestors in faith, persistent human folly leads to
disaster; therefore, we are challenged to remain faithful.

Exercise

Read 2 Chron 34:1–7. How does this passage view Josiah, the
boy king? What did Josiah do that was so good? Can you think
of any modern idolatries that stand in the way of our fidelity to
God? How can we rid our lives of these?

Ezra

Again we find that two books in our English Bibles exist as one in the Hebrew Bible. Ezra and Nehemiah are kept together as one in the Jewish tradition. Scholars believe they are the work of the Chronicler, the unknown author(s) of 1 and 2 Chronicles. But the name Ezra (from Hebrew, meaning "help") refers to a scribe to whom the book is attributed. The date is clearly after Cyrus's release of the Jewish exiles, perhaps in the late fifth or early fourth centuries B.C., depending on which King Artaxerxes is intended (7:1). Not much historical information is available about Ezra the scribe. He was of a priestly family. Later Jewish tradition considered him a prophet and attributed to him the writing of the Hebrew scriptures in general.

Structure and Content

Ezra can be divided into two segments. The first (1:1–6:22) summarizes the challenges of restoring Jerusalem and the Temple once King Cyrus had given approval for the Jews to return to their homeland from Babylon. Cyrus had conquered Babylon and adopted a more lenient attitude toward foreign peoples. Ezra includes a list of exiles who returned (ch. 2) and an assessment of the difficulties that the restoration entailed. The rebuilding of the Temple, in particular, met with resistance (ch. 4).

The second segment of the book (7:1–10:44) describes the mission of Ezra. He was a religious figure whose primary task was to encourage the rebuilding of the Temple and the reestablishment of a strong, healthy Jewish life in Jerusalem. One serious difficulty that arose was the existence of many mixed marriages (ch. 9–10). During the years of exile, many Jewish men had taken foreign wives. These Gentile-Jewish mixed marriages were highly controversial. Many Jews, especially the devout priestly leaders, viewed such marriages as a watering down of the heritage. In the end, the foreign wives and children were sent away.

Interpretation

This short book deals with both practical and theoretical issues. In practical terms, Ezra faced the enormous challenges of trying to rebuild the Temple, and thus the core of Jewish religion, with limited resources. The mixed marriages compounded this situation.

TITLE: The Book of Ezra

AUTHOR: Unknown, but attributed to Ezra the scribe

DATE: Ca. Late fifth–early fourth centuries B.C.

STRUCTURE:
      1:1–6:22   Restoration of Jerusalem
      7:1–10:44   The mission of Ezra the scribe

THEMES: Restoration, rebuilding the Temple, mixed marriages

The more theoretical issue was how to reestablish his people's love and respect for their religious traditions. After years of exile and contact with foreign cultures, this was also difficult to achieve. Yet Ezra felt God's strong call. He urged the people to remain focused on the primary challenges of rebuilding their faith. Prayer and fasting, entreaty and practical planning all went into the enterprise. Ezra shows what steadfast conviction can achieve.

Exercise

Read Ezra 7:7–10. Ezra desired above all else to study the Torah and teach it in his native land. Do you share in Ezra's enthusiasm for God's Word? What difficulties do you face in trying to live out this vision?

Nehemiah

Nehemiah is a continuation of Ezra. Nehemiah was the governor of the newly restored land of Judah. He was most concerned with rebuilding the walls of Jerusalem and the Temple. The book is written in first-person form as if it were a memoir. Scholars doubt that Nehemiah himself wrote it. More likely, it is the work of the Chronicler, written in the late fifth or early fourth century B.C. It is difficult to determine for which Persian King Artaxerxes (2:1) Nehemiah worked.

There is an overlap between Ezra and Nehemiah. One is the religious leader, the other the political leader, although they have a similar perspective on the rebuilding of Jerusalem.

TITLE: The Book of Nehemiah

AUTHOR: Unknown, but attributed to Nehemiah, son of Hacaliah

DATE: Ca. Late fifth or early fourth century B.C.

STRUCTURE:

1:1–7:73	Nehemiah's commission to rebuild Jerusalem
8:1–10:39	The call to obedience
11:1–13:31	Rebuilding the social and religious structure of Jerusalem

THEMES: Rebuilding Jerusalem, mixed marriages, renewed obedience to the Law

---

Structure and Content

Nehemiah can be divided into three sections. The first (1:1–7:73) describes Nehemiah's first governorship of Judah and his commission to rebuild the city of Jerusalem. Most importantly, he rebuilt the city's walls to afford protection. The work was completed despite serious opposition. At the conclusion of this section Nehemiah lists those who returned from exile, giving special notice to those associated with Temple worship.

The second section (8:1–10:39) is like an interlude. Ezra is the main focus of attention. He calls the people together to renew the covenant, celebrate the feast of Booths (see appendix D, p. 233), and confess their sinfulness. They take upon themselves the obligation to care for the Temple and to obey the Jewish traditions.

The final section (11:1–13:31) speaks of the reorganization of Jewish society after the return from exile. It includes a list of the priests and Levites who were charged with the care of the Temple. The problem of mixed marriages reappears here, as in the Book of Ezra. Nehemiah couches the problem as one of foreign influence that obscures Jewish ethnic identity.

Interpretation

Coupled with Ezra, Nehemiah argues for purifying Jewish traditions in order to maintain a pure ethnic identity. We might view this attitude as promoting exclusivity. It works against the inclusivity of other parts of the Jewish tradition, including Second Isaiah, which promoted the universal nature of salvation. We must, however, place Nehemiah in context. After the trauma of exile we can understand the desire to promote the purity of Jewish national identity. The exile nearly robbed the Jewish people of their heritage. Fortunately, scribes and priestly families preserved the traditions and collected them for posterity. Outside influences can threaten any closely knit society. Many immigrant groups have undergone similar challenges when emigrating to the United States. The real question is how to maintain faithful obedience without promoting intolerance.

Exercise

Read Neh 8:13–18. This passage describes the renewed festival of Booths, a Jewish commemoration of their wanderings in the desert after the Exodus. Have you experienced any religious festivals with such enthusiasm? Why do we celebrate religious festivals? Are there any that are tied to our very identity?

Tobit

Tobit is one of the OT apocrypha. Although it is included among the historical books, it is actually a fictional story set in the eighth century B.C. to promote personal faith in God among pious Jews. The story takes place after Assyria conquered the northern kingdom of Israel. It concerns two individuals, Tobit, son of Tobiel, and Sarah, daughter of Raguel. Tobit is a member of the tribe of Naphtali sent into exile to Nineveh, the capital of Assyria. Sarah lives in Media and is tormented by a demon. God sends the archangel Raphael in disguise to help these pious Jews who struggle in the Diaspora. Neither the author nor date of the work is known.

Structure and Content

I structure this book into five "acts," although it is possible to see each chapter as an individual division. The first act (1:1–3:16) gives the background for the story and identifies the main characters and their predicaments. Tobit is blinded accidently as he tries to elude Assyrians who seek him for unlawfully giving proper burial to dead Jews. He is reduced to poverty. Sarah is hounded

TITLE: The Book of Tobit

AUTHOR: Unknown

DATE: Perhaps ca. second century B.C.

STRUCTURE:

1:1–3:16	The predicaments of Tobit and Sarah
4:1–6:18	The journey of Tobias and Raphael
7:1–10:13	The marriage of Tobias and Sarah and the healing of Sarah
11:1–12:22	The journey home and the healing of Tobit
13:1–14:15	Tobit's prayer of thanksgiving and wise advice

THEMES: Personal faith, God's hidden messengers, the power of prayer

by a demon and is falsely accused of killing her seven husbands. God hears their separate prayers and sends a divine messenger, the archangel Raphael, disguised as a relative to help Tobit's son Tobias resolve these predicaments.

The second act (4:1–6:18) describes Tobit's instructions to Tobias to journey to Media to retrieve money he has left in the care of a friend there. Raphael guides Tobias on the journey and persuades him to stay at the home of Sarah, who is a relative of Tobias. In the third act (7:1–10:13) they get married, and with Raphael's instructions Tobias is able to heal her of the demon.

In the next act (11:1–12:22) Tobias takes Sarah back home with him, having recovered his father's money. Again, Raphael gives the youth instructions on how to heal his father's blindness, and the miracle is accomplished.

The last act (13:1–14:15) finally resolves the story. Raphael reveals his identity as God's special messenger; Tobit prays a lengthy prayer of thanksgiving and finally gives some sage advice to his son and grandchildren before he dies.

Interpretation

Tobit is meant to be read and understood as a whole. It is a story with a moral very similar to that found in OT wisdom literature. Maintain your identity, keep close to your traditions, remain faithful to God, and all will turn out well. In its original context

Tobit provided Jews who lived in the Diaspora hope that their lives were not being lived in vain. Maintaining Jewish identity in the dispersion was no simple matter. They faced many challenges, especially from the surrounding pagan cultures. Tobit also extended the hope that Jerusalem would one day gather Jews together again (13:15–17). It is a story that promotes Jewish pride while offering a tale that everyone can enjoy. The character of the angel in disguise, a frequent motif in ancient literature, has gained popularity today. You never no when the stranger in your midst (or even a relative!) might be just the right "angel" to help you.

Exercise

Read Tobit 3:11–15. This is Sarah's prayer to God in her misery. Have you ever felt like Sarah? How do you pray when you are in a dire situation? Do you believe God hears and answers such prayers? In what ways?

Judith

This is another book of the OT apocrypha. Judith tells the story of a Jewish widow who saves her hometown from an Assyrian invasion by cunningly killing the Assyrian general Holofernes. The book is set in the eighth century B.C., the time of the Assyrian empire, yet some of the details cause confusion. Some references are made to the later Babylonian and Persian empires and their kings. Nebuchadnezzar, for example, was Babylonian, not Assyrian.

Judith is thus probably intended as a fictional story that can be applied to various circumstances of oppression. Judith in Hebrew means "Jewess," and the book provides the Jewish people with another heroine of the stature of Ruth, Esther, and Miriam. The author is unknown. The date, however, can be fixed in the second century B.C. around the time of the Maccabeans.

Structure and Content

Judith has three main sections. The first (1:1–7:32) explains the circumstances that led to the Assyrian invasion. All the surrounding countries sue for peace; Judah alone refuses. The Assyrian king consequently dispatches his general Holofernes to besiege

---

TITLE: The Book of Judith

AUTHOR: Unknown

DATE: Ca. second century B.C.

STRUCTURE:
1:1–7:32	Assyrians besiege the Israelites
8:1–13:20	The story of Judith and Holofernes
14:1–16:25	The defeat of the Assyrians

THEMES: God's deliverance in times of trouble, strength and cunning in the face of an adversary, the power of prayer

---

Judea. Bethulia, Judith's hometown, comes under the siege, and the Israelites plead to God for help.

The second section (8:1–13:20) tells how Judith defeated Holofernes. After describing her impeccable piety, beauty, and virtue, the tale narrates how Judith addressed her town elders to be bold in defense of Israel. She prays eloquently to God for deliverance and develops a plan to trick Holofernes into trusting her. She allows herself to be captured by the Assyrians. Then, smitten by Judith's beauty, Holofernes throws a banquet at which he plans to seduce her. Alone with him in his chamber she beheads him and takes the head back to her town in a food bag.

In the last section (14:1–16:25) the Assyrians flee upon discovering the decapitated body of their general. Israel is saved once more by incredible heroism, and the entire people rejoice. Judith prays a final prayer of thanksgiving and praise. The conclusion describes Judith's honorable death many years later at the age of 105.

Interpretation

The story of Judith has inspired many portraits through history. The decapitation of Holofernes by an attractive young woman provides great material for artists. The main point of the story, of course, is that oppression requires both reliance upon God and human cunning to defeat it. The existence of inspiring heroines like Judith in the male-dominated Jewish tradition is of great importance. It provided role models for anyone in oppressive circumstances, and it testified to God's ability to raise up the least likely heroes in times of difficulty. In some ways, we might say Judith's story is a feminine version of David and Goliath. The underdog can indeed vanquish enemies by faith and wisdom. The canon naturally places Judith among the historical books because of its setting in the Assyrian period. It also accompanies the stories of other heroes that it precedes, Esther and the Maccabees.

Exercise

Read Judith 13:1–10. We might as well not pass up the most action-packed part of the story. What impresses you the most about Judith's actions? Does the passage condone murder? How would you judge your own ability to respond in a dire situation such as Judith faced?

Esther

This is a marvelous story that, unfortunately, has a difficult and confused history. The problem is that the book exists in two versions. The main version is part of the Hebrew Bible. The Septuagint, however, contains other additions to the book that are part of the OT apocrypha. Consequently, some English Bibles place the apocryphal additions in the place they were intended to supplement the Hebrew version. These additions supplied more of a religious character to the story because God is not mentioned in the original version. Is that confusing enough for you? Don't be alarmed if your text is different in structure from the way I treat it here. Some Bibles only print the shorter Hebrew version, while others print the longer edition with the Greek supplements.

Esther is the fictional story of another Jewish heroine. She became the queen of the Persian king Ahasuerus (the historical King Xerxes I). The book records how she and her uncle Mordecai defeated a plan by the king's advisor Haman to exterminate the Jews. Written probably in the Persian period in the late fourth or early third centuries B.C., the story gives the rationale for the Jewish festival of Purim (9:18–28; see appendix D, p. 238).

TITLE: The Book of Esther

AUTHOR: Unknown

DATE: Ca. fourth–third centuries B.C.

STRUCTURE:
   (with additions from the Greek Bible, A–F)
   A & B + 1:1–3:15   A plot to exterminate the Jews
   4:1–7:10 + C & D   The defeat of Haman and the advance-
                       ment of Mordecai
   8:1–17 + E   Esther saves the Jews
   9:1–10:3 + F   Enemies defeated and the Feast of Purim
                       established

THEMES: Feast of Purim, bravery in the face of adversity, avoiding
   pagan influence, human cunning and divine intervention

Structure and Content

The outline of the story is complicated by the six additions found
in the Greek edition. They are usually labeled with letters A–F.
I incorporate these additions in the outline by letter while maintaining the standard chapter numbers. (See the explanatory box
on p. 94.)

The first part of Esther (additions A & B and 1:1–3:15)
explains the plot against the Jews. Her uncle Mordecai had un-
covered a plan to harm the king. He was rewarded but earned
the jealousy of King Ahasuerus's wicked advisor Haman, who re-
solved to harm the Jews. In the meantime, the beautiful virgin
Esther, whose Jewish identity remained a secret, won the affection of the king above all the other women in his harem. She
is made the queen, but the king proceeds with Haman's plan to
harm the Jews.

The second part of the story (4:1–7:10 + C & D) reveals
that Esther resolves to help her people with her uncle's help.
Both Mordecai and Esther pray to God for assistance (addition
C). They are both received by the king and honored at a banquet where Haman's terrible plot is thwarted, and Mordecai is
commended.

The next section (8:1–17 + E) records how Esther intervened
with the king on behalf of her people. He issues a decree
exonerating the Jews and explaining the evil intentions of Haman.

THE ADDITIONS TO ESTHER

The additional material from the Septuagint is given both a letter and chapter/
verse designation. These correspond as follows.

A = 11:2–12:6   D = 15:1–16
B = 13:1–7   E = 16:1–24
C = 13:8–14:19   F = 10:4–11:1

The final act in the drama (9:1–10:3 + F) is the annihilation of those who had wished harm on the Jews and the establishment of the festival of Purim. The text explains that the name of the festival was derived from the casting of "lots" (*purim*) against the Jews.

Interpretation

Esther has the obvious flavor of a fictional drama in which an innocent, beautiful young heroine acts with great cunning to save her people. One can understand why the original (and shorter) version of the story caused concern among those Jews charged with translating their scriptures into Greek. God was left out of the picture. Only human ingenuity reigned supreme. The additions to the book obviously provided counterbalance by bringing in prayers to God to act on behalf of the Jews. As it stands now in the canon, Esther gives testimony both to human ingenuity and God's favor. Again, an unlikely heroine saves the day. For Jews living in the Diaspora the text also provided fair warning about pagan influences. They were dangerous and could threaten the very identity and well-being of the people.

Exercise

Read Esth 14:11–19 (part of addition C). Can you identify in any way with Esther's prayer to God? Do you find any evidence in it that brings together human capability with faithful reliance upon God?

1 Maccabees

First Maccabees is a history of the Maccabean revolt, covering the time period from 175 to 132 B.C. The name derives from a nickname for one of the revolt's leaders, Judas Maccabeus ("the hammer"), although they are more properly called the Hasmoneans. They fought against the dreaded Seleucids, who had succeeded Alexander the Great (1:1–9). The author is not known, but the book was composed somewhere around 100 B.C. or shortly thereafter.

Structure and Content

The book traces the linear history of the Jewish revolt against the Seleucids, especially the hated Antiochus IV. His subjects often derided him with the nickname *epimanēs* (madman) rather than his self-designation Epiphanes (God made manifest). First Maccabees begins with a record of Antiochus's terrible deeds (ch. 1). The most outrageous of these was the desecration of the (rebuilt) Temple in Jerusalem with Gentile images.

The next section (ch. 2) traces the beginnings of the revolt under Mattathias and his sons. Mattathias was from a pious priestly family who strongly resented the encroachment of pagan Hellenistic influences on Jewish society.

The third section (3:1–9:22) picks up after Mattathias's death with his son Judas leading the revolt. Judas achieved the nickname "the hammer," probably because of his fierce fighting tactics. The name stuck with his brothers and the family.

After Judas's death in battle, his brother Jonathan succeeded him. His exploits are detailed in the fourth section (9:23–13:30) until he is succeeded by another brother, Simon.

The final section (13:31–16:24) recounts the independence of Judea and the establishment of the Hasmonean rule under the leadership of Simon, whom the Jews make their high priest. The book concludes with Simon's assassination and the accession to leadership of his son John Hyrcanus.

Interpretation

Some readers may find it difficult to discern a religious message in the midst of the secular history narrated in 1 Maccabees. One must look a little deeper, however, than the surface story.

TITLE: The First Book of Maccabees

AUTHOR: Unknown

DATE: Ca. 100 B.C.

STRUCTURE:

1:1–64	Antiochus IV Epiphanes and the desecration of the Temple
2:1–70	Mattathias initiates a revolt
3:1–9:22	Judas Maccabeus leads the revolt
9:23–13:30	Jonathan leads the revolt
13:31–16:24	Independence and Hasmonean leadership

THEMES: Heroism in the face of adversity, trust in God

While this book contains important historical information about the time period it covers, it is also a record of the Jews' struggle against foreign pagan influences that threatened their faith. The Seleucids fostered Hellenistic culture, and many Jews found it attractive. Some Jews, however, rejected such "modern" ideas. The Maccabeans were in some ways idealists who wanted to preserve the most important of their traditions. They were willing to fight and die for these cherished ideals. The book recounts their deeds not simply from a human standpoint; it also shows how they relied on God to help them surmount the incredible odds against them. Ultimately, the message is to trust God entirely and be courageous in defending your faith.

Exercise

Read 1 Macc 3:1–9. What does this "song" say about Judas? Do you think it is factual? How are heroes generally remembered?

2 Maccabees

Second Maccabees is less unified than 1 Maccabees, but it picks up Jewish history in the time of the Hasmoneans. It covers roughly the twenty-year span from 180 to 160 B.C. The unknown author claims to summarize in one book a five-volume Jewish history by an otherwise unknown Jason of Cyrene (2:23). This

---

TITLE: The Second Book of Maccabees

AUTHOR: Unknown, but claims to digest a five-volume history by Jason of Cyrene

DATE: Ca. 100 B.C.

STRUCTURE:

1:1–2:18	Letters to the Jews in Egypt
2:19–10:9	The Maccabean revolt and the purification of the Temple
10:10–15:39	The leadership of Judas and the defeat of Nicanor

THEMES: Heroism in the face of adversity, trust in God, the glory of martyrdom, heavenly reward for the just

---

book was composed sometime after 1 Maccabees, around 100 B.C. or shortly thereafter. Although it covers some of the same incidents as 1 Maccabees, scholars generally judge 2 Maccabees less reliable for historical evidence.

Structure and Content

This book can be divided into three main sections. The first (1:1–2:18) records two letters sent to the Jews in Egypt from those in Jerusalem. These contain instructions on how to celebrate the feasts of Booths and Hanukkah.

The second section (2:19–10:9) introduces the contents of the book with a preface from the compiler (2:19–32). He explains his method and purpose and then sets out to record many incidents of the time period covered in his narrative. Most noteworthy in this section are the gory stories of martyrdom, especially of the old man Eleazar (6:18–31) and the seven brothers and their mother (7:1–42). This section climaxes with the purification of the Temple after the death of Antiochus Epiphanes.

The final section (10:10–15:39) records the many exploits of Judas and his ultimate defeat of Nicanor, the Seleucid general. A brief epilogue (15:38–39) rounds out the story with an apology of sorts: "If it is well told and to the point, that is what I myself desired; if it is poorly done and mediocre, that was the best I could do."

Interpretation

Despite the author's apology, many readers have found 2 Maccabees inspiring because of the tales of martyrdom. Early Christians, in particular, facing martyrdom themselves, could take some inspiration from the Jewish martyrs and all they endured to preserve their faith. An interesting aspect of 2 Maccabees is the notion that the just will receive an eternal reward for all they endure in this world. This idea, which prefigures the Christian teaching of an afterlife, emerged in late Judaism. The context for such a belief was the struggle to maintain their faith in the midst of the oppressive pagan influences of the Hellenistic world. Second Maccabees is really an attempt to encourage and inspire Jews facing such odds to remain faithful and courageous, for God will ultimately grant them victory.

Exercise

Read 2 Macc 6:18–31. How do you respond to the account of the torture and death of Eleazar? Do you find it heroic or foolish? How would you use such a story to make a point about faith?

Chapter 7

THE PROPHETS

The second major division of books in the Bible is the Prophets (Hebrew, *Nebi'im*). Fifteen of the forty-six books in the OT have the names of prophets in their title. Three of them are very large books: Isaiah, Jeremiah, Ezekiel. The remaining twelve are much smaller in size and are grouped under the heading, "the Minor Prophets" or "the Book of the Twelve." Despite their brevity, they are not minor in significance. Three other books are usually included among the Prophets — Lamentations, Baruch, and Daniel — even though they are different types of literature. The Jewish tradition included Daniel and Lamentations, for instance, among the "Writings" (see appendix A, p. 233). Daniel reflects a type of biblical writing called "apocalyptic" literature (described below, p. 102), while Lamentations contains five poetic laments about the destruction of Jerusalem. Before examining the individual books themselves, let's get an overview of prophecy and prophets.

What Is a Prophet?

Most likely we associate the notion of prophet with predicting the future. Most people think prophets have special knowledge to forecast the future. This understanding is not far removed from a palm reader, soothsayer, or seer. This aspect is only one small part of what the biblical prophets represent. More essential to the description is one who speaks for God. In fact, the Greek root of the word prophet (*prophētēs*) literally means "to speak for" (*pro* + *phēmi*). Prophets spoke "oracles," that is, oral pronouncements of God's Word. Even the root of the Hebrew word for a prophet (*nabi'*) relates to this sense, meaning actively to "call out" or passively to "be called." The biblical prophets were called by God to speak God's own word. That is their primary identity. True enough, the word they spoke to God's people sometimes concerned the future; it was not, however, a word directed to the indefinite future of thousands of years but to the immediate future.

We probably think of the OT prophets as rather stern men on the fringe of society who spoke harsh, condemnatory words. This stereotype does not exactly fit every case. First of all, some prophets were women. No prophetic book of the Bible bears a woman's name, but the Bible occasionally speaks of significant women prophets. For example, Josiah, the king of Judah, consulted a woman prophet named Huldah for God's Word, and she made a prophetic pronouncement about impending judgment (2 Kgs 22:14–20). She must have been fairly important, for one of the gates to the Temple Mount in Jerusalem eventually bore her name (the Huldah Gate). The prophetic books found in our Bible, however, all have male names attached to them, not surprising in a society dominated by men and a patriarchal perspective.

Another aspect of the normal definition of a prophet also is exaggerated. They were not always negative in their views. God's Word came to them at various times and under different circumstances. Sometimes the message was negative. They gave strict warnings to God's people to stop sinful activity and to keep God's laws (like Jer 9:1–5, the condemnation of corruption). At other times, however, the message was hopeful (like Jer 31:31–34, the new covenant). The prophets themselves insist that God's Word, whatever its content, applied to the current situation in an appropriate fashion. At times the word was *judgment,* at times *salvation.* Thus, the same prophet might receive and deliver a message of judgment one day, but a message of salvation another day. This is not fickle. Rather it shows God's ability to speak an appropriate word to people in any circumstance.

Another aspect of prophecy is that it frequently involved suffering and rejection. Society sometimes marginalized prophets, for the word they spoke was unacceptable. (Are we any different in the way we treat prophetic figures in our day?) Sometimes this opposition took the form of severe physical and psychological persecution. Amaziah the priest opposed Amos and told him to go home where he belonged (Amos 7:12–17). Jeremiah suffered considerable torment many times at the hands of persecutors (see his lament, Jer 20:7–18, and his arrest, Jer 37–38). The Jewish tradition developed a common belief that prophets were routinely persecuted and even put to death (for example, see the fate of Uriah, son of Shemaiah, Jer 26:20–23). The NT gives some evidence of this tradition, too, but it may be stated in exaggerated fashion (Matt 23:37). Prophets did not always have an easy life!

A final introductory comment concerns the writing of the prophetic books. Because prophets *spoke* the Word of God as it came to them in words or visions, we should not be surprised to find that their books were constructed from *oral* tradition. Oracles, the spoken word, are the building blocks of the prophetic books. Prophets did not write oracles but spoke them. Then their disciples or secretaries (scribes who could read and write) recorded the utterances for preservation. A good example is Baruch, who wrote for Jeremiah (see Jer 36:4). In the course of time these scribes would collect words of prophets pronounced over months or years. The prophetic books we have in our Bibles constitute the "classical prophets," sometimes referred to as the "literary prophets." When we read these books, we should keep this process in mind. This can help explain why one oracle might seem contradictory to another or why oracles can stem from entirely different periods of time. Scribes often placed prophetic sayings together according to related themes rather than their original context.

How Do You Recognize a True Prophet?

How do you tell true prophets from false prophets? This question was as crucial in biblical times as it is today. Or how do we know someone speaks *God's* Word rather than his or her own word? Some of the prophetic books themselves speak of conflicts between true and false prophets. The Book of Jeremiah describes the conflict between the prophet Hananiah and the prophet Jeremiah (Jer 28:1–17). Hananiah prophesies that God will break Babylon, the empire that oppresses Judah. Jeremiah, on the contrary, accuses Hananiah of speaking falsely and prophesies Hananiah's impending death. In the end Hananiah dies, and Jeremiah's prophecies are placed in the OT.

The solution the Bible offers to this quandary is the test of time. If a prophet's word comes true, then it is an authentic prophecy and it comes from God (Deut 18:21–22). If it doesn't come true, then it is a fraud. Of course, that's not much comfort in the midst of discerning who is telling the truth, is it? The ultimate test of prophecy is faith in God's Word. The fact that certain prophets' words made it into the Bible and others did not is the product of the Holy Spirit's guidance over time.

Reading the Prophets

Understanding the prophetic word doesn't just involve asking what it means to us today. It would be a mistake to think that the prophetic word was meant *only* for us in our time. Prophets, remember, originally spoke God's Word for their time. While the prophetic message is generally easy to apply to our lives, important clues to proper interpretation are found in the original circumstances that lie beneath the surface of prophetic oracles. To the extent possible, my approach will attempt briefly to place the prophetic books in their original historical context. From there it becomes easier to understand the prophetic words and apply them more adequately to our own day.

Apocalyptic Literature

Above I mentioned apocalyptic literature in connection with the Book of Daniel. We can understand why apocalyptic literature seems to belong to the world of the prophets. It focuses on the future, it predicts God's victory over evil, and it involves prophecies and their interpretation. The word "apocalyptic" comes from the Greek word *apokalypsis,* which means "revelation" or "unveiling." Apocalyptic literature made an early appearance in some prophetic books. In addition to Daniel, parts of Isaiah (Isa 24–27), Ezekiel (Ezek 38–39), and Zechariah (Zech 12–14) reflect an apocalyptic mindset. The NT also contains apocalyptic literature, such as Mark 13 and the Book of Revelation.

What makes this literature apocalyptic? The expression refers to the belief that God *reveals* (takes the veil from their eyes) to certain faithful individuals truths that transcend the immediate experience of suffering and hardship and foretell God's ultimate victory over all evil. Apocalyptic literature always appears in times of persecution, rejection, and severe hardship. Characteristics include:

- *dualism* — defining reality in only two contrasting terms, such as right and wrong, light and darkness, damnation and salvation, with it inevitably turning out according to God's plan;

- *determinism* — the belief that God has preordained history and human beings are helpless to change it;

- *symbolism* — the use of common, concrete images to represent a deeper spiritual meaning;

- *distant historical perspective* — the focus on the distant future rather than the immediate future, when God's victory will arrive and enemies will be vanquished;

- *eschatological judgment* — a belief that the end times (in Greek, *eschaton*) will bring God's day of judgment when the good will be rewarded and the evil punished;

- *pseudonymity* — the writing of literature in someone else's name, normally a hero or well-known figure from the past;

- *strong ethical teaching* — exhorting the readers to remain faithful, live upright lives, and endure whatever suffering comes their way.

If some of these ideas sound familiar to you, it may be because the teaching of Jesus in the NT includes many of these same ideas.

Jesus lived in a time when apocalyptic imagery was popular. It provided images of hope to a people who had suffered for centuries under various foreign rulers. Jesus adopts many of these images but gives them a unique twist reflecting his own intense relationship to God.

The main point is not to confuse apocalyptic literature with the prophets. Although there is a relationship, we must maintain the distinction in order to avoid misinterpretation as much as possible. The prophets very much focused on this world rather than the next.

Isaiah

Isaiah is one of the longest books in the Hebrew Bible. It has also been enormously influential in the history of biblical interpretation and theology. If you remember any of the words to Handel's *Messiah*, which is sung at Christmas and Easter time, you will recognize many of Isaiah's words immortalized in that music.

The prophet himself was an educated, aristocratic advisor to the kings of Judah. He prophesied in and around Jerusalem for forty years. He was married, probably to a woman prophet (8:3), and the names of his children were symbolic of his prophetic message (see 7:3; 8:3).

The Book of Isaiah is actually three books in one. The first part (ch. 1–39) originates from the eighth-century prophet whose name the book bears. But two other anonymous prophets from later periods of history have their words preserved in this book. Second Isaiah was a prophet of the exile about two hundred years after Isaiah of Jerusalem (ca. 540 B.C.). His words (ch. 40–55) focused on the promised restoration of Judah and Jerusalem after the Babylonian exile. Third Isaiah (ch. 56–66), whose real identity is also unknown, came along somewhat later when the restoration of Jerusalem was occurring. Why would these other two prophets have their words preserved in a book that originated with a much earlier prophet? The answer is probably that they and their hearers saw themselves in line with Isaiah's original prophecies. Many of the same themes are found in the three major sections of the book, even though they reflect different time periods.

TITLE: The Book of Isaiah

AUTHOR: Isaiah, son of Amoz, or Isaiah of Jerusalem

DATE: Ca. 740 B.C.

STRUCTURE:

1:1–39:8	Prophecies calling for fidelity
40:1–55:13	Prophecies of restoration (Second Isaiah, or Deutero-Isaiah)
56:1–66:24	Prophecies of vindication (Third Isaiah, or Trito-Isaiah)

THEMES: Holy One of Israel, universal salvation, trust in God, Zion as God's dwelling, hope, God as shepherd

Structure and Content

The three major divisions of the book reflect the three prophets and their respective historical situations. The first thirty-nine chapters stem from Isaiah of Jerusalem, who lived in the middle of the eighth century B.C. at the time of Assyria's rise to power. During his years of prophecy Isaiah constantly warned the kings of Judah against making alliances with foreign nations in order to save themselves from Assyrian rule. Many of Isaiah's prophecies call the people of Judah and their leaders to fidelity to God. "If you do not stand firm in faith, you shall not stand at all" (Isa 7:9). Isaiah sounds this warning despite the fact that at his calling God cautions that the prophetic word will fall on deaf ears (Isa 6:9–10). Isaiah also emphasizes the holiness of God (note a favorite expression, "the Holy One of Israel"). Although Isaiah warns that destruction will come to Judah because of the people's inability to trust wholly in God, his prophecies include magnificent visions of hope. Israel will one day live in light, justice will be established, and Israel will become a means for leading other nations to God (see Isa 9:1–17).

Second Isaiah's message (ch. 40–55) picks up on Isaiah's and applies it to his own day. To a people sitting in exile in Babylon, he speaks of the restoration of Jerusalem like a desert that blooms in spring. God will create a highway of salvation in the desert of suffering and will speak a message of comfort to the chastised people (Isa 40). Unique to Second Isaiah is a series of four "servant songs" (poems) about a mysterious figure whose suffering for the sake of others' sinfulness will restore integrity to God's people (see ch. 42, 49, 50, and 52–53). The exact identity of the servant for Second Isaiah is unknown, but Christians have always applied these songs to Jesus Christ. They are a perfect description of the one who "has borne our infirmities and carried our diseases" (Isa 53:4).

The content of the last chapters (56–66) is similar to Second Isaiah but reflects a slightly later period when the restoration of Jerusalem (symbolized by the name "Zion") was underway. Essentially, Third Isaiah envisions God creating anew ("a new heavens and a new earth," 65:17) and giving people a chance once more to live in righteousness, justice, and peace. The great vision of Isa 61:1–4 about liberty to captives, binding up the brokenhearted, and good news to the oppressed must have been well received by the Jewish exiles as they went home from Babylon to restore their lives.

Interpretation

Like so many of the prophetic books, Isaiah contains a vast number of useful prophecies for varied circumstances. Little wonder that Isaiah is one of the most quoted OT books in the NT. Early Christians found within it prophecies wholly appropriate to their understanding of Jesus. The famous Emmanuel passage (Isa 7:14) probably applied in its original context to King Ahaz's successor as king, but deeper reflection saw in it a foretelling of the birth of the messiah (see Matt 1:23).

We can say the same of other Isaian passages that honor the Davidic king (see Isa 9:6–7 and 11:1–9). The call of Isaiah (Isa 6:1–8) is also an inspiring passage. It sets forth the holiness of God as compared to the sinfulness of human beings. It also shows that God can so cleanse us from sin that we can be made bold, like the prophet, to set out on our own "mission impossible." People may well refuse for a time to listen to the prophetic word, but it is worth proclaiming. The tone of the entire book is ultimately one of hope. Despite the suffering of Israel, despite the tendency to trust in human resources rather than God, God's own power to restore will be victorious. In two other interesting metaphors, Isaiah also sees God as a "mother" who acts tenderly toward her children (46:3–4; 49:15) and a shepherd who gently tends the flock (40:11).

Exercise

Read Isaiah 55:6–11. What does this passage say to you about the power of God's Word? Has the Word ever had this effect in your life?

Jeremiah

Jeremiah is the longest of all the prophetic books of the OT. Jeremiah was from a priestly family from the village of Anathoth of the tribe of Benjamin. In both Jewish and Christian traditions Jeremiah has become the primary model of the suffering prophet. His prophecy led to severe mistreatment, ridicule, and imprisonment. He demonstrates that proclaiming the prophetic Word of God is not an easy task.

Personal information about Jeremiah is relatively abundant, thanks to his personal secretary, the scribe Baruch. Jeremiah was quite young when he received God's call to be a prophet (1:4–10). But he went on to have a lengthy career of more than forty years of prophecy. His legacy shows him to be the prophetic giant of the seventh century B.C. at a time when Babylon was on the rise and threatening Judah's independence. Jeremiah took the highly unpopular position of opposing overconfident reliance upon the Temple (see Jer 7:1–7). Strongly he exhorted the people of Jerusalem to reform their corrupt ways and to stop relying on empty practices of worship. Even the reforms begun by King Josiah in 609 B.C. were not sufficient, in Jeremiah's eyes, to ward off the destruction that was to come. Instead, he urged utter reliance upon God and conversion from within.

Structure and Content

Four large sections stand out in this book. The first part (ch. 1–25) is more autobiographical. Jeremiah's call (1:4–10) has some similarities to the call of Moses (Exod 3:1–4:17). He protests that he is too young and does not have the skill to speak God's Word. God's reply is to ignore the first protest altogether and to assure Jeremiah that God will provide the words for him to speak. No

---

Title: The Book of Jeremiah

Date: 627–585 B.C.

Author: The prophet Jeremiah, son of Hilkiah

Structure:

1:1–25:38	Autobiographical narratives and prophecies
26:1–45:5	Biographical narratives
46:1–51:64	Oracles against the nations
52:1–34	The fall of Jerusalem

Themes: Suffering prophet, power of God's Word, interior conversion, just punishment, new covenant

---

arguing with God when it comes to a prophetic call! He was also very visual in his prophetic ministry. He used concrete images to illustrate his message, such as the good and bad figs (24:1–10) and the cup of wrath (25:15–29).

The next section (ch. 26–45) contains biographical narratives about Jeremiah. Jeremiah's prophecies about the Temple and the coming Babylonian exile did not win him many friends. He suffered greatly for the sake of God's Word, being imprisoned and thrown into a cistern (37:11–38:6). The third section (ch. 46–51) collects together many of Jeremiah's oracles that pronounced judgment upon the nations that opposed Israel. The final passage (ch. 52) was not originally part of the book. It is actually an excerpt from the historical books (2 Kgs 24:18–25:30) that recounts the fall of Jerusalem in 587 B.C. in vivid detail.

Interpretation

Such a large book is difficult to summarize succinctly. Although Israel sometimes tormented its prophets, Jeremiah is remembered most as *the* suffering prophet. His message was often unpopular, and he paid a price for remaining faithful to God's prophetic call. The Babylonian exile was unthinkable to pious Israelites, and it ended up being a terribly traumatic experience. We should not, however, think of Jeremiah only in rather bleak terms. Two other aspects of his prophecy are worth noting. One was the power of his words. One look at the Temple sermon (ch. 7) shows us that Jeremiah could be very specific and very bold. Jeremiah did not mince words. We might consider him a "straight shooter," someone who tells things the way they really are.

Another aspect of his prophecy is the ingrained hope in his oracles of salvation. His famous "new covenant" passage (31:31–34) is a powerful vision of the newness that God can effect in people's lives. In the midst of the exile the Israelites probably thought of the new covenant as a pipe dream, some pie-in-the-sky that is almost impossible to imagine. But Jeremiah spoke of it in intimate terms. God would not need an external agreement written on tablets of stone, but an internal one written on their hearts. The NT makes use of this prophetic concept in the ministry of Jesus (Luke 22:20). Christians believe that Jeremiah's prophecy has come to complete fulfillment in Jesus Christ. The Letter to the Hebrews exploits this imagery extensively, quoting the full passage of Jeremiah (Heb 8:8–13). We can truly say, then, that Jeremiah's influence was far reaching.

Exercise
Read Jer 31:31–34. What image of God does this passage evoke for you? How do you understand Jeremiah's words in the context of your own life? Can you describe ways God has begun anew with you?

Ezekiel

The prophet Ezekiel is one of the most bizarre prophets of the OT. Reading his book requires entering a stranger world than most of the rest of the Bible. Ezekiel is the most visual of the prophets. His book records many *visions,* some of them so strange that some have wondered about the prophet's sanity. But Ezekiel was quite sane, and so is his message. Its strangeness is due rather to the symbolic style of writing found in the book.

Ezekiel, son of Buzi, was a prophet during the exile from about 598 to 571 B.C. He prophesied in Babylon (called the "land of the Chaldeans" in 1:3) where the people of Judah had been taken in exile after the fall of Jerusalem in 587 B.C. He came from a priestly family and may have been deported to Babylon as early as 598 B.C. when the Babylonians carted off some of the elite of society. In exile, of course, the people of Judah no longer had

---

TITLE: The Book of Ezekiel

AUTHOR: Ezekiel, son of Buzi

DATE: 598–571 B.C.

STRUCTURE:
1:1–24:27	Initial prophecies
25:1–32:32	Oracles against the nations
33:1–33	Disaster in Jerusalem
34:1–39:29	Restoration
40:1–48:35	New Temple and new people

THEMES: Sinfulness and repentance, destruction and restoration, eschatological hope, God the shepherd

---

access to the Temple and its entire scheme of worship. Hence, the focus of their religion shifted to the Word of God. Ezekiel is part of that focus on the Word; his words, however, describe not merely sayings or oracles but visions about God's plans for the chosen people.

Structure and Content

This long prophetic book can be divided into five distinct sections. The first section (ch. 1–24) contains the initial prophecies, including Ezekiel's magnificent call by God (1:1–3:11). The immediate effect is to be invited into an almost psychedelic world of strange heavenly creatures, sights, and sounds. The second section contains oracles against foreign nations (ch. 25–32). These are similar to other prophetic oracles that pronounce judgment against the foes of Israel and Judah. The third section is a chapter on coming disaster (ch. 33), but it is followed by several chapters on hope and restoration, constituting the fourth section (ch. 34–39). The final section (ch. 40–48) describes in exquisite detail the new Temple and new community that God will create once the exile is past.

Interpretation

The biggest challenge in understanding Ezekiel is to know the nature of *apocalyptic literature* that I described above in the introduction to prophetic literature (p. 102). This prophetic book contains primarily a message of hope that God delivers through the prophet to the exiles. In their most dire circumstances God tells them through this prophet that they will be restored. From the beginning of this book Ezekiel shows himself to be God's spokesperson. God tells Ezekiel to eat the Word written on a scroll (3:1–3). The Word becomes a vital part of the prophet himself. It tasted sweet as honey but the message was sour indeed: the people are stubborn and do not listen well to God's Word (3:7–9). Note that God addresses Ezekiel frequently as "son of man," translated in the NRSV as "mortal." In Hebrew it is a designation meaning "human being." In Ezekiel it emphasizes the prophet's weak humanity as compared to God's all-powerful divinity. Yet how significant that humans can become vehicles for God's Word! Later in Judaism this expression became a type of messianic title. The Gospels portray Jesus as cryptically referring to himself as "Son of man" in a manner very different from Ezekiel (e.g., Matt 8:20; 9:6).

Over and over again Ezekiel describes being taken by God's Spirit (i.e., God's creative power) to the heavenly realm where he witnesses incredible sights. Angelic beings (called cherubim), spinning wheels, symbolic creatures, and various visions of the siege and destruction of Jerusalem occupy the pages of this prophet. He is the "sentinel" of God (3:17; 33:1–9) who is to give God's warning to Jerusalem because of the peoples' sinfulness (4:1–17; 33:21). Ezekiel is given various images of destruction such as the sword that cuts like a barber's razor (5:1) and the vine thrown into the fire (15:1–8).

Yet there are also marvelous images of hope. The purpose of God's destructive actions against the people of Judah is not to destroy them wholly but to ensure their repentance (33:10–11). Since the traditional shepherds (i.e., kings and religious leaders) of Israel have failed, God asserts that he will shepherd the people (34:1–31). The most striking image of hope in Ezekiel is the valley of the dry bones (37:1–14). God's spirit takes Ezekiel to a valley of destruction, a scene of dried up bones representing the people of Israel. There the prophet witnesses the miraculous resuscitation of the bones as flesh and muscle reappear and God breathes the spirit of life into them. No scene is more earthy. The dead bones come to life, representing the complete restoration of God's chosen people. The image became important in later Christian tradition as a foreshadowing of the resurrection. The plan of the new Temple in ch. 40–48 is less a blueprint than it is a detailed assertion that God will reestablish authentic Temple worship in an even more glorious fashion than before the exile.

Exercise

Read Ezekiel's dramatic story of the dry bones (37:1–14). What similarities and what differences do you see between this story and the Christian belief in the resurrection of the dead? Have you ever tasted the restorative power of God in your life?

Hosea

Hosea was one of the four great eighth-century B.C. prophets, a contemporary of Isaiah, Micah, and Amos. He prophesied to the northern kingdom of Israel at a time when the threat of Assyrian invasion was great. The temptation to abandon the religious traditions of Israel was strong. Hosea warns the people to remain faithful. He emphasizes, moreover, that God is the one who ultimately remains faithful, even when the chosen people go astray.

The most striking feature of this book is Hosea's use of his own experience of marriage as a symbol of Israel's relationship to God. He combines this experience with covenant language for a moving portrait of how God is the ever-faithful one.

Structure and Content

The book divides into two sections of unequal portion. The first section (1:1–3:5) contains biographical and autobiographical information about Hosea and his marriage to Gomer. God instructs the prophet to marry a harlot (1:2–3). Despite her infidelity, the couple had three children, each of whom is given a symbolic name. They name the first son Jezreel (1:4–5), a reminder of the valley where numerous bloody conflicts had taken place. Hosea sees the site as symbolic of Israel's impending defeat. The next child, a daughter, they name Lo-ruhamma (1:6–7). The name means "not pitied," and it represents the state of the people if they abandon their faith in Yahweh. The last child is a son named Lo-ammi which means "not my people" (1:8–9). This child sym-

---

TITLE: The Book of Hosea

AUTHOR: Hosea, son of Beeri

DATE: Ca. 750–735 B.C.

STRUCTURE:
      1:1–3:5   Personal reflections
      4:1–14:9   Oracles of judgment and salvation

THEMES: Covenant, God's faithfulness, idolatry, marriage as a
     symbol of covenantal love

---

bolizes the breaking of the covenant relationship with God. They
will no longer be God's people. These negative images are re-
versed once God decides to initiate another "love affair" with
Israel despite their infidelity (2:14–23).

The second section of the book (4:1–14:9) contains oracles
that alternate between messages of judgment and salvation. They
are less personal than the contents of the first section but no less
potent in their message. Hosea employs strong language to try to
persuade the people to remain faithful to Yahweh and to avert
disaster.

Interpretation

The most distinctive feature of this prophetic book, the marriage
symbolism used for the covenant with God, has great potential.
It also contains a danger for modern ears. Hosea's experience
of the infidelity of his wife is not an indictment against faithless women *as women*, as if men do not themselves go astray.
While God is portrayed as the male wounded party, betrayed by
a faithless harlot wife (Israel), the point is God's faithfulness despite this situation. The highly charged sexual imagery associated
with this section of Hosea is not a description merely of adultery.
Rather, symbolically it represents Israel's flirtation with pagan religious practices that involved the use of cultic prostitutes. This
was an age-old problem in Israel's history — reversion to former
pagan ways. Hosea strongly condemns such practices, using his
own marriage as a symbol of them.

Exercise

Read Hos 2:14–23. The language describes a "seduction" by
God, an attempt by God to allure Israel once more, to put the
spark back in their relationship. How does this passage speak to
you of God's seeking you out? Does God ever speak to your heart
to attract you?

Joel

Not much is known of the prophet Joel, son of Pethuel. This book
is also difficult to date. It reflects a postexilic period but without
many clues as to the specific time and place of its origin.

Joel presents a series of powerful images for reflection. Some
are rather stern apocalyptic images, such as the day of judgment
(1:15), the consuming fire of God (1:19; 2:3), and the call to arms
(3:9). Others more directly exhort, such as the various calls to
repentance (2:1–16). In both instances Joel stands firmly in the
prophetic tradition.

Structure and Content

Joel begins with a lament over the destruction of the land (1:2–
12). This picture fits neatly into the period of the postexilic return
of the people to Judah from Babylon. Yet the text moves quickly
into calls for repentance. Joel calls for traditional signs of repentance to be used, such as fasting and dressing in sackcloth and
ashes (1:13–14). The first part of the book (1:1–2:27) concentrates on this call to conversion. It requires an acknowledgment
of one's sin and a firm resolve to do better in the future.

The second part (2:28–3:8) promises that God will pour out
the Spirit upon the people. Its effect will be to transform their
lives totally. God's Spirit will transfigure young and old, men and
women, even slaves. Heavenly signs (2:30–31) will accompany
this great act, and it will result in the restoration of Judah and
Jerusalem.

The final section of Joel shouts out a call to prepare to do battle
with the forces of evil (3:9–21). It presents an image of a vengeful
God who is willing to oppose the chosen people's enemies in a
holy war.

Title: The Book of Joel

Date: Uncertain; probably ca. 500–350 B.C.

Author: The prophet Joel, son of Pethuel

Structure:

1:1–2:27	Call to repentance and prayer
2:28–3:8	God's Spirit
3:9–21	Holy war

Themes: Repentance, judgment, God's Spirit

Interpretation

The book of Joel presents an example of how tricky biblical interpretation can be sometimes. The section that calls for war preparation (especially 3:9–10) can be very troubling. How are we to understand the words "Beat your plowshares into swords, your pruning hooks into spears" (3:10)? These words seem directly to contradict those of two other prophets, Isaiah and Micah (see Isa 2:4 and Mic 4:3). But this is exactly where we need to exercise caution.

First, the historical context of each passage is different. Isaiah and Micah writing in the eighth century B.C. did not face the same situation as did Joel in the sixth or fifth century B.C. Second, even though the words are the same, the tone is different. The oracles in Isaiah and Micah are an anticipated vision of a future time of peaceful and harmonious existence. Joel's words are a direct call to battle the forces of evil in the "valley of Jehoshaphat," a traditional symbol of judgment. In the desperate postexilic setting of restoration, the people of Judah needed to hear words of encouragement and courageous calls for strength to endure. In each era God provided specific oracles through specific prophets to meet the needs of the day. The words may or may not apply in our own day in the same fashion, but they represent God's faithful presence.

More understandably, Christians use Joel (2:12–18) regularly on Ash Wednesday to initiate the Lenten call for repentance and prayer.

Exercise

Read Joel 2:12–18. How does this traditional call for repentance resound in your own life?

Amos

This short prophetic book is the earliest book of the "classical" prophets of the OT. Amos was a shepherd from Tekoa (1:1; 7:14) in the southern kingdom of Judah. God's Word commanded him to go to the northern kingdom of Israel to prophesy.

Two words easily summarize the basic message of Amos: social justice. Perhaps more than any other prophet, Amos's message is the need for social reform. At the time of his prophetic ministry both kingdoms were in a period of relative political stability and economic security. A chasm had developed between rich and poor. Middle-class business people were abusing their customers. Amos loudly complains that they oppress the weak and abuse the needy (2:6; 4:1), cheat and sell inferior products (8:4–6), accept bribes and promote injustice (5:12). He catalogues the sins of *all* the nations, but he reserves special harsh words for the people of Israel: "You alone have I favored, more than all the families of the earth; therefore I will punish you for all your crimes" (3:2). In other words, Israel's position as God's chosen people does not yield privileges but even greater moral responsibility.

Structure and Content

The book divides neatly into four sections. The first section (1:1–2:16) is a collection of oracles against the surrounding pagan nations. It also includes words of judgment against Israel and Judah for their crimes. The oracles against the nations indicate that God's moral law applies not only to the chosen ones but to all nations. Amos uses the image of fire to represent God's judgment against the nations, symbolizing the Assyrian destruction of the lands. Notice repeated phrases about judgment: "I will not revoke my word"; "Yet you returned not to me"; "on that day." Little wonder that Amos comes across as "Mr. Doom and Gloom" among the OT prophets.

The second section (3:1–6:14) contains various words and

TITLE: The Book of Amos

DATE: Ca. 750 B.C.

AUTHOR: The prophet Amos of Tekoa

STRUCTURE:
1:1–2:16	Oracles against the nations
3:1–6:14	Words and woes
7:1–9:8	Visions
9:9–15	Epilogue

THEMES: Social justice and ethical responsibility, judgment, "the day of the Lord"

---

pronouncements of "woe" against the people of Israel. In each instance Amos singles out the multiple ways in which Israel has violated God's laws. The third section (7:1–9:8) records several symbolic visions. God gives the prophet these visions to symbolize the fate of Israel (locusts, fire, measuring line, ripe fruit). The final section (9:9–15), an epilogue, provides a more hopeful vision of the restoration of Israel, but it stems from a later time when the sensitivities of scribes preferred Hollywood-like positive endings to biblical books.

Interpretation

Amos clearly has a sobering view of moral responsibility. Jews and Christians alike respect his message for its strong social content. Accepting that the epilogue is a later addition to the original book, its message is more hopeful in tone than the rest of the book. We can thus summarize the main teaching of Amos as judgment against all who do not practice their religious beliefs by leading an ethical way of life. Amos warns that a day of reckoning will come. The "day of the Lord" will be a day of judgment and darkness (5:18, 20). He cautions against taking refuge in religious practices alone. Offering sacrifices to God does not suffice (5:21–25). We must practice what we preach. "If you would offer sacrifices, then let justice surge like water ... " (5:24). There can be no separation between God's demands and human actions, between religion and social responsibility.

Some readers might be upset at the thought that Amos

preached a pretty negative word. His focus is on judgment rather than salvation. But he couches his message in the context of repeated calls for conversion (5:4, 6, 14). Amos also seems to hold out the possibility that a small remnant of Israel (the *anawim*) will be found faithful and will not suffer total destruction (3:12; 5:3). Yet we have to admit that Amos's prophetic oracles sound dire warnings to those who fail to exercise justice in their lives.

Exercise

Read Amos 5:21–27. How do these words apply to your own life today?

Obadiah

Obadiah is the shortest book in the Hebrew Bible. It contains only twenty-one verses. The book enunciates a vision of God's judgment that will come upon Edom, a neighboring country southeast of Judah. The date is about the time of the destruction of Jerusalem (587 B.C.).

The sentiments expressed in this book are similar to parts of Jeremiah (Jer 49:7–10, 17). Edom may have assisted the Babylonians in the destruction of Jerusalem, or at least benefited from it by taking over territory that had once belonged to Judah (11; note that Obadiah contains no chapters, only verses). The real hurt in this action is that the Edomites were related to ancient Israel through Esau (Gen 25:30; 36:1). The prophet Obadiah is not otherwise known in the Bible, even though a number of other biblical personages have the same name. His name probably means "servant of Yahweh," an apt description of his self-identity.

Structure and Content

The book contains no narrative preface to set the context for the oracles contained in it. Instead, the phrase "the vision of Obadiah" begins the book (1).

This small book can be divided into three sections. Section one (1–14) contains the oracle against Edom. Edom's proud and haughty attitude will end in destruction. The prophet cries out:

TITLE: The Book of Obadiah

AUTHOR: Obadiah

DATE: 587 B.C.

STRUCTURE:

Vv. 1–14	Oracle against Edom
Vv. 15–16	Oracle against the nations
Vv. 17–21	Victory of house of Jacob

THEMES: Betrayal brings judgment, ultimate victory of God's people

---

> Though you soar aloft like the eagle,
> though your nest is set among the stars,
> from there I will bring you down, says the LORD. (4)

The prophet envisions a day (remember the "day of the Lord" from Amos) on which God will not only punish Edom for its mistreatment of God's chosen people, but also all the nations will be punished. This latter oracle is the second part of the book (15–16). Finally, the last section (17–21) tells of Israel's ultimate victory. God will reestablish Mount Zion as a dwelling, and the exiles shall return victorious.

Interpretation

Obadiah is generally not regarded as an important prophetic book. It lacks the appeal of many other prophetic books, yet we should not relegate it to oblivion. Its prophetic message is primarily directed to a foreign nation. It indicates that God's law ultimately applies in broad ways beyond the boundaries of Israel. Obadiah thus provides some testimony to the universalism of God's message, which entails both responsibility and accountability.

Exercise

Read Obad 10–14. It describes events during the destruction of Jerusalem. Note the use of the term "brother" throughout. Have you ever felt betrayed by a close relative or friend? How does this passage speak to such situations?

Jonah

Jonah traditionally is numbered among the minor prophets. Many have questioned whether it is accurately seen as a prophetic book. Is it not better understood as a symbolic fictional story? Scholars have not ascertained that Jonah was a real, living prophet. The book exhibits a fictional quality to it. There are certainly some humorous elements. The whole idea of a prophet jumping on a ship to run away from God, then being tossed overboard and swallowed by a great fish, and finally fulfilling the task only to have the people of Nineveh repent and God's judgment averted — all this may have had an audience of OT Jewish folk laughing heartily as the story was told again and again.

We cannot assign a firm date to the book. Sometime after the exile is likely, but this is purely an educated guess. The story is coherent and very literate. Its message has not only entertained through the ages but has also inspired.

Structure and Content

Think of the story of Jonah as a mini-play in four scenes. Each chapter constitutes a scene. Scene one (ch. 1) shows Jonah fleeing from God's request to preach repentance to the people of Nineveh. We must remember that Nineveh was the ancient capital of the dreaded Assyrian empire that had destroyed the northern kingdom of Israel in the eighth century B.C. The task would indeed be daunting for a Jewish prophet to go preach repentance in the heart of the enemy camp. But God punishes the prophet's attempted flight by having him swallowed by a "large fish" (not necessarily a whale).

In scene two (ch. 2) Jonah pours out his heart to God in a prayer of supplication from the belly of the fish, and God speaks to the fish, which spews him out on dry ground. Scene three (ch. 3) shows Jonah finally doing what God had asked all along. He goes to Nineveh, a huge city, crying out for repentance. Lo and behold, the entire city puts on the clothes of repentance, from the greatest (the king) to the least (even to the animals!). Seeing this conversion, God repents of the intention to destroy Nineveh.

The final scene (ch. 4) brings God and Jonah once more in direct confrontation. Jonah complains of God's mercy. He had been sitting on a hill awaiting a great fireworks of destruction, only to

---

Title: The Book of Jonah

Author: Unknown, perhaps Jonah son of Amittai, a prophet

Date: Unknown, perhaps postexilic ca. fifth century b.c.

Structure:

1:1–17	Jonah's flight from God
2:1–10	Jonah's prayer and rescue
3:1–10	Nineveh's repentance
4:1–11	Jonah's response and God's mercy

Themes: Repentance, prophetic tasks cannot be avoided, God's universal mercy

---

be sorely disappointed. But God chastises Jonah's anger. God reminds him: "And should I not be concerned about Nineveh, that great city, in which there are more than a hundred and twenty thousand persons who do not know their right hand from their left, and also many animals?" (4:11) (Doesn't this bring at least a smile to your face?)

Interpretation

Varying interpretations of Jonah abound. Its primary teaching is that God's mercy knows no boundaries. Our desire to see justice done against the wicked simply does not conform to God's mercy. I think of this book also as a humorous reflection on the difficulty of being prophetic. Prophets are not always dour people, overly serious and stern. Prophets often preferred to decline God's command — especially in cases of pronouncing judgment against a haughty people. But you cannot escape God's call. As in Francis Thompson's poem "The Hound of Heaven," God hunts us down and makes us confront our own weakness and insecurity. If you think of Jonah as a parable-like story, I believe you will find wonderful riches to reflect on. Even the most wicked of people might just find a conscience and repent.

Exercise

Read the entire book of Jonah. It is very short. Think of times when you may have fled or been tempted to flee from God. How did it feel? How did God finally seek you out?

Micah

Micah was the last of the great eighth-century B.C. prophets. Some of the materials in his book resemble those from his contemporaries, Isaiah and Amos. Micah came from the small village of Moresheth in the hill country, but his message was directed broadly to authorities, such as political and religious leaders (ch. 3) and to all who engaged in unjust practices. Jeremiah (Jer 26:18) mentions Micah briefly as the prophet who predicted to King Hezekiah that Judah would one day be destroyed.

Structure and Content

After the brief introduction (1:1) that identifies the prophet and his times, the book is divided into two sets of oracles (1:2–5:15; 6:1–7:17). Thematically, they are very similar. They alternate between judgment and salvation. On the one hand, Micah bemoans the social ills that afflict the nation. He decries unjust business practices (2:1–2; 6:11–12), and he warns against trusting any human beings because of their utter corruption (7:1–7). On the other hand, he believes that God will ultimately make Israel and Judah victorious over their enemies. Even if Assyria should triumph (as it did over Israel a few years later), still God will raise up the people once more and restore their fortunes (5:5–6).

One aspect of Micah's complaints against the people is the form they take. In the style of a lawsuit brought against a criminal, God pleads his case in the presence of creation ("mountains" and "hills"). This form of prophetic literature, called a lawsuit (Hebrew *rib*), is a moving image (see 6:1–5):

> O my people, what have I done to you?
> In what have I wearied you? Answer me!

The book concludes on a positive note with a prayer addressed directly to God (7:18–20). It praises God's faithfulness and God's ability not to remain angry forever.

Interpretation

Typical of the prophetic literature, the book alternates with messages of judgment and salvation. Like Amos, Micah was concerned about social injustice (ch. 2 and 7). In light of this situation, Micah has given us the classic response about what God's

---

TITLE: The Book of Micah

AUTHOR: Micah of Moresheth

DATE: Ca. 725 B.C.

STRUCTURE:

1:1	Title
1:2–5:15	First set of oracles of judgment and salvation
6:1–7:17	Second set of oracles of judgment and salvation
7:18–20	Prayer of God's fidelity

THEMES: Just judgment for sins, the faithful remnant, God's fidelity

---

expectations really are. Rather than empty sacrifices and hollow rituals, something more important should rule our behavior:

> He has told you, O mortal, what is good;
>   and what does the LORD require of you
>   but to do justice, and to love kindness,
>   and to walk humbly with your God? (6:8)

Can you think of any better shorthand summary of moral responsibility in the sight of God?

One of the most beautiful passages in Micah (4:1–4) also is found in Isaiah (Isa 2:2–4). It is the famous passage that speaks of the reestablishment of the Lord's mountain and a universal time of peace among all nations. The verbal similarities are so close that some have wondered which prophet copied from the other. This may be an example of how prophetic oracles could get confused over time and would be incorporated into a different setting. Regardless of which prophet originated the oracle, it remains a beautiful vision of world peace.

Exercise

Read Mic 4:1–4. Use your imagination to visualize how the prophet views the establishment of peace in some future time. Is the vision realistic? Can you find any role for yourself in this vision?

Nahum

Nahum is a single-minded prophet. His singular preoccupation
was the destruction of the dreaded enemy of Israel and Judah,
Assyria. Prophesying in 620 B.C. that Assyria would be destroyed
by God, the prophecy came true in 612 B.C. when Babylon
overwhelmed the weakened Assyrian empire.

Little is known of Nahum of Elkosh. The book is entitled both
an "oracle" and a "vision" (1:1). Nahum assures his audience
that God's vengeance will take place against Assyria, symbolized
by the capital city, Nineveh.

Structure and Content

I divide the book into three parts in addition to the title (1:1).
The first part of the book begins with an *acrostic poem,* that is,
a poem that uses the letters of the alphabet to begin each verse
(1:2–11). The poem may be incomplete, but it asserts that God
is by nature an avenging God. Although slow to anger, God ultimately will act against evildoers because God is all-powerful.
The second part (1:12–15) is an oracle that promises that Judah
will not have to fear enemies any longer. The third and final part
(2:1–3:19) is the extended oracle that foretells the destruction of
Assyria. In vivid detail the prophet describes the sack of Nineveh
(2:3–9; 3:2–3, 13–15).

Interpretation

Keeping in mind that Assyria was one of the cruelest and most
feared empires in the ancient world, the prophet's angry words
against the Assyrians are fully understandable. The Assyrian destruction of Israel in 721 B.C. was still a sore remembrance for the
people of Judah a century later when Assyria was on the decline.
In OT theology God is indeed vengeful. This means that God ultimately acts on behalf of God's chosen people. Vengeance is God's
(not ours!) because it is part of the bargain of covenant. Thus to
call God "a jealous and avenging God" (1:2) is to assert God's
desire to protect God's chosen people.

TITLE: The Book of Nahum

AUTHOR: Nahum of Elkosh

DATE: 620 B.C.

STRUCTURE:

1:1	Title
1:2–11	Poem on God's vengeance
1:12–15	The hope of Judah
2:1–3:19	Destruction of Assyria

THEMES: God is vengeful against the chosen people's enemies, destruction of Nineveh

---

Exercise

Read Nah 1:2–5. How does this description of God coincide with your own understanding of God? Can you find positive images in this passage that can be applied to God?

Habakkuk

Habakkuk is explicitly labeled a prophet twice in the book (1:1; 3:1). As with many of Israel's prophets, little personal information is known of him. He prophesied immediately before the exile, around 608–598 B.C. Unlike Nahum and Zephaniah, who specifically prophesy against Assyria, Habakkuk's oracles are more general. He prophesied near the end of Assyria's power and at the beginning of Babylon's rise to power (1:6). Habakkuk's main concern seems to be why God allows evil to flourish while the people cry out for help.

Structure and Content

This book can be divided into three parts. After a title (1:1), the first part is the prophet's plea to God (1:2–2:1). He begins with a familiar complaint, "O LORD, how long shall I cry for help and you will not listen?" (1:2) Where are you when we need you, God? But he ends this part with a stance of patient expectation that God will answer his complaint (2:1).

TITLE: The Book of Habakkuk

AUTHOR: Habakkuk the prophet

DATE: 608–598 B.C.

STRUCTURE:
1:1	Title
1:2–2:1	Habakkuk's plea
2:2–20	God's response
3:1–19	Habakkuk's prayer

THEMES: The problem of evil, God's power, faith in times of crisis

---

The second part contains God's response (2:2–20). God gives the prophet a "vision" to share with the people (2:3). The advice contained in the vision is standard biblical advice to remain moral and upright in the sight of God.

The third part of the book is the prophet's prayer (3:1–19), which was to be accompanied by musical instruments (3:19). It is similar to some of the psalms. The prayer especially exalts God who is all-powerful and who controls even the forces of nature.

Interpretation

The tone of Habakkuk is somewhat similar to the wisdom litera-ture of Israel (see ch. 8 below). Like the sages Habakkuk wrestles with the perennial question of why God allows evil to flourish and good people to suffer despite their goodness. He complains, "The wicked surround the righteous — therefore judgment comes forth perverted" (1:4). Habakkuk's prayer is one of surrender to the grandeur of God even when we cannot finally understand God's ways. In the end the prophet speaks firmly of faith (3:17–19). This thought was not lost on St. Paul, who quotes Habakkuk 2:4 in the context of developing his understanding of justification by faith (Rom 1:17).

Exercise

Read Hab 3:17–19. How does this part of the prophet's prayer speak to you of the essential nature of faith?

Zephaniah

Zephaniah, son of Cushi, is another of the minor prophets about whom little is known. He prophesied in Judah around 640–622 B.C. at a time when the despised Assyrian empire was in serious decline.

With language reminiscent of Amos, Zephaniah speaks of "the great day of the Lord" that is near, when God will bring judgment (1:7, 14). He lived at the time of the beloved King Josiah. Josiah had initiated reforms in Judah to cast off idolatrous practices that had crept into Jewish religion at that time. Zephaniah, too, condemns similar idolatry (1:4–6).

Structure and Content

This short book contains several oracles directed to Judah and to Judah's enemies. After an introductory verse (1:1), the first part condemns Judah's idolatrous practices that have led the people away from God and warns of an impending day of judgment (1:2–18). The second part is directed to those who have threatened Israel in its history, and it also predicts doom (2:1–3:7). The prophet includes in this threatening vision, however, Jerusalem itself (3:1–7) because:

> It has listened to no voice;
>   it has accepted no correction.
> It has not trusted in the LORD;
>   it has not drawn near to its God. (3:2)

The final section sounds a more positive note (3:8–20). The punishment of the nations will actually bring about conversion (3:8–13), leading the prophet to proclaim a song of joy that God will once more restore the fortunes of the chosen people (3:14–20).

Interpretation

Although Zephaniah is not one of the major voices in prophecy, this book has proved inspirational in history. The famous section on judgment (1:15–16), which in the Latin Vulgate translation reads "Dies irae, dies illa," inspired Mozart, for instance, to write the magnificent hymn by the same title in his requiem. The tension between the awesome day of judgment that will come

TITLE: The Book of Zephaniah

AUTHOR: Zephaniah, son of Cushi

DATE: Ca. 640–622 B.C.

STRUCTURE:

1:1	Title
1:2–18	Judgment against Judah
2:1–3:7	Judgment against Israel's enemies and Jerusalem
3:8–20	Cleansing of the nations and the joy of restoration

THEMES: The great day of God's judgment, the joy of God's mercy

and the promised cleansing that it will bring has made for intensive reflection among both Jewish and Christian interpreters. Both stances are part of God's message. Zephaniah's own words describe the tension well:

> That day will be a day of wrath,
>   a day of distress and anguish,
> a day of ruin and devastation,
>   a day of darkness and gloom,
> a day of clouds and thick darkness,
>   a day of trumpet blast and battle cry....
>
>   (1:15–16)

> Sing aloud, O daughter Zion;
>   Shout, O Israel!
> Rejoice and exult with all your heart,
>   O daughter Jerusalem!
> The LORD has taken away the judgments against you....
>
>   (3:14–15)

Exercise

Read Zeph 3:11–13. This passage speaks of becoming humble before God. How does humility relate to Israel's sin of idolatry? Do you see any connections in your own life?

Haggai

Rarely in OT studies can one date a prophet so precisely as Haggai. He prophesied during the postexilic period from August 28 to December 19, 520 B.C. How's that for precision? The historical situation after King Cyrus of Persia and his successors allowed the Jews to return to their homeland provides the rather secure dating of this prophet. Jewish leadership at that time centered on two figures, a governor named Zerubbabel and a high priest named Joshua. Haggai's prophetic words are directed to them specifically but also to the entire Jewish community that returned to Judah.

Haggai's prophecy concerned two realities. The first was the urgent but hopeful message to the postexilic community to focus on rebuilding the Temple in Jerusalem. The Persians had provided some financial assistance and the obvious encouragement of their freedom, but the task that confronted the exiles when they returned home was enormous. The city and the Temple lay in ruins. Their own livelihood had to be built up from scratch. God's Word to Haggai was that the Temple should be rebuilt first. Only then would full restoration arrive.

The second word was a warning to the leaders and to the people. Do not hold back from God if you want to be blessed. God will grant prosperity as in days of old (2:5), but the people had to live up to their responsibilities as well.

Structure and Content

Three sections comprise this little prophetic book. The first (1:1–2:9) is devoted to the task of rebuilding the Temple. Haggai's words could sound familiar in our own consumer-oriented society: "You eat, but you never have enough; you drink, but you never have your fill..." (1:6). The problem was that the people were too preoccupied with rebuilding their own lives rather than the Temple (1:9). Their focus was on themselves rather than on God. Haggai calls the people to task, but God goes on to promise not only a restoration to the "former glory" but a surpassing of it (2:9).

The second section (2:10–19) rebukes the people for withholding their gain from God but again ends in a promise that God will provide for the people's restoration. The final section (2:20–23) is an oracle of promise given to Zerubbabel the governor of

TITLE: The Book of Haggai

DATE: August 28–December 19, 520 B.C.

AUTHOR: The prophet Haggai

STRUCTURE:

1:1–2:9	Rebuilding the Temple
2:10–19	Warning and promise
2:20–23	Promise to Zerubbabel

THEMES: Hope in God, restoration, the Temple

Judah. He is a chosen instrument of God's work; he should thus have confidence in God.

Interpretation

The simplicity of Haggai's message might be deceiving. How easy it is in every age to become so distracted with making a living and getting ahead in life that we can forget the primacy of God. We can well imagine the urgency the Jews felt in attempting to rebuild their lives after the devastation of Babylon. Haggai reminds us that single-minded hope in God should be primary in all circumstances in life, then all else will fall into place. To the leaders and people together he cried out: "take courage" (2:4).

Exercise

Read Hag 1:2–6. How realistic in your life is it to put God's demands first?

Zechariah

Zechariah was the contemporary of Haggai. The historical circumstances are thus quite similar. He prophesied in the postexilic period when Judah was in the process of being restored with the permission of the Persian empire. Unlike Haggai's simple and rather clear prophecies, Zechariah's are more symbolic and visual.

Like some other books of the OT (remember Isaiah?), Zechariah is actually more than one book. Most likely it is compilation in two parts of two different prophets. The first part (ch. 1–8)

Title: The Book of Zechariah

Date: 520–518 B.C.

Author: The prophet Zechariah, son of Berechiah

Structure:

1:1–8:23	Visions of restoration
9:1–11:17	Oracles concerning judgment and the shepherds
12:1–14:21	Oracle of final victory

Themes: Restoration, judgment on Israel's enemies, true and false shepherds

---

stems from the prophet we know as Zechariah. The second part (ch. 9–14) comes from a later anonymous prophet whom scholars designate as Second Zechariah (Deutero-Zechariah). A brief comparison shows some important differences:

Zech 1–8	*Zech 9–14*
mostly prose	mostly poetry
visions	no visions
rebuilding the Temple	the Temple is not an issue
hope of Davidic king	no mention of Davidic king
Zerubbabel mentioned	Zerubbabel absent
Jerusalem is central	all of Judah is central

Structure and Content

The first part of the book (ch. 1–8) presents a series of eight visions interspersed with other messages and oracles. The visions are symbolic representations of aspects of the restoration of Jerusalem and the Temple. For example, the vision of the man with a measuring line (2:1–5) represents the length and breadth of the restored city of Jerusalem, which God is about to rebuild. Likewise, the vision of the two olive trees (4:11–14) depicts the two anointed ones blessed with oil (Zerubbabel the governor and Joshua the high priest) who will oversee the restoration.

The second section (ch. 9–14) is filled with oracles and other prophetic messages that the NT writers saw as applicable to Jesus. The coming of a humble messiah-king (9:9; see Matt 21:5) and one who would truly shepherd the people (11:4–17) but who would be struck down himself (13:7) are present images of hope that Christians quickly saw fulfilled in Jesus Christ. For the Jews returning from exile, these images represented God's promise to restore them and watch over them.

The final section (12:1–14:21) speaks of God's final victory in the last days when Israel will be vindicated and all its enemies defeated.

The tone of the entire book of Zechariah is different from much of the prophetic literature. With its visions and strong symbolism, it is more akin to apocalyptic literature, the literature of hope that developed later in times of severe persecution.

Interpretation

Zechariah presents a combination of hopefulness and stern warning. It moves between the encouraging words to flee from the tyranny of exile (2:6–13) to the depressing explanation that the people's own failure to keep God's commandments led to the experience of defeat under Babylon (7:8–14). The highly symbolic visions can be difficult to interpret apart from their historical circumstances. Nonetheless, the first part of the book focuses largely on the good news that God will restore Jerusalem fully, while the second part establishes a more distant hope that "on that day" (13:2; 14:1) God ultimately will be victorious over evil. If the separate sections originate with two separate prophets in two separate times, they are nonetheless soul mates with regard to their confidence in God's power.

Exercise

Read Zech 5:1–4. What do you think the flying scroll represents? Is it a sign of judgment or of hope?

Malachi

Malachi is the last book of "the Book of the Twelve Minor Prophets." It is also the final book of the Hebrew Bible. Its title does not actually represent a name but a function. The Hebrew word *malachi* means "my messenger." It may represent a generic understanding that the book stands in the prophetic tradition of God's messenger.

TITLE: The Book of Malachi

DATE: Unknown

AUTHOR: Unknown, probably postexilic

STRUCTURE:

1:1–2:17	Irresponsibility of the priests and people
3:1–4:4	The promised messenger and the day of judgment
4:5–6	Elijah will return

THEMES: Authentic worship, a coming day of judgment, responsibilities of religious leaders, Elijah will return

The book is difficult to date. It stems from the postexilic time after the restoration of the Temple when something had gone awry in the quality of worship. Its position at the end of the Old Testament became important in the formation of the canon. Note that it ends on a positive note of expectation: "Lo, I will send you the prophet Elijah before the great and terrible day of the LORD comes . . . so that I will not come and strike the land with a curse" (4:5–6). According to 2 Kgs 2:11, Elijah had been taken up into heaven in a fiery chariot, and the expectation of his glorious return gradually developed in Judaism. A later scribe sounded this hopeful note in Malachi so that the last word in the Hebrew Bible would not be one of judgment (see 4:1–4). The expectation of Elijah, of course, is exactly where the Christian scriptures pick up with the precursor of Jesus, John the Baptist as an Elijah figure. Thus, the last note heard in the OT is reprised as the first note in the NT.

Structure and Content

Malachi begins with a strong statement by God: "I have loved you, says the LORD" (1:2). Yet immediately the oracles turn to the disappointments that the chosen people have caused God. In particular, Malachi condemns the irresponsible actions of the priests (1:6–2:9).

The second part of the book (3:1–4:4) promises that God will come in judgment. Malachi accuses the people of failure to live up to the standard prophetic ideal of care for the orphan, the widow, the oppressed, and the stranger. Yet a call to repentance accompanies this stern message: "Return to me, and I will return to you, says the LORD of hosts" (3:7). At the end, the unremitting tone of warning of judgment is softened by the scribal addition of the promise of Elijah's return (4:5–6).

Interpretation

Two observations about Malachi are striking. One is the presence of strong words directed against the religious leaders of his day, especially the priests. Even though God had restored the Temple and sacrificial worship, those charged with the special duties of officiating at worship were not fulfilling their obligations faithfully. The very ones who should be most honorable had become the least trustworthy. "Oh, that someone among you would shut the temple doors so that you would not kindle fire on my altar" (2:10). I think any of us in positions of religious leadership might be a little nervous in Malachi's presence.

The second observation is the need for fidelity to the covenant. Malachi specifically mentions marriage and divorce (2:14–16) as a way of understanding the relationship between God and God's people. The prophet reminds the people not to be faithless (2:16).

Exercise

Read Mal 3:8–10. What does it mean to "rob God"? Can you think of examples how people do this today?

Lamentations

The Book of Lamentations has a most appropriate name. It is a collection of poetic laments over the fate that has befallen Jerusalem at the time of the exile. Traditionally assigned to the prophetic books, its form is more closely related to some of the psalms. What *we* mean by a lament or lamentation is not exactly what the Bible means. We tend to think of a lament as a complaint. We bemoan our fate, complain about our misfortune, argue angrily about our victimization.

In the Bible a lament is not merely a complaint. Rather, it is a faith-filled act in which people pour out their hearts to God and plead for God's mercy. A lament does not merely catalogue one's

TITLE: The Book of Lamentations

AUTHOR: Unknown, but traditionally attributed to Jeremiah by
means of his scribe, Baruch

DATE: Sixth century B.C., after the destruction of Jerusalem

STRUCTURE:

1:1–2:22	Lament for the fate of Jerusalem
3:1–4:22	God's eternal faithfulness
5:1–22	Plea for mercy

THEMES: Just punishment for sin, lament and plea for mercy, God's
faithfulness

misfortune. It places that reality in God's hands and concludes in
praise of God's grandeur, wisdom, and power that are beyond all
human comprehension. The author and date of Lamentations are
unknown, although the book is attributed to Jeremiah.

Structure and Content

This poetic book consists of lengthy lists of the trials endured by
God's people during the destruction of Jerusalem and the exile.
I divide the book into three segments. The first (1:1–2:22) de-
scribes the dire situation of the brokenness of life in the exile. It
concludes with the advice never to cease taking their feelings to
God:

> Cry aloud to the Lord!
>   O wall of daughter Zion!
> Let tears stream down like a torrent day and night!
>   Give yourself no rest, your eyes no respite! (2:18)

The second segment (3:1–4:22) changes the perspective. Although the afflictions are still present and very much on the
speaker's mind, nonetheless the statement of God's fidelity shines
clearly (for example, 3:22–24). Even in the midst of suffering, a
prayer of praise of God arises from the lips of those who are patient. The final segment (5:1–22) is a plea for mercy reminiscent
of the psalms of lament. "Remember, O LORD, what has befallen
us; look and see our disgrace!" (5:1). The speaker goes on to describe the dire situation, with a final plea for restoration if God
has not entirely abandoned the people.

Interpretation

The beginning of this book describes poignantly the situation of Jerusalem after the sack by the Babylonians: "How lonely sits the city that once was full of people!" (1:1). Many Americans might find it difficult to place themselves in the situation assumed and described by this book. Our country has never been invaded and leveled. Indeed, we have not known war on our own soil since the Civil War. The Jewish people, on the other hand, have had to endure a long, hard life of irrational persecution. This sad history stretches from the earliest days of anti-Semitism to the atrocities of the Holocaust (or Shoah, as the Jews call it) during World War II. Lamentations bears testimony to a people's anguish.

If we cannot identify fully with the pain of persecution on such a massive scale, on a personal level many people know the painful hurt of loss, depression, anxiety, or illness. Many have found themselves in situations in which they can only cry out: Why me (us), Lord? Have you forgotten me (us)? To enter the world of lament is to be able to feel pain and anguish. It is not to deny it, nor is it to revel in it and become masochistic. True lament is based upon an appreciation of the depths of human suffering while never losing sight of faith in God. Some readers might recall the musical and movie *Fiddler on the Roof*. The main character, Tevye, was an expert at lament. He could pour out his heart to God and complain bitterly about the evils befalling his family, and he was very aware of the challenges in life. Yet in the end, he would surrender his pleas to God — the essence of a lament.

Exercise

Read Lam 5:19–22. Can you find any trace of faith on the part of the speaker in this passage? Are you able to pour out your heart to God in times of difficulty in ways that show your continued faith in God? Do you find this easy to do?

Baruch

Baruch was a scribe who wrote for the prophet Jeremiah. Scribes were trained experts who could read and write. Prophets em-

TITLE: The Book of Baruch

AUTHOR: Unknown, but attributed to Baruch, son of Neriah, a scribe and companion of Jeremiah

DATE: Ca. 200 – 60 B.C.

STRUCTURE:

1:1–3:8	Explanation of exile
3:9 – 4:4	Poem in praise of wisdom
4:5–5:9	Poem of consolation and hope
6:1–73	The Letter of Jeremiah

THEMES: Just punishment, suffering, true wisdom, hope

ployed their expertise to record oracles. This book is styled by an anonymous author or authors to represent the time of the Babylonian exile. Actually, it is a collection of mixed writings that date from a later period. The book most likely originated during the time of the Maccabeans, between 200 and 60 B.C.

Structure and Content

The simplest structure for this book is in four parts. The first part is a prose description of how the scroll was read to the exiles in Babylon and was sent back to Jerusalem for public reading (1:1– 3:8). It contains a letter to the remnant of the people in Jerusalem explaining how the catastrophe of the destruction of Jerusalem and the subsequent exile was God's just judgment against Israel because of repeated sinfulness.

The second part (3:9–4:4) contains a lengthy poem more at home in the wisdom literature than among the prophets. It speaks in praise of true wisdom identified as the Law. The third part (4:5–5:9) is an oracle of consolation and hope that promises comfort for Jerusalem one day when the exiles are brought back. The final section (6:1–73) appears in some Bibles entirely separated from Baruch, as an individual item among the OT apocrypha. It contains a letter from the prophet Jeremiah sent to the exiles to bolster their courage. The prophet's words include a judgment against the idols of Babylon. He considers them ultimately powerless before the sight of God. (The Septuagint lists the Letter

of Jeremiah as a separate "book" placed between Baruch and
Lamentations.)

Interpretation

Baruch has never been considered a very important book in the
Bible. Protestants, of course, consider it one of the OT apocryphal
works. Although Catholics consider it inspired scripture, its significance is minor. The book testifies to the ancient form of letters
used for communication. It gives due recognition to the important function of a scribe like Baruch. Without scribes we would
not have the writings in the Bible. Many of the biblical writings,
in fact, initially took shape during the time of the exile. Baruch
also alludes to certain ritual practices that began to be refined at
that time: "And you shall read aloud this scroll that we are sending you, to make your confession in the house of the Lord on the
days of the festivals and at the appointed seasons" (1:14).

Exercise

Read Bar 2:6–10. What tone does this passage communicate?
What effect does the reading have on you, and how would
that compare to the effect upon the people in exile who heard
these words?

Daniel

Despite the title the Book of Daniel is not a prophetic book. Even
ancient tradition evaluated this book from two different perspectives. In the Hebrew Bible, Daniel is listed among the Writings,
not among the Prophets. In the LXX (and most English translations), it appears as the fourth major prophet. The truth is
that this book is the premier example in the OT of *apocalyptic
literature* (see the introduction to the prophets above, p. 102).

The historical context for the origin of this book is the time
of Antiochus IV Epiphanes, a wicked Seleucid king who persecuted the Jews in the second century B.C. (he ruled 175–164 B.C.).
Daniel is actually a tract that symbolically lays out God's victory
over tyrants such as Antiochus. In the guise of covering some four
hundred years of history, from the Babylonian exile to Antiochus,

TITLE: The Book of Daniel

AUTHOR: Unknown, but attributed to a young Jewish hero named Daniel

DATE: Ca. 167–164 B.C.

STRUCTURE:

1:1–6:28	Daniel's experiences in Babylon
7:1–12:13	Dreams and visions of Daniel
13:1–14:42	Other legends of Daniel

THEMES: Courage under pressure, dreams, God's victory over tyranny

the message resounds that God always raises up heroes to defeat tyranny.

Structure and Content

Daniel conveniently divides into three sections. The first (1:1–6:28) contains stories of heroism during the Babylonian captivity. Daniel is introduced as a "wise man," a great interpreter of dreams (2:19). He successfully interprets the Babylonian king's dreams and wins favor. But when the king demands that the Jews worship a golden idol, some of them refuse (ch. 3). The king has them thrown into a fiery furnace, but they miraculously survive and endure the torture, praising God in prayer. (*Note:* Protestants consider 3:24–90, containing the prayer of Azariah and the song of the three Jews, to be apocryphal. Protestant Bibles preserve them separately from Daniel.) Daniel also undergoes tests, such as being thrown into the lions' den (6:16–24) and miraculously surviving.

The second section (7:1–12:13) recounts Daniel's other exploits and his interpretations of various dreams. Daniel's own visions are highly symbolic but are clearly understood as divine interventions to give the people hope. The final section of the book (13:1–14:42) is actually an appendix. Protestant Bibles preserve these chapters separately among the OT apocrypha under two other titles, namely, Susanna, and Bel and the Dragon.

Interpretation

Who has not heard of and used the image of Daniel in the lions' den? It has become a stock metaphor for surviving severe trials or tests. As with all apocalyptic literature, the most important aspect of Daniel is the perspective of hope. It is a tale of heroism, endurance, and irrepressible hope. Just as Daniel could survive innumerable trials and tribulations, so can all who remain faithful to God.

Unfortunately, many interpreters through history have preferred to read Daniel like a blueprint for their own times. They see in the ornate symbolism, the animal imagery, the magical flavor of dreams and fiery tales, a specific prediction about the end of time. During the Cold War, some Americans interpreted this book along with the Book of Revelation as predictions about Communism and the Soviet Union. In approaching the year 2000, others have seen in Daniel and other apocalyptic works dire predictions about the end of the world. All of this is a misunderstanding of the nature of the book. Daniel provides an optimistic message. It portrays God's ultimate victory over evil forces. Such a message can apply to every age, not simply to one age. Yet the essence of the book is not in the details, but in the "big picture." Don't sweat the details, but maintain your faith even in the midst of struggles. God raises up heroes and dreamers in every age. The wisdom is to distinguish the authentic ones from the frauds.

Exercise

Read Dan 6:14–24. Can you identify with Daniel in the lions' den? Have others unfairly persecuted you? How did you survive, and how did God speak to you in this process?

Chapter 8

THE WRITINGS

Job	Song of Songs
Psalms	(Canticle of Canticles)
Proverbs	Wisdom of Solomon
Ecclesiastes	Wisdom of Ben Sira
(Qoheleth)	(Sirach)

The designation "Writings" is admittedly a catch-all expression. As the Bible took shape, the scribes recognized that some books did not fit the categories of Law or Prophets. So they created a general designation to accommodate all the remaining books, *Kethubim* (Hebrew for "writings"). As can be seen in appendix A (p. 233), the canons differ as to the contents of this section of the OT. For example, the Hebrew canon includes Ezra, Nehemiah, Esther, and 1 and 2 Chronicles in the Writings. Christians consider these part of the "historical books," a category that does not exist in the Hebrew Bible. In the Christian canon, the "Writings" simply include wisdom literature and poetry.

What Is Wisdom Literature?

The origins of wisdom literature are probably as early as the human ability to think and communicate. The biblical roots of wisdom literature begin in the basic structure of human society, the family. As with many other ancient cultures, Jewish families created ways of passing on collective wisdom about life from generation to generation. The building blocks of this wisdom were *proverbs,* short, pithy sayings that pass on insights about life and its meaning.

Much of the wisdom literature consists of proverbs and other

141

types of poetic devices that originated in oral tradition. Parents passed on to their children such wisdom within the context of the family. Families preserved collective wisdom within the clans and tribes. Eventually, once kingship evolved in Israel, a type of royal wisdom developed. Solomon became especially associated with this tradition, for he was remembered as exceptionally wise (see 1 Kgs 3:3–9 and 4:29–34). Boys from elite families would be schooled in wisdom and proper etiquette. Professionals emerged who preserved such wisdom and passed it on. These were the *sages,* and some of them (like Ben Sira) left written legacies of their wisdom. Probably in every era women and men who were viewed as "wise" were respected for their advice, but in Israel the position of "sage" was primarily a male institution.

If wisdom literature primarily consists of proverbs and poetry, it also contains other types of literature. The Book of Job, for instance, is a lengthy poetic reflection on the problem of innocent human suffering. The Book of Ecclesiastes (also called Qoheleth) is a highly skeptical or even cynical reflection on the futility of human existence. At first glance, some of the wisdom literature may seem quite secular or even anti-religious in outlook. As we shall see, that is an unwarranted prejudgment. If some Christian denominations especially have ignored this section of the Bible, it is due largely to a lack of appreciation of its true value. Its preservation in both Jewish and Christian canons is testimony to the respect it deserves as another aspect of God's Word.

Although some psalms are wisdom literature, the Book of Psalms is also unique. It represents the poetic, musical, and liturgical heritage of Israel that grew primarily out of its cultic life. Many psalms emerged from worship services in the context of the Temple in Jerusalem. Their preservation in the "Writings" is an acknowledgment that they fit no other category.

Job

Everyone knows Job. He is like the original "bad luck" figure for whom everything goes wrong. But in the end, God smiles on him and restores him to his former glory. It sounds like a formula for a Hollywood movie. Job, indeed, is everyman and everywoman.

TITLE: The Book of Job

AUTHOR: Unknown

DATE: Unknown, but perhaps sixth–fourth centuries B.C.

STRUCTURE:
1:1–2:3	Prologue
3:1–42:6	Poetic Dialogues
42:7–17	Epilogue

THEMES: Innocent suffering, divine retribution, faith, the mystery of God

---

From this perspective, it is uncertain whether Job was a real person or is a literary invention meant to model the typical human experience.

The land of Uz (1:1) is not known, but it probably represents Edom. Hence Job is not an Israelite. Yet he clearly models for Jewish and Christian scriptures alike the age-old problem of innocent suffering. How do we explain the fact that bad things sometimes happen to good people and good things sometimes happen to bad people? This problem is technically called "theodicy," the problem of the existence of evil in a world that our faith says was created by a good God.

Assigning a date and author for Job is very difficult. Sometime after the exile (ca. sixth–fourth centuries B.C.) is most likely. The original language of the poetic sections is quite challenging. The book itself is unique. It combines poetry and prose in the framework of a narrative, but there are no exact parallels to other ancient literature.

Structure and Content

The overarching structure of Job is like a sandwich. The meat of it is in a huge poetic middle section sandwiched between two short prose narratives. The first slim section, the prologue (1:1–2:3), sets the context for the story. It describes Job's very blessed life and Satan's bargain with God that he should test the reality of Job's faith by allowing evil to befall him.

The large middle section (3:1–42:6) consists of a series of poetic dialogues that describe Job's attempts to comprehend what has happened to him and why. Job's three friends (Eliphaz, Bildad, Zophar) first attempt to wrestle with their own explanations (ch. 3–31), but each gives unsatisfying answers. Then a young upstart named Elihu comes on the scene to offer his explanation (ch. 32–37), but he fares no better. In the midst of this section is a poetic reflection on the ultimate inaccessibility of God's wisdom (ch. 28).

In the final part of this section, God speaks to Job out of a whirlwind (38:1–42:6). The book concludes with a slim epilogue (42:7–17) that describes God's restoration of Job to his former glory with a storybook ending:

> After this Job lived one hundred and forty years, and saw his children, and his children's children, four generations. And Job died, old and full of days. (42:16–17)

Interpretation

The fairy tale tone of Job does not mean it is whimsical. On the contrary, Job wrestles with the eternal question of evil in the world. The fact that this book has appealed to enormous numbers of people in history, both believers and nonbelievers, is testimony enough to its universality. There is an endless parade of commentaries and books on Job trying to plumb its depths.

Although the book is a coherent whole when considered with its prologue and epilogue, one can get lost in the giant middle section. The poems in which Job's companions try to offer their explanations can get confusing. A brief summary of their arguments is a synopsis of traditional wisdom. If evil befalls you, then either you have sinned or your parents have sinned. Evil follows upon wickedness; the righteous don't suffer. This perspective, of course, is exactly the stance of traditional wisdom literature. It is very cut and dried; no gray areas allowed. Job is an attempt to move beyond that perspective.

So what is Job's answer to this universal problem? Interpreters vary in their judgments. Jewish interpreters will analyze Job from one perspective, Christians from another. Really there is no firm resolution to the problem of evil in Job. Instead, God's appearance on the scene and subsequent speech (38:1–42:6) send Job back squarely to the crux of the matter. God's plan remains from our human perspective a mystery. Regardless of your fate, do you

WHO IS SATAN?

The figure of Satan in Job might be easily misunderstood. Christians automatically equate Satan with the devil. That is not the image in Job. Rather, Satan is something akin to a prosecuting attorney for God. He is part of the divine council that advises God. His duty is to "patrol the earth" and check up on God's creatures. His challenge to God to test Job is just his job. This notion of Satan may have crept into the Bible from Persian religion. The image later developed, especially among Christians, into a full-fledged figure of evil — God's nemesis.

still have faith? Simple as it is, Job's statement at the beginning of his calamities summarizes the position well: "Naked I came from my mother's womb, and naked shall I return there; The LORD gave, and the LORD has taken away; blessed be the name of the LORD" (1:21). Justice is not always achieved in this world, but do we have enough faith to await justice in the next?

Exercise

Read Job 38:1–11. How does God's response to Job address Job's problem? How does this passage speak to you of awe in the sight of the grandeur of God?

Psalms

Psalms may be the most popular book in the OT. It is the only book in the Bible where God's Word to us is paradoxically phrased in our words directed to God. Psalms are hymns, songs, and prayers. Many were intended to be accompanied by musical instruments. (For example, look at the instructions "to the leader" for Pss 12, 54, and 76.) Ancient tradition held that David composed most of the psalms, and many are attributed to him in the Book of Psalms. He was reputed to have been gifted musically (1 Sam 16:18, 23). Actually, these hymns reflect different composers from many different periods in ancient Israel's history. Some are even adaptations of ancient Canaanite hymns.

TITLE: The Book of Psalms (Hebrew, *Tehillim,* meaning "praises")

AUTHOR: Unknown, but many different authors among whom King David is the most famous

DATE: Unknown

STRUCTURE:

Pss 1–41	Book I
Pss 42–72	Book II
Pss 73–89	Book III
Pss 90–106	Book IV
Pss 107–150	Book V

THEMES: Lament, praise, thanksgiving, repentance, joy, entreaty, among many others

Structure and Content

The structure of this book is artificially divided into five collections, or "books," to create an analogy with the first five books of the Bible. One cannot adequately summarize the contents of each book in such a short space. The themes are simply too diverse. Although there are some common themes within each section, the breadth of topics covered by the psalms precludes any real uniformity to the divisions of the book. In reality, they are sub-collections of psalms that may have circulated independently before being incorporated into the final form of the book (for example, the songs of Korah, Pss 42; 44–49; 84–85; 87–88, and the songs of Asaph, Pss 73–83).

In place of summarizing each section of the Book of Psalms,

Type of Psalm	Examples
Praise	Pss 34, 100, 104
Thanksgiving	Pss 30, 75, 105
Trust	Pss 23, 91, 131
Lament	Pss 22, 69, 137
Petition	Pss 54, 74, 80
Zion hymns	Pss 48, 84, 122
Royal psalms	Pss 2, 72, 110
Wisdom psalms	Pss 1, 32, 112

PSALM NUMBERS

You may notice that Bibles sometimes show different numbers for psalms. This can make it difficult to find just the psalm you want. The chart below provides a convenient guide. It also helps to explain that the numbering conflict is due to the differences in the way the Hebrew Bible and the Septuagint (followed by the Vulgate) divide the psalms. The Septuagint combines Pss 9 and 10 into one and Pss 114 and 115 into one, but divides Ps 116 and Ps 147 into two parts, respectively. Some Bibles print the alternative numbers in parentheses.

Hebrew Bible	LXX
Pss 1–8	Pss 1–8
Pss 9–10	Ps 9
Pss 11–113	Pss 10–112
Pss 114–115	Ps 113
Ps 116	Pss 114–115
Pss 117–146	Pss 116–145
Ps 147	Pss 146–147
Pss 148–150	Pss 148–150
	Ps 151

I offer a brief digest of the *types* of psalms in the chart on the previous page. Keep in mind that the categories are somewhat loose and may overlap. Some psalms, moreover, exhibit mixed literary characteristics.

Interpretation

Almost everyone knows a psalm or has a favorite among them. Funerals often evoke a reading of Psalm 23 ("The LORD is my shepherd...") even among those who are not particularly religious. People in the midst of guilt over some wrongdoing might well pray Psalm 51 ("Have mercy on me, O God..."). It is the prayer of one painfully aware of his sinfulness. It contains the following title: "A Psalm of David, when the prophet Nathan came to him, after he had gone in to Bathsheba" — an apt description of the context.

Virtually any human emotion can be found in the psalms. The ancient Israelites composed them in many different circumstances and settings. Frequently, as one would expect of hymns, they have a liturgical flavor. That is, they reflect Israel's Temple worship

---

HALLELUJAH!

Many of the psalms of praise and thanksgiving employ the Hebrew word *hallelu-jah*. It is a combination of the verb *hallel* ("sing praise") and *Yah* (shortened form of God's name, Yahweh). It means "God be praised" or "sing praise to Yahweh." It is a poetic word that begs to be sung.

(for example, Pss 24, 150). Some psalms are short (Ps 134 has 3 verses), some are long (Ps 119 has 176 verses). Some speak in the voice of an individual (Ps 34), while others express the unified voice of an entire community (Ps 137). One can easily under-stand how effectively the psalms functioned in daily prayer for Jews and Christians alike. Jesus himself is portrayed as having prayed a psalm or part of one during his passion (Mark 15:34; Matt 27:46). Regardless of the setting, you will find a prayer that expresses just the right sentiment for the specific occasion. More than any other biblical book, the Psalms are to be prayed.

Exercise

Read Ps 136. Into what category of psalms does this fit? If you composed a similar psalm for your own life, what items would appear on your list of reasons to give thanks to God?

Proverbs

Just as ancient tradition held that King David had composed most of the psalms, so it held that his son Solomon composed most of the proverbs. Solomon had a reputation for wisdom (see 1 Kgs 1–3), so it was natural to attribute wise sayings to him.

In reality the Book of Proverbs is a collection of wisdom lit-erature extending anywhere from the thirteenth to the seventh centuries B.C. Like the Psalms, this book is a compendium. Al-most every culture has proverbs. They are short, insightful sayings that summarize collective wisdom. Some of the proverbs are dis-tinctively Hebrew, but others show great similarity to wisdom literature in the ancient Near East. Ancient Egypt, for exam-

TITLE: The Book of Proverbs (Hebrew: *Mishlē,* meaning "proverbs" or "riddles")

AUTHOR: Unknown, but many proverbs attributed to Solomon

DATE: Unknown; compilation of proverbs from the thirteenth to the seventh centuries B.C.

STRUCTURE:

1:1–9:18	Wisdom Woman and her instruction
10:1–22:16	Proverbs of Solomon
22:17–24:34	Words of the wise
25:1–29:27	More proverbs of Solomon
30:1–14	Words of Agur, son of Jakeh
31:1–9	Words of Lemuel, king of Massa
31:10–31	Poem exalting Wisdom Woman

THEMES: Fear of the Lord, honesty, integrity, self-control, chastity, prudence, discipline, and many others

ple, had the words of the sage Amenemope, some of which are comparable to Prov 22:17–24:34.

Regardless of the social origin of some of the proverbs, they provide concise bits of wise advice passed on from parents to their children to train them properly for an upright life. We should note, however, that the text is written as if it were an instruction of a father to a son. Women and girls were not originally in view because of the standard patriarchal stance of Israelite society. Yet many proverbs can apply equally well to both genders. (Note that Prov 6:20 invokes obedience to father *and* mother.)

Structure and Content

This book may be divided into seven sections. The first (1:1–9:18) provides a poetic overview of the nature of wisdom. The "Wisdom Woman" (or Lady Wisdom) emerges as a side of God that embodies truth and willingly guides young men on their way to adulthood. The second section contains a collection of proverbs attributed to Solomon (10:1–22:16). The third section sets forth wise sayings that bear resemblance to common wisdom in the ancient world (22:17–24:34). Further psalms of Solomon appear in the fourth section (25:1–29:27), while the next two sections contain collections from two other wise figures, Agur, son of

Jakeh, and Lemuel, king of Massa (respectively, 30:1–14; 31:1–9). The book concludes with a beautiful poem that exalts the ideal woman (31:10–31), who may well symbolize the Wisdom Woman herself.

Sometimes the logic of this division is seen in the repetition of certain words or themes that recur throughout the section. These "catchwords" make natural connections between proverbs that originally existed as independent sayings but are now collected in convenient summary fashion.

Interpretation

Proverbs is not a book to be read from beginning to end. Rather, since it is a collection of individual sayings, it is better to take small sections at a time. In many instances, individual proverbs should be read and digested for their own sake. Many are contradictory, but that is to be expected in a collection that spans such a long period of history. Circumstances often demand different courses of action.

The book contains typical wisdom themes that recur over and over again. The overarching image is of Wisdom Woman issuing an invitation to all to listen to her advice. The young should strive to attain true wisdom. They should avoid the pitfalls and temptations of worldly evil and learn "the fear of the Lord" (1:7).

Standard human values like honesty, truth, integrity, hard work, humility, self-control, chaste living, and so on are the building blocks of authentic human existence. They reflect the orderly design of the universe that God intends. Human pride and sinful-

---

WHAT IS "FEAR OF THE LORD"?

This expression permeates the wisdom literature, but it may sound foreign to our ears. The basic principle in wisdom is that "fear of the Lord is the beginning of all wisdom" (Prov 1:7; 9:10; Job 28:28; Sir 1:14). Fear, however, does not simply mean quaking in one's boots. Fear means awe and respect, an appropriate reverence that human beings feel when in God's presence. In a way, the concept means knowing one's place as "creature" in relation to the one who is "Creator." While the idea includes a healthy dose of fear that occurs when people come into contact with the unknown, the predominant notion is adopting the attitude of reverent humility before God.

ness of all kinds interfere with this grand design. Obtaining God's true wisdom will keep one on the right path and will impart a satisfying life. Note that there is a certain simplicity to the perspective of many proverbs. The good will prosper, the wicked will stumble (10:24–25; 11:8; 12:2, etc.). This simplistic view sometimes contradicts our experience when bad things happen to good people. Proverbs does not tackle this question directly, but other wisdom books in the Bible do (Job, Ecclesiastes).

Exercise
Read Prov 6:6–11. The author sends the reader to study the ant. What can be learned from the behavior of ants? Why is this perspective important for what God wills for human beings?

Ecclesiastes

The standard Christian title of this book, Ecclesiastes, should not be confused with another book of wisdom literature, Ecclesiasticus (Sirach). Ecclesiastes, or Qoheleth, is a most unusual book to be in the Bible because it is filled with skepticism. Finding a faith perspective in it can be a challenge, though I believe there is one.

The title (from the Greek *ekklēsia*, gathering, and Hebrew *qahal*, assembly) is problematic. It may mean teacher or preacher in the sense of one who addresses those gathered together. The date of the book's origin is also difficult to pinpoint. The postexilic time when the wisdom books were being collected is most likely. The designation that this "Teacher" is the "son of David" (1:1) or "king over Israel in Jerusalem" alludes to Solomon. But this is done in deference to Solomon's reputation for wisdom, not as a factual identification of the author. The book's attitude toward royalty is actually rather negative. The identity of the author remains a mystery.

Structure and Content
The style of the book is a personal reflection by a sage on his experience in life. The perspective is one of an old man looking back over his life and feeling depressed over the sameness of it. After an introduction (1:1–11), Qoheleth recounts his attempts to

TITLE: The Book of Ecclesiastes (Greek), The Book of Qoheleth (Hebrew)

AUTHOR: Qoheleth, the Teacher

DATE: Ca. 300–250 B.C.

STRUCTURE:

1:1–11	Introduction
1:12–6:9	Investigation of life
6:10–11:6	Conclusions
11:7–12:8	Poem on old age
12:9–14	Added ending

THEMES: The futility of human life, human frailty, vanity, work

understand human existence. His investigation of life (1:12–6:9) yields a uniformly negative judgment: there is nothing new (1:9). His conclusions are summarized in the next section (6:10–11:6). Finally, the author adds a poetic reflection on the relation between youth and old age (11:7–12:8). The end of the book contains a short summary of Qoheleth's life written by someone else (12:9–14). Qoheleth is praised for his wisdom and his attempts to teach the truth plainly.

Interpretation

I will be honest with you. This is not a book to read when you are depressed. Qoheleth's skepticism is not likely to lift you out of the doldrums. However, Qoheleth has much to offer serious religious reflection. He sees life in repetitive cycles. Time and again he moans that there is "nothing new under the sun" (1:9; 2:11) and that life is a "vanity and a chasing after the wind" (2:26; cf. 1:2, 14; 3:19; 12:8). "Vanity," by the way, does not refer to narcissistic concern for one's looks but to utter futility or a waste of time. Qoheleth provides a realistic antidote to those who are overly optimistic in their assessment, but his is not a totally pessimistic assessment. There is faith-filled acknowledgment, be it ever so slim, that God is in charge of existence (1:13; 3:10; 5:2, etc.). Qoheleth's problem is that human beings cannot ultimately know what God's plan is all about. We must surrender to a power greater than ourselves. Even wisdom can offer delusion if one is not careful (2:19; 9:1).

Exercise

Read 3:1–8, the famous poem on the diversity of seasons in human existence. How do you fit this poem into the author's skeptical view of life? Do you find it uplifting or troubling?

The Song of Songs

This book is known by different titles. It is called the Song of Songs, the Canticle of Canticles, or the Song of Solomon. The first two titles are simply different English renderings of the same Hebrew expression. To label something the "song of songs" or the "book of books" is a Hebrew way of saying it is the best or greatest of that class of objects. There is none like it. The last title indicates that the author was by ancient tradition thought to be Solomon. As with so much of the wisdom literature, Solomon is unlikely to be the real author of the text, but he provides the inspirational model of the ideal lover (1:4, 12; 3:11).

This book is unique in the Bible. It is an unabashed exaltation of physical beauty and human sexuality. The book can be difficult to follow at times without a script, but it is essentially a series of dialogues and monologues between two lovers, a woman and a man, who are obviously enamored of each other. There are also chorus parts that refer to various aspects of love. The origin of some of the text might well be in secular love poetry from the ancient Near East, but its preservation in the Bible assures us that there is also a deeper meaning to appreciate.

Structure and Content

Ideally, one should have a translation that identifies the different "voices" that speak in the course of this extended poem. Few translations offer these identifications. The Song is most likely a collection of independent love poems combined into one. That makes structuring the book especially challenging. It focuses on a wedding between Solomon and his bride.

For the sake of simplicity, I structure the text into two parts. The first part (1:1–3:11) offers reflections on the beauty of human love. The marriage setting is not clear, but tradition has interpreted the text as praising marriage as a covenant relationship.

TITLE: The Song of Songs (or the Canticle of Canticles, or the Song
       of Solomon)

AUTHOR: Unknown, but traditionally attributed to Solomon

DATE: Unknown

STRUCTURE:
          1:1–3:11   Reflections on human love
          4:1–8:14   Conversations on human love

THEMES: The beauty of human love and sexual attraction, physical
        beauty, marriage as symbol of God's love

The second section (4:1–8:14) records a series of conversations
between the bride and groom and the "chorus" of other women
who assist the bride. Some of the poems quite explicitly exalt the
physical beauty of both the bride and groom. Other poems speak
in more general terms of love.

Modern readers may have trouble understanding some of the
language of the Song. It is filled with much imagery, names of
fruits and flowers (pomegranate, palm, fig, rose of Sharon, etc.),
exotic foods and spices (apple, raisin cakes, saffron, cinnamon,
etc.), and all kinds of animals (gazelle, leopard, horse, stag, etc.).
We also may find it curious, if not hilarious, to describe the
beauty of our beloved in the language of the poem. What bride
would like to have her hair described as "a flock of goats" (4:1)
or her neck like "the tower of David" (4:4)? But if the imagery
is somewhat antiquated, the intention is easy to comprehend. The
object of one's love is scrutinized in great detail for his or her
physical beauty. Not that the person is reduced to physical characteristics alone. Each of the lovers appreciates the personality of
the beloved as well as the interior disposition. Yet the text gives
the impression that both lovers are star-struck, infatuated entirely
with one another — in other words, bowled over by love!

Interpretation

Two main types of interpretation of this book exist, the literal and
the allegorical. They do not have to be in conflict with one another. On a literal level, the text exalts human sexual attraction.
This perspective can also be found in other parts of the Bible (Gen

2:4–25; Prov 5:15–19; 30:18–19). No other text so beautifully and poetically expresses this reality. The text presumes a marriage context, but its praise of physical attraction is an assertion that human sexuality is good in its essence. This belief contradicts some other perspectives, ancient and modern, that view human sexuality as essentially bad.

Interpreters through history have always appreciated deeper levels of the text. Rabbinic interpreters saw in this love relationship the symbol of God's covenantal love for Israel as his bride. Some prophets used this image as well (Hos 2:14–23). Christian interpreters picked up on this deeper symbolism, seeing in the book the allegory of the relationship of Christ to his church. These views are not contradictory but complementary.

Exercise

Read Song 2:10–15. Who speaks these lines? Who is the object of the speaker's affection? How do you understand the gift of human sexuality from the perspective of your faith?

The Wisdom of Solomon

The Wisdom of Solomon, also known simply as the Book of Wisdom, is another collection of proverbs and wisdom instruction. An anonymous Greek-speaking Jew writing in the name of King Solomon authored the book somewhere between 100 and 28 B.C., probably in Alexandria, Egypt.

The tone of this book of wisdom literature is different from other books of wisdom. Although it is written from a Jewish perspective, the author has also incorporated influences from Hellenistic Platonic (Greek) philosophy into his teachings. The result is not merely a repetition of Jewish traditions but a transformation of them into practical advice for Greek-speaking Jews living in the Diaspora. This perspective is quite at home in Christian thought as well. Christians can identify, for example, with the notion of immortality after death explained in ch. 1–5. This idea did not appear in Judaism until late in OT history, shortly before the birth of Jesus.

Title: The Wisdom of Solomon

Author: Unknown, but a Greek-speaking Jew writing in the name of King Solomon

Date: Ca. 100–28 B.C.

Structure:
1:1–6:21	Wisdom and immortality
6:22–11:1	Solomon and wisdom
11:2–19:22	The Exodus explained

Themes: Immortality and the reward of the righteous, Wisdom Woman, human folly vs. divine wisdom, God as liberator

---

Structure and Content

One can discern three distinctive divisions in this book. The first (1:1–6:21) teaches at length about the immortality that God will bestow on those who remain faithful and who suffer unjustly in this life. The second division (6:22–11:1) assumes the stance of King Solomon giving first-person instruction to his audience about the nature of true wisdom. At numerous points the author identifies wisdom with God's Spirit (e.g., 7:22–25), but it is also seen as a gift that God grants to those who seek it properly.

The final division (11:2–19:22) explains how Yahweh, Israel's God, is the God of liberation. God's greatest act of liberation was the Exodus event when God led the Israelites out of slavery in Egypt to a life of freedom in the promised land. The author identifies Wisdom as the guiding light in this process. The text also repeats standard warnings about the continual dangers of idolatry that had affected the Israelites in their history. God alone can be the object of their worship and affection.

Interpretation

Wisdom is supposedly addressed to the "rulers of the earth" (1:1). The author assumes the identity of Solomon to instruct foreign kings in true wisdom. The real audience is anyone who would seek to live righteously according to God's wisdom. The book maintains that human perceptions can be deceiving. Death, for example, only seems to be a permanent departure, but in reality it leads to one's eternal reward (3:1–9). Like metal tested by fire, suffering makes a person strong (3:5–6).

Another interesting aspect of Wisdom is its combination of salvation history motifs with those from traditional wisdom material. This is typical of late Jewish wisdom literature, but it is quite extensive here. Wisdom is God's right-hand power that has guided Israel's entire history, including the all-important Exodus event (ch. 10–11). Seeking the Wisdom Woman is the beginning of true knowledge. This powerful feminine image requires that one recognize the need to learn. The timeless lesson to empty oneself in order to be filled by something greater still applies to our lives today. In an age of self-reliance and independence, recognizing our own limitations is not always easy. Christians have gleaned many rich insights from this Jewish book that presages many Christian themes.

Exercise

Read Wis 5:15–20. What image of God comes out of this reading? Do you find it comforting, mystifying, exhilarating?

The Wisdom of Ben Sira (Sirach)

This book is the longest book of wisdom literature in the Bible (fifty-one chapters). Protestants consider it one of the OT apocrypha, but Catholics have revered the book for its practical advice on many matters. It is not found in the Hebrew Bible but exists only in the Septuagint, whence comes its Greek title, Ecclesiasticus (not to be confused with Ecclesiastes). Ecclesiasticus (from the Latin Vulgate translation) means "church book," testimony to its frequent use in the Catholic Church's tradition.

Unlike many books in the Bible, we know the name of the author of Ecclesiasticus. It is given in the prologue written by his grandson. The prologue tells us that Jesus ben Sira (whom we call Sirach) was a sage who used the wisdom in this book to provide wise instruction to boys in Jerusalem around 180 B.C. His grandson then translated the work into Greek for the Greek-speaking Jews of Alexandria in Egypt around 132 B.C.

TITLE: The Wisdom of Ben Sira (Sirach) or Ecclesiasticus

AUTHOR: Jesus ben Sira (Sirach)

DATE: Ca. 180 B.C. and 132 B.C.

STRUCTURE:
      Prologue by grandson of Ben Sira
      1:1–43:33   Wisdom and the wise
      44:1–50:21   Praise of the ancestors
      50:22–29   Conclusion
      51:1–30   Appendix

THEMES: True wisdom, duties of parents and children, frugality,
      death, friendship, ancestors

Structure and Content

Outlines and versification of this book vary widely because of
the different textual traditions. I divide the book into five parts,
the first being the prologue, which contains no numbers for the
verses. The prologue introduces the purpose of the book and indicates the difficult task of translating. (That is still a tough job
for scholars.) An interesting hint of the threefold division of the
Hebrew Bible is given in the prologue. It mentions the Law, the
prophecies, and "the rest of the books." The second and largest
section of the book (ch. 1–43) is a collection of typical proverbs.
They cover a multitude of themes, often topically arranged. Sirach places much emphasis on learning proper manners and good
behaviors since it is primarily directed to children and young
people.

The next section (44:1–50:21) is a lengthy poem in praise
of the great heroes of Israel. This is unusual for wisdom literature. Normally wisdom literature only makes slight allusions
to the salvation history of Israel. But Sirach takes a point of
view that looks back over the history of his people and recounts
the wonderful deeds done by their ancestors under God's guidance. The list of male heroes is selective but contains many of
the famous and popular figures we have come to know (Abraham, Moses, David, Solomon, etc.). The original conclusion to
the book (50:22–29) is a benediction accompanied by the transla-
tor's wish that readers may benefit from the wisdom of the book.

An appendix added at a later time rounds out the book (ch. 51). It contains Sirach's prayer of thanksgiving and praise to God and a first-person poem spoken about the magnificence of wisdom.

Interpretation

Like so much of the wisdom literature, Sirach is best read in small doses. The proverbs describe common sage advice on how to flourish in this life by doing righteous acts that conform to God's will. This book presents the traditional view of wisdom. There is a right path and a wrong path to follow. The righteous shall prosper; the wicked shall fail. The viewpoint could be considered at that time in history as "conservative," espousing tried and true sayings in order to foster standard obedience. This perspective is understandable in the context in which Sirach lived and worked. At that time the Seleucids ruled Palestine. They continued Alexander the Great's promotion of Hellenistic culture and the values of the Hellenistic world, which were attractive to the youth of Jerusalem. Sirach felt that they had to be countered. His book is a compendium of sage advice from the ages to bolster the traditional values of his society and his faith.

The book begins in praise of wisdom. "To fear the Lord is the beginning of wisdom" (1:14). Then it moves to duties toward God (ch. 2) and duties toward parents (ch. 3) and on to many other practical pieces of advice. Of particular interest is Sirach's insistence that human beings bear their own responsibility for their actions (15:11–20). In a society such as ours where people look for others on whom to place blame, these words are a powerful reminder of the free choices that God allows human beings to make.

Exercise

Read Sir 30:14–17. How does Sirach's advice concerning wealth and health compare with your own values? Do you agree or disagree? Is his advice meaningful to the young as well as the aged?

Part III

INTRODUCING
THE NEW TESTAMENT

Chapter 9

GENERAL ORIENTATION TO THE NEW TESTAMENT

The various Christian denominations view the NT more uniformly than the OT. It is consequently easier to categorize the twenty-seven books of the NT. Four divisions are apparent:

- The Four Gospels

- The Acts of the Apostles

- The Letters

- The Book of Revelation

As was the case with the OT Law, the Gospels are preeminent among all the books of the NT. Because they tell the story of Jesus of Nazareth, the church has held them in higher regard than all the other NT books, although the entire collection is viewed as God's Word. They are placed first in canonical order for this reason. Among Catholics the practice of standing for the proclamation of the Gospel during the Mass is a sign of this honor. The Orthodox also accord the Gospels special recognition in their liturgies.

There is a logic to the ordering of the books of the NT, although it is not always consistent. Matthew comes first among the Gospels partly because of an ancient tradition that it was written by Matthew the tax collector, one of the twelve apostles. The early church fathers indeed quoted Matthew most frequently of all the Gospels. Among the letters Romans is first. Although one could view this as recognition that it is a most significant letter, it is probably rather due to its length. Note that generally among the letters the larger ones come first, the smaller ones follow. They are also grouped together according to author. The Book of Revelation appropriately comes last. It speaks of "the last things" and presents a vision of God's ultimate victory over evil.

◆   ◆   ◆

Most of my introductory comments for the OT world apply to the NT. The writers of the NT lived in that OT world. For them, the only scriptures were the writings of the OT. There is no need to repeat that information here, but I will add some pertinent comments on the world of the NT that will place these writings in their historical and cultural context.

1. *The Roman empire.* The largest cultural influence in the NT world was certainly the Roman empire. None could escape the influence of Rome. This relationship had both positive and negative effects. Positively, the Jews benefited by obtaining special privileges from Rome to avoid military service, to maintain many of their religious practices, and to be relieved of some taxation. The Roman road system and the ability to travel in relative safety throughout the empire greatly facilitated the rapid spread of Christianity. In the early NT period, the Roman peace (*pax romana*) prevailed. Negatively, some of the Roman overseers were cruel to the Jews, among them Pontius Pilate. Later persecutions also arose against Christians. The Romans often interfered politically in Jewish affairs, causing further disruption and capitalizing on intra-Jewish disagreements.

2. *Hellenistic culture, philosophy, and religion.* Another major influence stemmed from the Hellenistic world. *Hellenism* (from *hellēnē* meaning "Greek") is the name given to the cultural influences that began with Alexander the Great (fourth century B.C.). Since he thought Greek culture was the most advanced in the world, he wanted to share it with every people he conquered. The impact was felt for centuries afterward. Hellenistic institutions such as the gymnasium, where athletic contests were conducted in the nude, changed the course of life. Such developments offended the religious sensitivities of the Jews. This world also fostered innumerable philosophies and religions that attempted to solve life's problems. Greek philosophers developed the notion of the division of the body and the soul that influenced later OT writings and the perspective of the NT. Various cults arose that offered strong temptations to believers among both Jews and Christians. Later gnostic philosophies and religions also made an

impact on Christian beliefs. The NT shows awareness of some of this influence, and some of the NT writers strongly opposed such pagan ideas. Yet none could escape the general atmosphere of the Hellenistic world.

3. *Social institutions.* Certain Hellenistic-Roman institutions, requiring separate emphasis, exerted influence on later NT documents. The cultural world of the NT had preconceived understandings of society's basic structures. The family was the primary foundation of society. Each member of the family had distinct roles. In a patriarchal world, men had distinctive roles, often apart from the home, and women had their own roles, usually in the home. Children had their own duties and responsibilities, and there were set patterns of behavior between masters and slaves. Slavery, in fact, was accepted by most as an essential aspect of society. All life was hierarchically oriented.

We should not be surprised, then, that such an organizational structure shaped greatly the Christian church as it developed. This is why some of the later NT letters speak of the "household of God" and delineate distinct roles for each member of this household, including slaves. The church took nearly twenty centuries to recognize fully the moral degradation of slavery. Today, questions are being raised about other cultural patterns, e.g., the role of women in society. Most important for us is to recognize that some of the NT developments are due to cultural influences. Naming the NT God's Word does not mean that every single passage applies today in the same way it might have in the early church. God's Word finds expression in human concepts that themselves are shaped by time-conditioned cultural values. Learning to separate what is culturally predetermined from what is eternal truth is not easy, but we should be alert to the cultural values that so strongly molded the final shape of the NT.

4. *Relations with the Jews.* One of the more difficult areas to deal with is how relations with the Jews deteriorated throughout much of the NT period. Jesus himself was a Jew. Originally, of course, many Christians were Jews who accepted Jesus as the messiah. The Jewish leaders eventually expelled these people from the synagogue, probably around A.D. 90. After the fall of Jerusalem in A.D. 70 the Jews who escaped fled to Yavneh (also called Jamnia) and began to pull their lives together by collecting and organizing their scriptures. Christians did the same thing but fled

to Pella (in the Jordan valley). The NT shows that relations between these two groups in the wake of Jerusalem's destruction
were sometimes highly volatile. Although this topic is quite complicated, I believe we must acknowledge its presence in the NT.
Later history saw the unfortunate development among Christians
of anti-Semitism in an irrational and highly immoral way. It led
ultimately to the terrible Holocaust (known to Jews as the Shoah)
by the Nazis during World War II. I don't believe that the NT
itself fosters this attitude intentionally, but excessive Christian
interpretations throughout history led to these intolerable developments. When reading the NT, Christians should be careful not
to use anachronistic labels.

5. *Complexity of first-century Judaism.* A corollary to the previous point is that we sometimes have misconceptions about the
nature of Judaism in the time of Jesus. Contrary to popular opin-
ion, Judaism was not a monolithic religion in Jesus' day. There
were many different types of Jews, and disagreements about how
best to live out the Torah were frequent and sometimes violent.
Judaism consisted of many different groups, at least up until the
Roman destruction of Jerusalem in A.D. 70. The Sadducees were
allied to the Temple and favored compromise with the Roman
government. The Pharisees, a lay movement of pious Jews, fought
for flexibility in applying the Torah and developed beliefs that
were often in conflict with the aristocratic Sadducees. Another
group, the Essenes, fled mainline religion in Jerusalem and established a more rigorous, monastic lifestyle near the Dead Sea.
Other groups, such as the Zealots, espoused violent revolution
against Rome later in the first century. They were not reluc-
tant to murder even some of their fellow Jews if they opposed
them forcefully. The Gospels, unfortunately, do not present this
complexity in any clear fashion. Written after the destruction of
Jerusalem, all of the Gospels tend to give a naive view of Judaism
that more reflects the post-70 environment of conflict between
Jews and Christians. We should keep this background in mind
as we read the NT.

6. *Miracles and magic.* The Gospels, in particular, exhibit a lot
of interest in miracles. Sometimes Christians wonder why Jesus
would not have been accepted by most people in his day, given
the many wondrous deeds he did. But herein lies the problem.
Miracles and magic were stock parts of the Hellenistic-Roman

world in Jesus' day. There were many other wonder-workers, both Jewish and Gentile, who developed great reputations. Some even claimed to be the messiah. How could one tell a fraud from "the real thing"? Miracles by themselves did not prove Jesus' identity, nor did they necessarily lead people to faith. There were many hucksters in the ancient world, and it was not always easy to discern the truth in the midst of commonplace events. The Hellenistic-Roman world conceived of miracles and magic somewhat on the same terms. They could be signs from God, or they could be deceptions. The ultimate test, as even Jesus' miracle stories in the Synoptic Gospels show, is the faith prior to the miracle. In reading the Gospel miracles we have to avoid two exaggerations: (1) automatic skepticism because of our modern scientific mindset; (2) uncritical acceptance of the literal details of such stories. The fact is that Jesus and his followers gained reputations for being able to effect wondrous deeds of healing and exorcism. The power is always attributed to God, not to them alone. When we read the Gospels, we should not prejudge such stories but analyze each one according to its own merits.

These six additional observations point out only the most obvious influences on the NT world, coupled as they are with the OT background given in chapter 4 above. As with any book, the NT developed in its own context. It is best understood with that context clearly in view if we truly want to understand it on its own terms.

Chapter 10

THE GOSPELS

Matthew	Luke
Mark	John

The Gospels are likely the most familiar part of the Bible to the majority of Christians. Even if you have never read the Bible directly yourself, you have encountered the Gospels whenever you heard stories about Jesus. Many people consequently assume that the Gospels are biographies about Jesus of Nazareth written by some of his closest associates. This was, in fact, the assumption in history for hundreds of years. Then in the seventeenth century some scholars began to study the Gospels in a more sophisticated and scientific manner. What they discovered was a far more complex picture of what the Gospels represent.

Of the four Gospels in the NT, it is easy to see that three of them are very similar. These three — Matthew, Mark, and Luke — are called the *Synoptic Gospels*. The Greek word *synoptikos* means that they can be viewed "with one eye." That is, they correspond so closely to one another that they can be set down in parallel columns and viewed simultaneously. All three tell a comparable story of Jesus but with different details and emphases. To show just how similar they can be in detail, let's look at an excerpt from a "synoptic" story from the passion of Jesus (see the comparison on the following page).

Note how closely the words in these three stories match one another. Such verbal similarity cannot be accidental, nor is it due to the same oral tradition. Scholars have determined that such similarity in the Synoptics is accounted for by one of three reasons: either they used common written sources, they copied off

Matthew 21:1–3	*Mark 11:1–3*	*Luke 19:28–31*
And when they had come near Jerusalem and had reached Bethphage, at the Mount of Olives, Jesus sent two disciples, saying to them, "Go into the village ahead of you, and immediately you will find a donkey tied, and a colt with her; untie them and bring them to me. If anyone says anything to you, just say this, 'The Lord needs them,' and he will send them immediately."	And when they were approaching Jerusalem, at Bethphage and Bethany, near the Mount of Olives, he sent two of his disciples and said to them, "Go into the village ahead of you, and immediately as you enter it you will find tied there a colt, that has never been ridden; untie it and bring it. If anyone says to you, 'Why are you doing this?' just say this, 'The Lord needs it and will send it back here immediately.' "	After he had said this, he went on ahead, going up to Jerusalem. When he had come near Bethphage and Bethany, at the place called the Mount of Olives, he sent two of the disciples, saying, "Go into the village ahead of you, and as you enter it you will find tied there a colt that has never been ridden. Untie it and bring it here. If anyone asks you, 'Why are you untying it?' just say this, 'The Lord needs it.' "

one another, or a combination of the two. For centuries it was assumed that Matthew was the earliest Gospel since it was thought to have been written by the apostle of that name (Matt 9:9). Since the nineteenth century, however, the best explanation for the interrelationship between the Synoptic Gospels has been the theory that Mark is the oldest Gospel. Matthew and Luke came afterward and used Mark and another unknown source of Jesus' sayings (simply known as Q), supplemented by other independent sources arbitrarily labeled M and L, for their story of Jesus. This theory is called "The Two Source Hypothesis." It can be diagramed as follows:

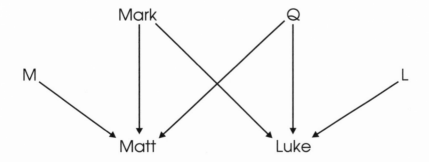

WHAT IS Q?

Q is the letter designation for the unknown and hypothetical source that under-lies the Synoptic Gospels. It derives from a German word, *Quelle*, which means "source." The Q document consists of the material common to Matthew and Luke and *not found* in Mark (about 220 verses). Most of this material is com-prised of sayings and teachings of Jesus. Some scholars make extravagant claims for Q and the hypothetical community that supposedly used it. Despite the media hype, such claims are greatly exaggerated.

We need not go into the technicalities of this hypothesis. Note that I emphasize that it is only a scholarly theory, albeit the best one currently available to explain the relationship of these three Gospels.

The fourth Gospel is another matter. Compared to the Syn-optics, the Gospel of John is extremely different. It has been recognized since the earliest days of Christianity as an unusual Gospel. It does not tell the story of Jesus in the same manner as the other three. A quick comparison can give us a general picture of these differences:

Synoptic Gospels	*Gospel of John*
• Public ministry appears to be one year	• Public ministry is as long as three years
• Jesus goes to Jerusalem once, for his passion, death, and resurrection	• Jesus frequently goes to Jerusalem, especially to celebrate Jewish feasts
• Cleansing of Temple takes place at the end of the public ministry	• Cleansing of the Temple takes place at the beginning of the public ministry
• Jesus frequently performs miracles	• Jesus seldom performs miracles; rather, he accomplishes "signs"
• Jesus accomplishes exorcisms	• Jesus does no exorcisms
• Jesus speaks in parables	• Jesus never speaks in parables but in long discourses
• Jesus speaks frequently of the Kingdom of God	• Jesus seldom speaks of the Kingdom of God but often of himself in various roles
• Last Supper words of institution of the Eucharist	• No words of institution at the Last Supper, but Jesus washes his disciples' feet

DATING THE GOSPELS

The best scholarly theories use the following estimates to date the four canonical Gospels. Keep in mind that Jesus' life extended approximately from 4 B.C. to
A.D. 30. Consequently, the earliest Gospel would date in written form nearly forty
years after Jesus' death and resurrection.

Mark	ca. A.D. 66–70
Matthew	ca. A.D. 80–90
Luke	ca. A.D. 80–90
John	ca. A.D. 90–100

Even this cursory look shows us that they are very different
Gospels. Although some have tried through the centuries to har-
monize these stories and place them in a sequential order, no one
has been successful at this endeavor in a satisfactory way. The reason, I think, is that they were never meant to be taken together as
a whole. Rather, each Gospel originated in a particular Christian
community that told the story of Jesus in its own way and for its
own purposes. This does not mean that all four Gospels do not
contain historical remembrance. On the contrary, since the origin
of the Gospels is in oral tradition, there is a historical nucleus that
undergirds them. Yet they are not biographical records of Jesus.
After all, the evangelists didn't have camcorders!

Each Gospel is a theological interpretation of Jesus and his
significance. They cannot be harmonized naively into one continuous story. Early Christians recognized this. They applied, in
fact, a passage from the Book of Revelation (Rev 4:7) to the four
Gospels, assigning each one a distinctive image to represent it.
Matthew was the "human" image, Mark the "lion," Luke the
"ox," and John the "eagle." These artistic representations have
survived through the ages and are symbols often applied to each
Gospel. Taken together the four Gospels provide not a unified
picture of Jesus but four different snapshots taken from different
angles. This multiplicity should not make us anxious. Instead, it
is a gift of diversity to the church. Chances are, as you read the
Gospels you will find that one is more appealing than the others.
Favorites are fine to have, provided that you remember there are

three other stories of Jesus that may provide alternative ways of understanding him.

Matthew

Matthew's Gospel was the favored Gospel of the early church. It was the most frequently quoted, and its large sections of teaching material may have made it useful for catechetical purposes. From Matthew we receive the forms of the Beatitudes and the Lord's Prayer that have become practically Christian ID badges.

Originally Matthew was thought to be the oldest Gospel because its author was supposed to be Matthew the tax collector (Matt 9:9; cf. Mark 2:14 and Luke 5:27), but modern scholarship has cast doubts on that identification. The titles of all the Gospels date only from the second century A.D. The author of Matthew appears to be a Jewish Christian. He views the world with Jewish eyes, having utmost concern for the fulfillment of the Law and for the need to lead a righteous life before God. The place of origin of Matthew is difficult to pinpoint. The Gospel shows evidence of tense relations with synagogue Jews (note references to "*their* synagogues") at a time when Christianity was beginning to appear as an altogether different religion. An urban environment, like Antioch in Syria, is perhaps a likely spot for such a situation.

Structure and Content

Many have noted that Matthew possesses a tendency to use parallelism. There are neatly balanced sections to the Gospel. For instance, the infancy narrative (ch. 1–2) parallels somewhat the passion/resurrection narrative (ch. 26–28). Both use "dream motifs," and an overarching theme that Jesus is Emmanuel, "God-with-us" (1:23), is reprised in the risen Jesus' promise to be "with" his disciples until the end of the ages (28:20). Yet one should not overlook that this Gospel tells a *story*, the story of Jesus, the messiah and obedient and faithful Son of God.

The first section of the Gospel (1:1–4:16) establishes the identification of Jesus, placing him in the context of Israel's history. Jesus is the fulfillment of the prophetic promises, he is in David's messianic line, and he, unlike Israel of old, will be faithful and

TITLE: The Gospel according to Matthew

AUTHOR: Unknown Jewish Christian, but tradition identifies him as Matthew the tax collector (Matt 9:9)

DATE: Ca. A.D. 85

STRUCTURE:

1:1–4:16	Origins of Jesus
4:17–11:1	Initial ministry
11:2–16:20	Growing opposition
16:21–28:20	Passion, death, resurrection

THEMES: Righteousness, prophecy and fulfillment, judgment, Emmanuel, Jesus the obedient and faithful Son

obedient to his Father's will. The second section (4:17–11:1) begins Jesus' ministry in Galilee. His preaching of repentance picks up John the Baptist's mission (4:17; cf. 3:2), but soon his own special teaching comes to the fore. The magnificent Sermon on the Mount (ch. 5–7) shows Jesus to be the messiah in *word*. It is the first of five great discourses interspersed throughout the Gospel (ch. 5–7; 10; 13; 18; 23–25), each of which ends with a repeated phrase ("And when Jesus had finished... ").

Then Jesus demonstrates that he is the messiah in *deed* by the mighty miracles he effects (ch. 8–9). After he instructs the disciples on the meaning of discipleship (ch. 10), serious opposition begins to appear in the next section of the Gospel (11:2–16:20). Certain Jewish leaders oppose Jesus, and tension builds in the story throughout this section as Jesus continues his ministry of preaching, teaching, and healing. The final section (16:21–28:20) shows that the increased hostility leads to actions against Jesus, actions that ironically demonstrate Jesus' authentic fulfillment of his Father's will even to death on the cross. The resurrection vindicates Jesus who, in turn, appears to his disciples in Galilee and commissions them to go forth and evangelize the whole world (28:16–20).

Interpretation

There are many problems to address in the interpretation of Matthew. If the author is a Jewish Christian, why does the Gospel seem to commend Gentile believers and to orient the gospel mission toward the Gentile world? Similarly, how could an author of Jewish heritage use such offensive language to describe Jewish leaders as hypocrites and whitewashed sepulchers (ch. 23)? How can Matthew maintain that Jesus came to fulfill the Law and not eradicate it (5:17), and yet show Jesus deliberately advocating rules that go far beyond that Mosaic Law ("you have heard it said, but I say to you...")?

There are many apparent contradictions in this Gospel. They are not easy to resolve. Some of them may be due to the preservation of different traditions from different times. Others may stem from levels of editing that the Gospel underwent. As you read Matthew, I suggest you concentrate on the flow of the story. Watch the development of the tension between Jesus and his opponents and the tentative growth of the disciples in their faith. Listen to the large tracts of teaching material as if it applies to you. It does. The ethical teaching of this Gospel is timeless, and as we read of Jesus teaching his disciples in the five great discourses, it's as if we are present listening at the same time.

Exercise

Read Matt 5:1–12, the Beatitudes. How do you understand them: as impossible ideals, as goals to be achieved, as wishful blessings upon those who suffer, or as hallmarks of God's kingdom when it arrives? Why?

Mark

Mark's Gospel is the shortest of the four Gospels. Ancient tradition held that a companion of Peter was the author and that he was writing from Rome. Nothing in the text identifies the author as a companion of Jesus, but there are indications that the author or his community was Gentile because Jewish terms and customs are regularly translated.

The brevity of this Gospel belies its impact. It tells the story of Jesus almost breathlessly. Events take place with great speed, one after another. Mark is fond of saying "and immediately" this or that happened. There is only one instance of Jesus speaking at length, the parables discourse (ch. 4). Otherwise, Mark describes

TITLE: The Gospel according to Mark

DATE: Ca. A.D. 66–70

AUTHOR: Unknown; tradition says a companion of Peter

STRUCTURE:

1:1–8:26	Jesus' Galilean ministry
8:27–16:8	Passion, death, resurrection
16:9–20	Later ending

THEMES: Secret of Jesus' identity, faith and fear, the cross, true discipleship

Jesus as performing miracles and exorcisms. In these activities he shows himself to be a great "teacher" (1:22, 27).

Structure and Content

The simplest division of this Gospel is into two parts. The first part (1:1–8:26) sets forth the identity of Jesus for the readers. He is God's Son (1:1) who comes in power that is paradoxically made effective in the willingness to suffer. In his powerful deeds and parables he reveals God's kingdom. The problem is that not even his disciples understand. A distinctive feature of Mark is that the human characters in the story don't know Jesus' identity. It remains a secret. Even after witnessing miracles, they ask: Who is this, how does he have such powers? (4:41). Only demons scream out his true identity (1:24; 3:11).

In the second part of the Gospel (8:27–16:8) the true nature of Jesus' identity is made clear. As Jesus instructs his disciples he tries to explain the meaning of discipleship, but they consistently misunderstand him. Being God's Son doesn't mean privilege but the willingness to offer one's life for the sake of others. Only as one gazes at the cross does the meaning of Jesus' mission become clear. A Gentile soldier confesses his true identity: "Truly this man was God's Son" (15:39).

The final section (16:9–20) is a later addition describing resurrection appearances.

Interpretation

A strong feature of Mark is the teaching about the nature of discipleship. If you were ever tempted to become rather proud that you are a Christian, you might be startled by Mark's portrayal of the disciples. Despite their privileged position of being in Jesus' presence, they are the original "people unclear on the concept." Time and again Jesus must remind them to pay closer attention to the essentials. Even after the double multiplication of the loaves, they do not comprehend. Even after a lengthy teaching that discipleship entails suffering (8:22–10:52) they argue over who will get the best places at the heavenly banquet. But Jesus never gives up on them. The message at the empty tomb is directed to the disciples (16:7). They are sent back to Galilee, where Jesus' own ministry had begun.

Another distinctive feature of Mark is the ending. You might consider it the first "interactive" media. You get to choose your ending. Do you want the shorter ending, the longer ending, the Freer ending (referring to a manuscript at the Freer Art Gallery in Washington, D.C.), or the startling ending of 16:8: "they went out and told nothing to anyone"? The last possibility was obviously unsatisfying to some early Christians because alternative endings sprang up early. Yet I believe 16:8 could be the intentional ending. The reader knows that someone broke the silence about the resurrection and the empty tomb. Otherwise we would not be Christians. The curious ending places the reader squarely in the presence of the messenger at the empty tomb. Go to Galilee, and you will encounter the Risen Lord. That is, sink yourself into the mission, and the Risen Lord will be there. Our faith is not in an empty tomb but in a Risen Lord whose presence is no longer restricted to physical presence.

Exercise

Read Mark 10:46–52. Why is blind Bartimaeus a better disciple than Jesus' own chosen ones? Where would you situate yourself in the story?

Luke

Luke is the only Gospel that is the first of two volumes. The same author also wrote the Acts of the Apostles. Yet because of its similarity to Mark and Matthew, Luke is often studied in relation to them.

From Luke we have received many memorable scenes captured by artists through the ages. The Annunciation (1:26–38), the Visitation (1:39–45), the Prodigal Son (15:11–32), the Emmaus story (24:13–32) all come from this Gospel. Some famous prayers also derive from Luke, like the Magnificat (1:46–55), Zechariah's Canticle (1:68–79), and Simeon's Canticle (2:29–32). In short, Luke is a storehouse of Christian imagery.

Luke is also the only Gospel to provide us a rationale for his enterprise. His prologue (1:1–4) self-consciously reflects an attempt to place Jesus and the story of Christianity in the broader context of history. Note, too, that the prologue presumes the writer is at least a second-generation Christian, for he relies upon "eyewitnesses and ministers of the word" rather than identifying himself as one (1:2). His audience was probably largely Gentile. Some have suggested that the purpose of Luke was apologetic. In other words, maybe he was trying to defend Christianity in the eyes of the Romans as a nonthreat to the Roman empire or vice versa. Regardless of that intention, Luke provides yet another interpretation of Jesus of Nazareth and his significance.

Structure and Content

Luke can be divided into five parts. The prologue (1:1–4) sets the context and is paralleled by a similar prologue in Acts (Acts 1:1–5). Luke writes to a certain Theophilus in order to set the record straight. Who was Theophilus (Greek = "lover of God")? We don't know. He probably was a real person, perhaps a recent convert. Some scholars think he is a literary invention, an idealized image of Luke's community. The point is that Luke is attempting to put into writing *his* understanding of Jesus while acknowledging that others have done likewise.

The second section of the Gospel (1:5–9:50), like Matthew, sets forth Jesus' identity and origin and describes his ministry in Galilee. His mission is clearly stated at the synagogue in Nazareth when Jesus quotes the Book of Isaiah (Isa 61:1–2): "The Spirit of

TITLE: The Gospel according to Luke

DATE: Ca. A.D. 85

AUTHOR: Unknown; tradition held him to be a companion of Paul

STRUCTURE:
1:1–4	Prologue
1:5–9:50	Ministry in Galilee
9:51–19:27	Travel narrative
19:28–21:38	Ministry in Jerusalem
22:1–24:53	Passion, death, and resurrection

THEMES: Jesus the Savior and reconciler, prayer, forgiveness, role of women, the Holy Spirit

the Lord is upon me..." (4:18–19). Jesus goes about his ministry, teaching and healing and always a source of reconciliation. The third part is laid out as a travelogue (9:51–19:27). At 9:51 Jesus prophetically "sets his face" toward Jerusalem, the city of his destiny. For many chapters Jesus is "on the way" to Jerusalem, all the while instructing his disciples about God's kingdom and fulfilling his mission. This section is often called the "travel narrative." Once Jesus is in Jerusalem, Luke devotes a section to Jesus' ministry there (19:28–21:38), which shows his great concern for the city's fate and the climactic events that will come upon it.

The final section (22:1–24:53) recounts the passion, death, and resurrection. While there are many similarities in this section to Mark and Matthew, Luke also contains unique details. Jesus appears before both Herod and Pilate to be declared innocent (23:4, 15). Even while he is being judged he reconciles these two enemies (23:12) and expresses forgiveness for his persecutors (23:34). Jesus even promises "paradise" to the repentant thief (23:42–43). His ministry of mercy thus shows no bounds from beginning to end.

Interpretation

To grasp Luke's Gospel, one must get "the big picture." I mean that one must understand that Jesus' life and ministry, death and resurrection, and even the birth of the church are part of God's grand design guided by the Holy Spirit. Practically everything in Luke happens under the Holy Spirit's guidance. Jesus accomplishes his mission because he is filled with the Spirit. Jesus also has inner reserves of strength that derive from prayer. He teaches his disciples about prayer and its necessity. He also teaches that reconciliation and forgiveness are the hallmarks of God's kingdom. Frequently Luke shows Jesus at meals with a variety of people. Luke's Jesus is a real party-lover! Meal-time is a social event and a time for healing. He even eats with Gentiles, tax collectors — the scum of the earth. Such scandalous behavior in the eyes of his "religious" opponents shows how far God's healing power extends. Not that Luke's Jesus is a wimp. He makes demands on his disciples, but the more difficult message to get across is the necessity to forgive even one's enemy.

Exercise

Read Luke 15:11–32 several times. Each time place *yourself* in the position of a different character in the story (the prodigal, the elder son, the father). Does each perspective change your understanding of the story?

John

Right from the start this Gospel soars above the other three. Its grandiose beginning sets the backdrop of a cosmic event. The eternal Word of God becomes flesh and comes to dwell with his people. The rest of the Gospel plays out this story in all of its glory.

From the earliest days of Christianity believers have recognized the uniqueness of this Gospel. In fact, it had trouble being accepted in all quarters of Christianity for centuries. Some saw in it a particular danger — it could lead someone to the heresy of rejecting the incarnation, the idea that God would deign to become one like us. Simultaneously it could overemphasize the otherworldly nature of Christian teaching. Fortunately, even though some Christians fell for these misinterpretations of the Gospel's message, the church retained it in the canon.

Ancient tradition held that this Gospel originated with one of the twelve disciples of Jesus, John of Zebedee. He was identified as "the beloved disciple" who is otherwise unnamed in the

TITLE: The Gospel according to John

AUTHOR: Unknown, but traditionally identified as John, son of
     Zebedee

DATE: Ca. A.D. 90–100

STRUCTURE:

1:1–51	Prologue
2:1–12:50	The Book of Signs
13:1–20:31	The Book of Glory
21:1–25	Epilogue

THEMES: Word made flesh, light and darkness, truth and falsehood,
     signs and glory, Bread of Life, Good Shepherd, Vine and
     branches

Gospel (see 19:26; 21:20, 24). Scholars have reason to doubt this
identification. The Gospel shows signs of being composed at a
later period in Christian history, near the end of the first century.
The beloved disciple was probably a real, historical figure who
followed Jesus and whose authority lies behind the Gospel because he was important in the Johannine community. But he did
not compose the Gospel. Whoever the author was, he had a gift
for drama, for this Gospel contains some of the most memorable
stories about Jesus ever told.

Structure and Content

The large structure of John is fairly simple. It consists of two main
parts, a "Book of Signs" and a "Book of Glory," enveloped by
a prologue and epilogue. The Gospel begins with a poetic prologue and historical introduction (1:1–51). It describes in cosmic
dimensions how the eternal "Word became flesh" and came into
the world and how John the Baptist prepared for this coming.

The first main part of the Gospel, the Book of Signs (2:1–
12:50), shows how Jesus reveals himself and his relationship to
God, his Father, by a series of "signs" that affect his audience
in two ways. These signs lead some people to faith but make
others direct enemies of Jesus. The second part of the Gospel
(13:1–20:31) describes how Jesus receives glory from his heavenly Father by his obedience even to death. The glory foretold in
the first part of the Gospel comes to its fullness in the second part.

Jesus gloriously embraces his fate on the cross as a good shepherd who lays down his life for his sheep, only to take it up again (10:11, 17–18). A careful reader will notice that John 20:30–31 sounds like a conclusion to the Gospel. Scholars believe, indeed, that the epilogue (ch. 21) was added by a later hand that genuinely stems from the Johannine tradition. It rounds out the story of "the disciple whom Jesus loved" as a model disciple even while acknowledging the preeminence of Peter among Jesus' disciples.

Interpretation

The eagle is the ancient symbol for John's Gospel. It is so appropriate. This Gospel soars like an eagle. To read John one must enter a different world, one in which themes are repeated over and over again but in a rising, cyclical fashion. Like an eagle on the hunt, the Gospel flies higher and higher in circular fashion. The more one ascends, the deeper the understanding of what its message holds.

The most important teaching contained in John is that Jesus is the incarnate Word, God-become-flesh, who came to show us the way to the Father (1:1–3, 10–14). He came down from heaven for a time but then ascended back to God's glory. We can visualize this movement with a diagram.

Pre-existent Word with God   *Word returns to Father in Glory*

↘   ↗

Word made flesh, dwells in world

As the story unfolds John describes a series of personal encounters with Jesus. As Jesus performs signs that demonstrate his true origin, people are either drawn to him or are repulsed by him. They must make a decision to believe and to follow him in discipleship. The characters are quite memorable: a Jewish teacher of the Law (Nicodemus, 3:1–21), a Samaritan woman (4:1–42), a crippled man (5:1–18), a man born blind (9:1–41), and a friend named Lazarus (11:1–44).

On the surface, these stories are simple encounters. But notice that each of them contains lengthy dialogues and monologues that treat deeper religious issues. The message takes on new complexity. Hence, the Nicodemus and Samaritan woman stories speak subtly of baptism. The story of the man born blind speaks of conversion as movement from darkness and blindness to light and sight. And the Lazarus story speaks of resurrection and eternal life. The reader can discover many new insights into the essentials of Christian living by a careful reading of these stories.

Exercise

Read John 9:1–41. What symbolism is most striking to you in this story? Using your imagination, where would you place yourself in the story? That is, with what character(s) would you identify? Could your role change from time to time as your own faith develops?

Chapter 11

THE ACTS OF THE APOSTLES

Acts is unlike any other book of the NT. It tells a story no one else recounts — the birth and growth of the infant Christian church. The author is clearly the same as the author of the Third Gospel, for the prologue mentions the intended reader Theophilus and refers to the first volume of his work. The goal is also clear. Luke wants to recount his understanding of how Christianity came to be in the months and years following Jesus' death and resurrection. It is like the open-ended second act of a two-act play.

Structure and Content

Acts can be structured rather simply according to an important geographical reference. Acts 1:8 describes the command of the risen Jesus to the apostles to be "my witnesses in Jerusalem, throughout Judea and Samaria, and to the ends of the earth." The plan of the book basically follows that geographic spread of the gospel. After a prologue (1:1–5) that reminds the reader of the relationship of Acts to Luke's Gospel, the story begins with an evangelizing mission in Jerusalem (1:6–8:3), proceeds to Judea and Samaria (8:4–9:43), and eventually extends to the Rome (10:1–28:31). Since Rome was the center of the empire (from and to which all roads led), Rome may well symbolize the "ends of the earth." Hence, Acts demonstrates how the promise of the risen Jesus comes to fruition in the growth of the church.

Such a large and complex book contains many themes. An important one to notice is the function of the Holy Spirit throughout the book. Jesus in Acts calls the Spirit "the promise of the Father" (Acts 1:4; see also Luke 24:49). The Spirit is at one and the same time God's powerful presence at work in the church and the ongoing presence of the Risen Christ in the Christian community. For Luke, everything that happens is due to the power of the Spirit mysteriously present and active among the Christians as they proclaim their message all over the world.

183

TITLE: The Acts of the Apostles

AUTHOR: The author of the Gospel of Luke, called Luke

DATE: Ca. A.D. 80–90

STRUCTURE:

1:1–5	Prologue
1:6–8:3	Mission in Jerusalem
8:4–9:43	Mission in Judea and Samaria
10:1–28:31	Gentile mission to the ends of the earth

THEMES: Holy Spirit, growth of the church, apostolic preaching, bearing witness to Christ

Interpretation

From one perspective this book is wrongly titled. It could easily be called "The Acts of Peter and Paul." They are the only two prominent characters in the book. Peter dominates ch. 2–12 while Paul dominates ch. 13–28. Other apostles and Christian preachers, of course, are mentioned, but none receives the limelight like Peter and Paul. From Luke's perspective they sum up the essence of how Christianity became a world religion. Flawed characters though they were (one denied Jesus, the other persecuted the church), they became key vehicles for the spread of the gospel message.

Another comment is necessary concerning the nature of Acts as history. Acts reads like a history book, but we must be careful to understand how this history is presented. As with his Gospel, Luke tells the story of the church the way he wants it understood. It has its own intensely theological perspective. It is not intended to be read as objective modern history. Consequently, interpreters have had to read Acts carefully for information regarding Paul, for instance, and compare that information with what is known from Paul's own letters. Sometimes the perspectives are quite different. One cannot always be certain whose viewpoint is more historically accurate. This should not distress us. Acts, like all the books of the NT, is a faith document. We are to understand the birth of the church as a miracle that God's grace has wrought with the cooperation and hard work of the apostles and their successors through time.

WHO IS THE HOLY SPIRIT?

Christians identify the Spirit as the third person of the Blessed Trinity, but we often forget that it took centuries for that insight to develop into an official Christian doctrine. Traditional images of the Spirit are impersonal: wind, breath, fire, a dove. The Spirit is portrayed in the OT as a powerful, intangible aspect of God. The Spirit is present at creation as a great wind that brooded over the waters (Gen 1:2). The Spirit also inspires prophets to speak God's Word and breathes new life into Israel (Ezek 37:14). In the wisdom tradition the Spirit is identified at times with the Wisdom Woman (Wis 1:5-7; 7:24-25), another mysterious presence of God.

In the NT Luke-Acts makes the most frequent use of the image of the Holy Spirit. The Spirit is God's guiding power that directs the plan of salvation in accomplishing God's will (Luke 1:35) and in wind and fire enables the birth of the church (Acts 2:1-4). The Spirit appears in other documents as well. Only Matthew uses a trinitarian formula tied to baptism (Matt 28:19), but all the Synoptic Gospels show Jesus himself receiving the Spirit at his baptism and being empowered to defeat evil (Matt 3:16; Mark 1:10; Luke 3:22). John's Gospel provides the most unique image of the Spirit as the Paraclete — an advisor or counselor who defends Christians in time of difficulty and provides a comforting presence in Jesus' absence (John 14:16-17, 26). In short, the biblical understanding of the Holy Spirit is as a multifaceted, powerful, creative, and mysterious divine presence that guarantees that God's plan will ultimately come to fruition.

Exercise

Read Acts 2:1–13, the Pentecost story. The strong images of wind and fire and Holy Spirit appear. What gave the apostles courage and strength to proclaim their message? What elements of the story speak of the universal mission of the church? How do you participate in this mission?

Chapter 12

THE LETTERS

Letter writing is an ancient activity. It should not surprise us that the NT itself includes letters. Letters were an important means of communication to the early Christians. They could make contact with one another and share ideas from various parts of the Roman empire. Some people make a distinction between a "letter" and an "epistle." Although epistles tend to be more formal, the epistolary form in the NT is basically the same as the letter. So for our purposes the words can be used interchangeably.

Numerically the letters comprise the lion's share of the NT. Twenty-one of the twenty-seven books of the NT are letters. Yet most of them are small in size, as one might expect of letters. They are organized in the NT according to authorship and size. Paul's letters come first. This is most appropriate because he wrote most of the NT letters, and he composed the earliest book of the NT, 1 Thessalonians. His letters were probably the first NT books to be collected as the NT "canon" began to take shape.

How do we modern people go about writing a letter (if we have not entirely lost the art)? If I remember my elementary school training correctly, all letters have a simple three-part outline:

- Salutation (greeting or opening)

- Body

- Closing

Of course, there are variations on this outline as determined by circumstances and type of letter. One does not write to one's friends the way business letters are composed. But the basic outline of letters has changed little over the centuries. In Paul's day the outline of a typical Hellenistic-Roman world letter was:

- Salutation (greeting)

- Thanksgiving

- Body

- Closing

The only added feature that we do not include in our letters is the formal word of thanks to the addressee(s), usually accompanied by flowery wishes for blessings from the gods. Paul's letters follow this outline but with special reference to the Christian God. He also regularly added a word about his travel plans (he traveled a lot visiting his congregations and founding new ones) and specific instructions about ethical behavior. These new sections could be added in various locations of the letter, but often Paul placed his ethical instructions in a separate part of the body of the letter. Hence, a typical Pauline letter has the following outline:

- Salutation (greeting)

- Thanksgiving

- Body

- Ethical instruction (sometimes scattered throughout the letter)

- Closing

As you read Paul's letters, pay attention to these distinctive sections of the letter. You may be surprised at how easily you can pick them out.

Everyone knows the story of Paul, especially his dramatic conversion on the road to Damascus (see Acts 9:1–22). Once he received his commission from the Risen Christ to proclaim the gospel to the Gentiles, he set off to evangelize throughout the Roman empire. He became the itinerant evangelist par excellence. He went throughout Asia Minor and then into parts of the European continent founding Christian communities. His extensive travels required some form of easy communication; the letter suited perfectly. He could use some of his many companions as couriers. At times he would also hear oral reports from people who had passed through some of his congregations. He also used letters to stay in touch during his many imprisonments. These letters are collectively sometimes called "the prison epistles" (Phil, Phlm, Col, Eph). Paul normally used the services of a scribe to write (technically called an *amanuensis*), but he occasionally added his own personal touch (1 Cor 16:21). Paul always was concerned about his communities. He saw himself as their pastor, their father, their personal "apostle." His letters were not merely casual communications. Rather, they were instructions and formal communications, and he intended them to be read by the entire community (1 Thess 5:27). They were his substitute presence. His congregations, fortunately, recognized the import of his writings and preserved them for all time.

Not all the letters are *true* letters, that is, direct communications between friends, associates, and acquaintances. A few NT "letters" are masquerading. The Letters of James and Hebrews, for instance, are probably theological treatises or homilies dressed up in letter fashion. Scholars sometimes call NT letters that have a more general characteristic "the General Epistles" because they apply to the church at large rather than to specific congregations. This situation sometimes makes it difficult to determine exactly who wrote such a "letter" to whom, and when and why. Even some of Paul's letters are suspect. Scholars have determined that at least seven of his letters genuinely stem from him (Rom, 1 and 2 Cor, Gal, Phil, 1 Thess, and Phlm), but that leaves six that are disputed (2 Thess, Eph, Col, 1 and 2 Tim, Titus). Contrary to our practice, ancient peoples did not think it improper to write a letter in someone else's name. All the more acceptable, too, if they wrote as someone well-known, like Paul. His name could lend authority to the letter. Younger colleagues or disciples often wrote materials in the name of their master. Fortunately, we do not have to address each of these issues in order to appreciate the NT letters. As you begin the letters, think of yourself eavesdropping on ancient conversations about weighty matters of faith and the Christian life. It's a bit like reading someone else's mail that is also useful for you.

Romans

Everyone would agree that Romans is Paul's greatest literary achievement. It is his most theologically informed letter, and its influence in Christian thought is immeasurable. From Augustine to Luther, from John Calvin to Karl Barth, Romans has had an impact. Its tone is more formal than the rest of Paul's letters. For this reason some label it an "epistle." I prefer to see it as a personal letter, but one written in a more refined and thoughtful manner. Paul's primary purpose was to introduce himself to a community that he did not found and knew only by reputation. In the course of his introduction, he gives an overview of his understanding of Christian faith and how it relates to the experience of the largely Gentile Roman community. In doing so, he has given us a masterful treatise on the significance of Jesus Christ for the world.

Paul wrote Romans from Corinth around A.D. 57–58. It is the last of his letters. He directed it to the Christians in Rome where, tradition says, Christian faith began with the preaching of St. Peter and his companions.

Structure and Content

Although the tone of the letter is formal, it does divide well into the normal letter format we have seen for Paul's letters. The greeting (1:1–7) and thanksgiving (1:8–15) are a little lengthier but easily recognized. The body (1:16–11:36) contains more extensive argumentation than some of Paul's letters. He begins with an analysis of both the Gentile and Jewish worlds (ch. 2 and 3). It contains both good news and bad news. The bad news is that

---

TITLE: The Letter of Paul to the Romans

AUTHOR: St. Paul

DATE: A.D. 57–58

STRUCTURE:

1:1–7	Greeting
1:8–15	Thanksgiving
1:16–11:36	Body
12:1–15:33	Ethical instruction
16:1–27	Closing

THEMES: Justification by faith, Christian freedom, the Law under Christ, the Holy Spirit, Christ the new Adam, fate of Israel

---

both worlds are corrupt and in need of salvation. The reality of sin abounds. The good news: God has sent Jesus Christ as a savior for the whole world, to Jews and Gentiles alike, without any fee or charge. But the key is faith, sheer trust in God's mercy, the kind of faith that Abraham displayed in his life (ch. 4). Paul also contrasts Christ with the original Adam (ch. 5) and speaks of the need to let go of the Law and embrace the new life in Christ (ch. 6–7).

After a beautiful chapter on life in the Holy Spirit (ch. 8), Paul engages in a lengthy and complicated discussion of how the people of Israel are to be saved since they rejected Jesus as the Christ (ch. 9–11). To put it too simply, God's mercy will embrace them in the end. They will be brought into the fold paradoxically by the example of the Gentiles.

The ethical instruction of Romans is scattered throughout the letter, as in all of Paul's letters. A specific section (12:1–15:33) exhorts the community to love one another and not to judge others. Paul admits that he writes "rather boldly" (15:15), but he is compelled by his ministry in Christ Jesus.

The final chapter (ch. 16) looks like an exceptionally long closing. It lists many women and men whom Paul greets. A difficulty has always been that some ancient manuscripts leave out this chapter in Romans. A careful reader will note that Rom 15:30–33 sounds suspiciously like a closing. Did someone else add an extra chapter not original to Romans? It is possible, but no one knows for sure. One can question how Paul would have known so many people in a church he did not found and had not yet visited. Regardless, ch. 16 is probably Pauline material, even if it did not originally belong to Romans. It illustrates the great care Paul took with some of his communities.

Interpretation

If you are hungry to get acquainted with Paul, Romans is not the place to quench your appetite at first. Like eating at a smorgasbord, you may find yourself overstuffed. I suggest you savor it after you have sampled some of Paul's lighter fare, something more practical and less theoretical, like Philippians or 1 Thessalonians. Even Paul knew not to feed babies solid food until they were ready for it (1 Cor 3:2).

The most "meaty" issue that Paul tackles in Romans is the notion of justification by faith alone. This used to be a dividing line between Catholics and Protestants. Supposedly, Catholics thought you could earn salvation by good works, while Protestants thought it was a gift of God that required nothing else. Both positions were inaccurate, nothing more than caricatures. Fortunately today, Catholics and Protestants alike have a more nuanced appreciation of Paul. Romans does teach that justification by faith is God's free gift, but Paul also insists that people must live out that faith by their good actions. Christian freedom, in fact, is not the license to do whatever you will but to do God's will freely because it is the right thing to do. Paul instructs us to "put on the Lord Jesus Christ" (13:14) and it will transform our lives.

Exercise

Read Rom 7:14–25. Notice how many times the personal pronoun "I" is used in the passage. Who is this person, Paul himself or Paul speaking for all humanity? Do Paul's words confirm at times your own experience of inner conflict and inability to make the right choices?

1 Corinthians

Paul wrote several letters to the community he founded in Corinth, only two of which survive in the canon. Paul was quite fond

TITLE: The First Letter of Paul to the Corinthians

AUTHOR: St. Paul

DATE: A.D. 56

STRUCTURE:

1:1–3	Greeting
1:4–9	Thanksgiving
1:10–15:58	Body
16:1–18	Ethical instruction
16:19–24	Closing

THEMES: Unity and diversity, the body of Christ, Christian virtues, sexuality and marriage, the Lord's Supper, love, resurrection

of this community. He viewed it as his showcase community in the province of Achaia (now Greece), but he became disturbed when he learned that there were deep divisions among them. The primary purpose of his correspondence was to heal the divisions and keep the Corinthians focused on Christian essentials.

He wrote what we call 1 Corinthians around A.D. 56 from Ephesus in Asia Minor. The letter responds to two sets of information Paul had received, an oral report from "Chloe's people" (1:11) and a letter from the Corinthians themselves seeking advice on several matters (7:1). In this letter we see Paul at his best as a pastor. He alternates between scolding them for their sinfulness and tenderly entreating them to put Christian love into action.

Structure and Content

The letter follows somewhat loosely the basic structure of a Pauline letter. After a standard greeting (1:1–3) and thanksgiving (1:4–9), Paul launches into the first of his concerns, the report he has received from Chloe's people about divisions in the community. The body of the letter actually contains many diverse topics. These include true wisdom, apostolic ministry, sexual immorality, lawsuits among Christians, marriage and family, celibacy, meats offered to idols, conduct at the Lord's Supper, the nature of resurrection, and so on. They seem to follow one another in random order, yet one can discern Paul's main concern. Divisions hurt the body of Christ, the church. Christians are not supposed to be so attached to the individuals who may have brought them to faith, no matter who they are, but to Christ and his new community.

The ethical instruction typical of Paul's letters is scattered throughout the body of the letter. But immediately before closing (16:19–24) Paul offers other practical admonitions (16:1–18) that include his request for financial support of the poor in Jerusalem (16:1–4) and his travel plans (16:5–9). The practical side of Paul the pastor comes out even in the midst of important religious issues.

Interpretation

One of the most powerful and influential images to emerge from the Corinthian correspondence is that of the church as the body of Christ. We should keep in mind that for Paul the word "church" (Greek *ekklēsia*) meant a local community. Later theology would envision it in a more universal sense. Paul, employing a familiar term from his Hellenistic background, uses the image of the human body (Greek *sōma*) to explain the mystery of unity and diversity in the church. Just as a body has many different parts but remains a single body, so does the church (12:1–31). Every individual part of the body plays a unique role in its healthy functioning. Yet the body itself becomes a separate entity. Paul applies this image to the church as the way the Spirit mysteriously provides unity while respecting individual diversity.

For Paul, this notion was not simply good theology. It was also of practical importance to the Corinthians. They had split themselves into factions, each rallying around a hero and defending their own turf (1:10–17). Paul insists that Christ cannot be split this way. The unfortunate testimony of Christian history, however, shows sadly that this has happened many times. Surely one of the scandals of Christianity continues to be the periodic schisms that have split the body of Christ into multiple entities. Paul's challenging words to Corinth ring true today.

Exercise

Read 1 Cor 13:1–13, the great ode to love. This passage is often used at wedding ceremonies. How do you apply it to your own life, whether you are married or not?

2 Corinthians

Paul's Second Letter to the Corinthians most likely is a composite document. That means it consists of excerpts from several different letters of Paul that were put together as one letter in the canon. It is more disjointed than 1 Corinthians, but one can discern easily Paul's ongoing relations with that community. The relationship was obviously a rocky one. On the one side was their mutual love and admiration. On the other was the Corinthians' squabbles among themselves and Paul's frustration when they ignored his advice. Sound familiar? I think many a pastor has felt the same in similar situations.

Paul probably wrote the main parts of this letter around A.D. 57 from Macedonia. Part of the letter is intensely personal. It shows Paul's defensive side in light of attacks on his personal integrity and his apostolic ministry (10:1–11:33).

Structure and Content

After the standard opening (1:1–2) and thanksgiving (1:3–11), Paul begins with a personal matter over the postponement of a visit to Corinth. Some in the community interpreted this as vacillation on Paul's part, as if he was fearful to visit them and risk confrontation. Paul speaks of a "painful visit" (2:1), indicating just how tense his relationship with the Corinthians had become.

Paul devotes the lion's share of the body of the letter (2:12–12:21) to the issue of apostleship and ministry. Paul was keenly aware that "false apostles" were afoot in Corinth. They had challenged his authority with severe attacks. The tone of the letter is somewhat like "damage control." To defend himself Paul recounts his exploits as a missionary apostle. His credentials, that is, his call by Jesus Christ and his numerous sufferings, are inferior to no one else's (ch. 11).

Despite these tensions, Paul speaks in this letter most eloquently of the reconciliation that comes in Jesus Christ (5:16–21). Human disagreements, arguments, fights, and the like are no match for the reconciliation that God has achieved in his Son, Jesus Christ. Paul concludes his letter with some practical instructions (13:1–10) and a standard closing (13:11–13).

TITLE: The Second Letter of Paul to the Corinthians

AUTHOR: St. Paul

DATE: A.D. 57

STRUCTURE:

1:1–2	Greeting
1:3–11	Thanksgiving
2:12–12:21	Body
13:1–10	Ethical instruction
13:11–13	Closing

THEMES: Apostleship and true ministry, treasure in earthen vessels, new creation, reconciliation

Interpretation

Second Corinthians clearly relates to 1 Corinthians. One can tell that they are directed to the same community. Yet the issues in 2 Corinthians are distinctive. The alternation between the stern sections and the parts on reconciliation have led scholars to suggest a sequence of visits that Paul conducted to Corinth. His painful visit resulted in hurt feelings and misunderstanding. A later visit finally achieved reconciliation. The result is a view of both the painful and hopeful realities of Christian ministry.

A confusing feature of Paul's letter can be his understanding of "boasting in the Lord" (ch. 11). At times Paul can sound like he is proud as a peacock (11:17–29). He ridicules some of his opponents sarcastically as "super-apostles" (11:5). Whatever happened to them, Paul seemingly experienced it far greater! In spite of the appearances, Paul believes he is not boasting on his own accord but boasting in the Lord. What he means by this can be seen in the contrast between true weakness and true strength. Enduring suffering is not weakness, according to Paul. It is actually real strength (12:10). It shows one's ability to put the things of God first and to see human values as quite secondary. Paul thereby is not encouraging people to go out to seek such sufferings. Rather, should they come your way, trust solely in God's grace and that will suffice (12:8).

Exercise

Read 2 Cor 4:7–10. Paul uses the image of clay jars to describe the fragility of being an apostle of Jesus Christ. Have you ever had to suffer because of your faith? Does Paul think that fragility implies the inability to flourish as an apostle of Jesus Christ?

Galatians

Galatians is closely related to Romans with regard to themes. As an earlier letter of Paul, written around A.D. 54 from Ephesus, it nonetheless contains many of the basic religious ideas that he developed more fully in Romans near the end of his career.

Scholars have found it difficult to determine just to whom Paul was writing this letter. Galatia covered a large area in Asia Minor (modern Turkey). It is uncertain where Paul evangelized, whether in the more rural area to the north or in the urbanized Roman colony of Galatia to the south. In any case, Paul makes it clear that he is extremely upset with this community that he founded. They have allowed themselves to be led astray by false apostles. These opponents of Paul were preaching against him and corrupting his message. In the letter Paul challenges them with very strong language in order to set the record straight for his Galatian community.

Structure and Content

Galatians has a traditional Pauline greeting (1:1–5), but do you notice what is missing in the outline? There is no thanksgiving section. Paul launches directly into an impassioned complaint against the Galatians that they have forsaken the gospel message he gave them. It's as if Paul felt that he did not have much to give thanks for in their case.

The body of the letter (1:6–5:26) discusses Paul's major concerns. First, some opponents have questioned his apostleship, so Paul defends his apostolic credentials with vigor (ch. 2). He insists that he is as much an apostle as the great leaders, Peter and James the brother of the Lord. With equal strength he maintains that Peter had agreed that Paul could preach to the Gentiles without requiring their conformity to the Law (2:10–14). Then he

TITLE: The Letter of Paul to the Galatians

AUTHOR: St. Paul

DATE: A.D. 54

STRUCTURE:

1:1–5	Greeting
1:6–5:26	Body
6:1–10	Ethical instruction
6:11–18	Closing

THEMES: Gospel, Law, Christian freedom, apostleship

claims Peter got cold feet and hypocritically gave in to factions from Jerusalem that were insisting on circumcision for the Gentiles. The rest of the letter spells out the implications of Paul's understanding. Paul accuses the Galatians of reverting to slavery to the Law when they should be living out the freedom of the Gospel. So upset does he get that he angrily wishes his opponents would castrate themselves rather than impose circumcision on others (5:12). He also employs in a complicated fashion an OT image of Sarah and Hagar (see Gen 21:8–21) to explain the difference between being a slave and being free (4:21–31).

After specific ethical recommendations (6:1–10), Paul closes the letter in a personal manner (6:11–18).

Interpretation

Galatians is a letter that combines strong personal feeling with sophisticated religious ideas. I think we can identify with Paul somewhat. He experienced a call from the Risen Lord to preach the gospel to the Gentiles, yet he was being attacked for his ministry. Furthermore, his opponents were insisting on circumcision for Paul's male Gentile converts. The Jewish requirement of circumcision was one element that prevented many Gentiles from converting to Judaism. Paul came to realize it was not required to be Christian. But old customs die hard, especially when they are attached to one's very identity.

Paul's message in Galatians is quite radical. Christian freedom does away with the minimalistic rules of the Law. Christ has replaced the Law. "For freedom Christ has set us free. Stand firm, therefore, and do not submit again to the yoke of slavery" (5:1). He also warns the Galatians not to be fooled by those who claim to have another gospel (1:8–9). The gospel cannot be split. There is only one gospel message, and Paul had proclaimed it authentically when he converted them. Galatians is testimony to the firmness of Paul's convictions. It also demonstrates how radical the gospel message is. The old ways of the flesh must die and new ways of the Spirit must be born.

Exercise

Read Gal 5:22–26. What does Paul mean by "fruit of the Spirit"? What types of actions oppose the work of the Spirit and what types promote the work of the Spirit?

Ephesians

Experts are divided on the question of the authorship of this letter. Some hold that Paul himself wrote the letter. If so, he would have done it in the mid-60s of the first century A.D. Because of style, language, and content, the majority of scholars believe this letter is pseudonymous, that is, written by someone else late in the first century. Since some ancient manuscripts lack the designation "to the Ephesians," there is even a question about the intended audience.

Despite these uncertainties, Ephesians remains a beautiful and instructive letter. It uses familiar Pauline themes but develops them differently.

Structure and Content

Even though Ephesians can be structured like a standard Pauline letter, its tone is more universal and general. Its message could have been addressed to different congregations in different circumstances. This is why some prefer the designation "epistle" for Ephesians. There is little in the letter that speaks of specific circumstances that would relate to the city of Ephesus in Asia Minor (now Turkey) in Paul's day.

The author speaks in the letter as if he were Paul in prison writing instructions to one of his churches. He especially wants to emphasize that the church is the body of Christ. Christ is the

TITLE: The Letter of Paul to the Ephesians

AUTHOR: St. Paul or more probably a later unknown author writing
in Paul's name

DATE: Unknown, but probably ca. A.D. 80–100

STRUCTURE:

1:1–2	Greeting
1:3–23	Thanksgiving
2:1–3:21	Body
4:1–6:20	Ethical instruction
6:21–24	Closing

THEMES: The church as the household of God, the body of Christ,
and the bride of Christ

head of the body (4:15–16). Just as a household has a structure,
so does the church of God (5:21–6:9). All should use their God-
given gifts to build up the body and to promote unity (4:12).
Most importantly, Ephesians speaks of the incorporation of the
Gentiles, the non-Jews, into this special family of faith (3:1–6).
God has established in the church through Christ a new unity,
one that surpasses the covenant community of Israel.

The ethical section (4:1–6:20) emphasizes especially the need
to put away pagan temptations and to devote oneself thoroughly
to instruction in faith. It contains a striking image of the Christian
soldier who does battle with evil and withstands the attacks of
the devil (6:10–17).

Interpretation

Ephesians contains some magnificent reflections on the nature of
the church. Building upon Paul's basic insight, that the church
is the body of Christ, Ephesians enlarges the notion into a cosmic, all-embracing image of unity. Gentiles and Jews alike belong
to the one family of God. Family is understood in terms of the
standard Hellenistic-Roman world. Each family member had a
distinct role to play. But herein comes a problem for modern ears.

Whenever the passage on the role of husbands and wives (Eph
5:21–33) is read, some hearers quickly misinterpret it. The difficulty is the expression "wives be subject to your husbands"
(5:22). This command gives no one permission for the abuse of

wives or the subjugation of women. The same letter speaks of
slaves and masters (6:5–9), yet would we accept such instruction
at face value? We now recognize slavery as evil. The author of
Ephesians viewed it simply as part of the structure of society. My
point is not to go overboard in our interpretation of such difficult
passages. The stronger point is not to minimize the role of women
in society, even though such was the reality in the first century
A.D. The main instruction is that *everyone* should "be imitators
of God, as beloved children, and live in love, as Christ loved us
and gave himself up for us..." (5:1). These words overshadow
the other roles and place them in their proper context.

Exercise
Read Eph 3:14–21. It is a prayer of the author (Paul?) for the
readers. Pray this prayer very slowly. Can you call to mind those
for whom you would recite such a prayer?

Philippians

Philippi was a seacoast town in the Roman province of Macedonia (modern Greece) named after Philip II of Macedonia, the
father of Alexander the Great. It was the site of the first European converts to Christianity. Paul went there around A.D. 50 at
the urging of a vision in which he saw a "man of Macedonia"
beckoning him to come and preach the gospel (Acts 16:9–10).
Whether because it was his first European site or because of the
special attention he received from the Philippians themselves (Phil
4:14–15), Paul had a tender spot in his heart for this community.
   Paul wrote this letter from prison (1:13) probably in Ephesus
around A.D. 56 or from Caesarea Maritima (Palestine) a couple
of years later. The tone of the letter is extraordinarily joyful in
spite of the setting.

Structure and Content
The greeting (1:1–2) and thanksgiving (1:3–11) are standard for
Paul. The thanksgiving, however, is full of tenderness for the
Philippians as Paul explains his longing for them. The rather short
body of the letter (1:12–4:1) combines ethical exhortation with
some practical information about Paul's co-workers, Timothy and

TITLE: The Letter of Paul to the Philippians

AUTHOR: St. Paul

DATE: A.D. ca. 56

STRUCTURE:

1:1-2	Greeting
1:3-11	Thanksgiving
1:12-4:1	Body
4:2-20	Ethical instruction
4:21-23	Closing

THEMES: Joy, suffering, humiliation and exaltation of Jesus Christ

Epaphroditus. The frequency with which Paul mentions joy and rejoicing sets the tone in the midst of Paul's imprisonment. Since Paul views suffering as part of the gospel of Jesus Christ, his experience will not dampen the joy that he finds in maintaining his faith.

The ethical section (4:2–20) exhorts two women in the Philippian community to stop their bickering (4:2–3) and urges the Philippians to "keep on doing the things that you have learned" (4:9). Paul concludes with a brief closing using the common early Christian self-designation "saint." The early Christians referred to themselves as "the saints" not to imply their perfection, but their election as followers of Jesus Christ.

Interpretation

Philippians is a remarkable letter. Given the context of Paul's imprisonment, the note of joy that is sounded with such regularity throughout the letter is striking. Paul also gives us an extraordinary inside look at his Jewish background (3:4–6). In spite of his blessed Jewish heritage, he counts everything else in his life as rubbish compared to what he has gained in Christ (3:7–8). So committed is he to this new way of life that nothing else matters. That is why he feels he can endure any kind of suffering and hardship that comes his way.

The most important passage in the letter is the cosmic hymn of praise to Christ (2:5–11). Here Paul adopts and adapts an early Christian hymn (probably familiar to his readers) that makes

Christ a model of human behavior. We are to make the attitude of Jesus Christ our own. Though he was in the form of God, he did not grasp at power but surrendered himself like a common slave and endured death, even death on a cross. This humble surrender earned him God's eternal exaltation. The NT contains no greater summary of the message of the cross than this hymn. Paul uses it to instruct the Philippians about their obligations and in doing so provides us a model for all time.

Exercise

Read Phil 4:4–7. Why does Paul advise his readers to "rejoice in the Lord always"? Do you find it easy to follow Paul's recommendation? Are there ways you can improve to conform to Paul's vision?

Colossians

The Letter to the Colossians bears Paul's name, and it may have been written by him. A majority of scholars, however, think that someone else wrote it much later. The language and style of the letter is different from much of Paul's authentic letters. If Paul did write it, it would date from the early 60s. If someone else wrote it, it would be dated to the 80s.

Colossae was a city in the Lycus Valley in Asia Minor (modern Turkey). Paul did not found this church. Their founder was one of their own, Epaphras, who is mentioned in the letter as a companion of Paul (4:12). There is a close relationship thematically between Colossians and Ephesians. Both speak in exalted terms of Christ and the church.

Structure and Content

Even if Paul did not write this letter, the unknown author imitated Paul's style fairly well, and he presents himself as Paul. The letter begins with a standard greeting (1:1–2) and thanksgiving (1:3–8). The body of the letter (1:9–3:17) speaks of some concerns Paul has come to know from Epaphras while he sits in prison. Some pagan elements have crept into the Colossian community (2:16–19). Paul emphasizes that the focus of their faith must be Christ. He uses a hymn of praise to Christ (1:15–19) to teach

TITLE: The Letter of Paul to the Colossians

AUTHOR: Unknown, but attributed to St. Paul

DATE: Ca. A.D. 80–90

STRUCTURE:

1:1–2	Opening
1:3–8	Thanksgiving
1:9–3:17	Body
3:18–4:6	Ethical instruction
4:7–18	Closing

THEMES: The cosmic Christ, Christ as head of the body

the exalted nature of Christ and to remind them of their responsibilities of living the new life of faith they received from Christ (3:12–17).

The ethical section (3:18–4:6) instructs the Colossians about the nature of the household of God. Each member has distinct duties, wives, husbands, children, masters, and slaves. All are to contribute to maintaining harmony and peace. This structure is not to rob any of them of their human dignity, for Paul insists that all are one in Christ and Christ is in them all (3:11). The closing (4:7–18) contains an extensive list of greetings that names some of Paul's close associates.

Interpretation

Colossians contains many passages worthy of lengthy reflection. Like Ephesians it emphasizes God's mysterious plan that unfolded in time and revealed Jesus Christ as the universal savior. In him all things have come into being. In him all things will find their ultimate meaning. For Christians, these words are commonplace. For others, these words might sound arrogant or exaggerated. The intention of Colossians is to promote harmony, but it does so by reminding the faithful of their duties to one another and to outsiders. We are to seek the things above and not the things on earth (3:1–2). Keeping our perspective balanced, we will be able to remain faithful and allow God's mysterious plan to unfold before us.

Exercise

Read Col 1:15–20. This is an early Christian hymn of praise to Christ, the creator of all. What image of Christ emerges from this reading for you? What powers are attributed to Christ? Does this image conform to Christ as you have come to know him?

1 Thessalonians

First Thessalonians is Paul's earliest letter. It is, in fact, the earliest written document in the NT. Paul went to Thessalonica in Macedonia (now Thessaloniki in modern Greece) after being driven from Philippi (see Acts 16:39–17:1). He wrote the letter from Corinth in A.D. 50–51 upon receiving news that the Thessalonians needed some advice.

According to Acts (17:2), Paul stayed only a short time in Thessalonica before opposition forced him to leave for Athens. This letter is not known for its great Pauline themes, but its tone is filled with sentiments of thanksgiving for the community and gentle reminders of what their lives should reflect as Christians.

Structure and Content

The letter follows the format of most the Pauline letters. The greeting (1:1) and thanksgiving (1:2–10) sections open the letter. A careful eye notices that Paul mentions in his greeting his co-workers Silvanus (Latin form of the Greek name, Silas) and Timothy as co-authors (1:1). Paul's letters are not always exclusively his.

A curiosity in this letter is the presence of another thanksgiving (2:13–16). Some scholars think this section has been added by a later hand. Perhaps, or it may simply indicate how grateful Paul is to this community for their faithfulness. The primary focus of the body of the letter (2:1–3:13) is to reinforce the fidelity of the Thessalonians in spite of the challenges that sometimes appear. The ethical section (4:1–5:22) focuses primarily on the question of Christ's second coming. The Thessalonians were worried about Christ's promise to come again. Some of them spent considerable time trying to work out the details of that promise. Others were concerned about those in the community who had already died.

TITLE: The First Letter of Paul to the Thessalonians

AUTHOR: St. Paul

DATE: A.D. 50–51

STRUCTURE:

1:1	Greeting
1:2–10	Thanksgiving
2:1–3:13	Body
4:1–5:22	Ethical instruction
5:23–28	Closing

THEMES: Thanksgiving, Christ's second coming

What would become of them since they would not be around when Christ would come again? Paul puts these concerns in perspective. He tells the Thessalonians not to get so upset about these matters because they are in God's hands. Their task is to live like children of the light and to go about their business in faithfulness. Paul then concludes with his standard closing (5:23–28).

Interpretation

A striking feature of 1 Thessalonians is the reinforcement that Paul provides the community. Repeatedly in the letter Paul uses phrases like "as you know," "you already know" or "as indeed you are doing." This is truly a pastoral letter. I mean that Paul takes the position of a pastor who both tenderly reinforces the positive aspects of his community but delicately challenges them to go further. Paul compares himself to a gentle nurse (2:7) and to a tender father who cares for his children (2:11).

One difficulty seems to have been that some in the community were not doing their fair share of work. Paul reminds them that he always worked for a living in the midst of his ministry so as not to burden them (2:9). He also urges the idle in the community to get to work (5:14). For Paul, faith is not merely a matter of sitting back and waiting for your reward. It requires hard work in the midst of observing one's moral obligations in faith.

Exercise

Read 1 Thess 4:9–12. What impression does this passage give you about Paul's treatment of the Thessalonians? Is Paul's advice

to them sound? Does it apply equally well to your life today? If
so, how?

2 Thessalonians

Scholars are divided on whether 2 Thessalonians was written by
Paul himself or by a later unknown author. If the former were the
case, it would be dated to around A.D. 51–52. If the latter is the
case, the author and date would be mere guesswork. I myself am
torn. Sometimes I read it and think Paul wrote it to the Thessalonians he knew so well. At other times I am convinced Paul would
not have spoken to them that way.

The tone of the letter is very different from 1 Thessalonians.
Its perspective on the end times is also very different. These are
two important reasons to raise the question of authorship. The
question of tone is crucial. First Thessalonians is so warm and
personal, and 2 Thessalonians is so cold and impersonal. Could
Paul have written them to the same community? Regardless of
the answer, we can still take something of value from this short
letter.

Structure and Content

The letter begins with a standard opening (1:1–2) and thanksgiving (1:3–12). Compared to 1 Thessalonians, the thanksgiving
sections are skimpy. The body of the letter (2:1–3:5) is devoted to
the question of coming judgment. The letter speaks of "the law-
less one" who will be condemned by Jesus Christ on the day of
judgment (2:1–12). One can taste the apocalyptic flavor throughout the letter. The wicked will meet their end on the day of
judgment. We, in contrast, are to remain steadfast and faithful.

The ethical section (3:6–15) concentrates on the notion of
work. As in 1 Thessalonians, Paul reminds them that he worked
for a living rather than relying on their charity. He urges everyone
to imitate him. They are to work if they want to eat (3:10–12).
The closing mentions a type of signature (3:17) that Paul made in
all of his letters. It could be taken as an overstatement of someone
trying to authenticate the writing in Paul's name.

Title: The Second Letter of Paul to the Thessalonians

Author: Unknown, but attributed to St. Paul

Date: Late first century A.D.

Structure:
1:1–2	Opening
1:3–12	Thanksgiving
2:1–3:5	Body
3:6–15	Ethical instruction
3:16–18	Closing

Themes: Christ's coming judgment, working for a living, remaining faithful

---

Interpretation

This letter lacks the personal flavor of 1 Thessalonians. It may reflect a later time in Christian history when persecution was beginning to mount. Apocalyptic literature reappeared in this environment (see p. 102 above). The split between good and evil is most apparent in this letter. Evil forces from outside the community try to undermine it. The need to remain steadfast and faithful becomes all the more important in this situation. Imitation of Paul also figures significantly here. The letter is a great illustration of the need to preserve ancient tradition and to follow ancient example. "So then, brothers and sisters, stand firm and hold fast to the traditions that you were taught by us, either by word of mouth or by our letter" (2:15).

Exercise

Read 2 Thess 2:13–15. What is meant by being "the first fruits for salvation"? To whom is the expression addressed? In what way is this a privilege and in what way is it a challenge?

1 Timothy

The First Letter of Paul to Timothy is the first of three letters that belong together. They are collectively called "the Pastoral Epistles," 1 and 2 Timothy and Titus. This designation derives from

TITLE: The First Letter of Paul to Timothy

AUTHOR: Unknown, but attributed to St. Paul

DATE: Ca. Late first century A.D.

STRUCTURE:

1:1-2	Greeting
1:3-6:19	Body
6:20-22	Closing

THEMES: Ministerial roles in the church, guarding the faith

the unknown author who writes in Paul's name. He is called "the pastor" (or shepherd) because of the ministerial roles addressed in these letters. Scholars consider all three letters to be pseudonymous, written at a later time in Paul's name. They purport to be Paul writing to his co-workers, Timothy and Titus respectively, about their pastoral ministries.

Timothy was Paul's "beloved and faithful child in the Lord" (1 Cor 4:17) whom Paul had had circumcised because of his mixed Jewish/Gentile ancestry (Acts 16:3). He frequently acted as a courier for Paul, taking letters or oral reports back and forth between Paul and some of his congregations.

The primary reason scholars judge these letters to be Deutero-Pauline is the language and the situation envisioned by the letters. By this time, the church already had well established ministerial roles beyond what we see in the genuine Pauline letters. These letters are evidence of the increasing institutionalization of the church late in the first century A.D.

Structure and Content

The letter format is still apparent in 1 Timothy even if it does not conform exactly to Paul's usual structure. The greeting (1:1-2) sounds familiar, but the body of the letter conveys a more formal and institutional tone than usually found in Paul's letters. The main concern of the letter is to protect authentic teaching and to ward off false teaching.

It also speaks of distinct roles in the Christian community, designating those who are bishops and elders (Greek *episkopoi* and *presbyteroi*) and those who are deacons (Greek *diakonoi*). We should not confuse these roles with those of similar titles in various Christian churches today, but they are distinctive leadership roles in the later Pauline communities. Sections of the letter instruct these pastoral ministers in their duties (3:1–13; 5:17–23). The letter also speaks of the need to assist widows and even hints that older widows constituted a distinctive ministry in the community (5:3–16). The closing (6:20–22) exhorts Timothy with a summary warning to guard the faith.

Interpretation

The pastoral tone of this letter is seen most clearly in the practical advice offered to Timothy. His biggest challenge is to guard what has been given to him and to teach it to others (6:20). Some have made a "shipwreck of their faith" (1:19). The temptation is great to listen to what is only human advice rather than to follow God's laws. Furthermore, by the time of this letter, the institutional setup of the Christian community was reflecting more and more the wider secular environment. Societies were built on households, and households had their organization to maintain. Everyone had his or her own obligations to fulfill. As with any good organization, the Christian community's effectiveness depends upon loyal fulfillment of each one's duties. Primary among them is the proper exercise of faith and the respectful treatment of fellow Christians as sisters and brothers in Christ (5:1–2). Organization in this letter is not for its own sake but for the proper managing of what has been entrusted to the church's ministers. The issue is not whether our own church polity conforms to 1 Timothy's to the letter but whether we maintain the same spirit of trying to promote a faithful and loving community.

Exercise

Read 1 Tim 4:11–16. It evokes an older, wiser pastor giving advice to a younger, less experienced colleague. How would you feel about this advice addressed to you? Would you find it encouraging? Challenging? Upsetting? Is the advice still applicable today?

2 Timothy

Like 1 Timothy, 2 Timothy pretends to present to Paul's younger colleague, Timothy, some practical and sound advice about how to shepherd the Christian community. Despite its order in the canon, this letter may have preceded 1 Timothy in origin. It also may contain some fragments of genuine Pauline material, as seen in some of the intensely personal greetings (see 4:9–15).

Structure and Content

This letter follows the basic pattern of Pauline letters. The greeting (1:1–2) and thanksgiving (1:3–7) speak in tender terms of Paul's close relationship to Timothy. Paul is in prison and longs to see his friend again in person.

The body of the letter (1:8–3:17) is concerned with many of the same matters that are found in 1 Timothy. Adhering to sound doctrine and not getting involved in philosophical disputes is very important to Paul. The letter compares the task of maintaining the gospel message to the rigors of athletic training and competition (1:5; 4:7). Typical virtues are extolled and evils are listed that are to be avoided (3:2–5; 2:22; 4:5).

In the section on ethical instruction (4:1–18) Paul speaks quite personally of being harmed by some people in their opposition to him and being deserted in his imprisonment. But he also expresses his confidence that the Lord will bring him safely home to the heavenly kingdom. The closing (4:19–22) mentions a few of Paul's other co-workers, some of whom were associated with him at Corinth.

Interpretation

The practical nature of the advice in this letter has provided much fruitful reflection over time. The list of problems to be encountered by people "in the last days" sounds like a complaint list in any age (3:2–5). Equally valid is the advice to Timothy to maintain his own commitment to his ministry in spite of hardships (4:5). Knuckle down and do your work, and don't worry about what evil lurks in the hearts of others. A pastor should not become discouraged by his or her flock's (or colleagues') failures.

Perhaps the most important passage in this letter concerns the nature of sacred scripture (3:16–17). These words have been

---

TITLE: The Second Letter of Paul to Timothy

AUTHOR: Unknown, but attributed to St. Paul

DATE: Late first century A.D.

STRUCTURE:

1:1–2	Greeting
1:3–7	Thanksgiving
1:8–3:17	Body
4:1–18	Ethical instruction
4:19–22	Closing

THEMES: Sound doctrine, remaining faithful in the task of ministry

---

very influential especially among some evangelical fundamentalist interpreters. They take this passage to provide proof of the
inspiration of sacred scripture. It does insist on the inspiration of
sacred writings, but it never defines or describes *how* inspiration
functions. To assert the inspired nature of scripture is something
universal to all Christians. The text nowhere connects such an
assertion with the inerrancy of the Bible as regards historical or
scientific matters — that is, that the Bible contains no errors of
any type. Consequently, for many Christian churches the doctrine of inspiration is not necessarily tied to a doctrine of literal
inerrancy on the basis of this passage.

Exercise

Read 2 Tim 4:6–8. Does this passage sound like the words of
someone at the end of a long career of ministry? Do you think
Paul is tired of his work? How would you describe Paul's tone?
Why? Have you ever felt like that?

Titus

Titus was another of Paul's Gentile co-workers. This letter, the
third of the Pastoral Epistles, is supposedly written by Paul to
Titus as he ministers on the island of Crete. Titus is presented
as a presbyter-bishop who administers the church and appoints
other leaders in the community.

TITLE: The Letter of Paul to Titus

AUTHOR: Unknown, but attributed to St. Paul

DATE: Late first century A.D.

STRUCTURE:

1:1–4	Greeting
1:5–3:11	Body
3:12–15	Closing

THEMES: Sound doctrine, faithful administration of Christian ministers

Structure and Content

This short letter addresses some of the same issues we found in 1 and 2 Timothy. The main concerns are with church ministers, adherence to sound Christian doctrine, and maintaining an upright Christian life. After the greeting (1:1–4) the body of the letter addresses these issues in a forthright manner. Tensions between the Jewish and Gentile Christians are apparent (1:10). The community has some problems, and the letter instructs Titus to exercise his authority properly. The instruction lists many different qualities necessary in an effective Christian minister (1:6–9). In somewhat shorter form, the letter also addresses individual roles in the community, such as older men and women, younger men and women, and slaves (2:1–10). Nobody is excluded. Even obedience to lawful secular authorities is encouraged as a way of exercising influence in the social world around them (3:1). The closing (3:12–15) mentions more of Paul's co-workers and exhorts all to devote themselves to good works.

Interpretation

The relationship of Titus to the other two Pastoral Epistles is very clear. They exhibit similar situations in which the church has evolved ministerial roles to help keep Christians focused properly on spiritual and moral responsibility. Titus also emphasizes that God is the responsible agent who has transformed Christian life (2:11–12). Paul acknowledges that "we ourselves were once foolish" and gave in to evil desires, but the appearance of Jesus Christ as has changed all that (3:3–7). The outcome is Christian responsibility to the world and to everyone in the community. Paul urges Titus to be a model for others in the exercise of his duties. Actions, as we all know, speak louder than words.

Exercise

Read Titus 2:11–14. What attitude does this passage convey to you about the Christian life? How would you describe it?

Philemon

No one would consider this letter one of the theological high points of Paul's teaching. This tiny letter is one of Paul's most personal. He directed it primarily to a certain Philemon who owned a runaway slave named Onesimus. Yet Philemon's community is also mentioned (v. 2; *note:* no chapters, only verses).

Dating the letter is not easy, but it is likely one of Paul's last letters, perhaps written in the early 60s during his captivity in Rome. The brevity of this letter should not allow us to overlook its importance. Although the issue seems simple enough, the implications of Paul's advice to Philemon are revolutionary.

Structure and Content

Paul uses the standard opening (1–3) and thanksgiving (4–7) and immediately gets to the heart of the matter in the body (8–20). Paul wants Philemon to receive his runaway slave back not as a slave but as a fellow Christian. Paul had converted Onesimus during a mutual imprisonment (10). Paul artfully argues for Philemon's cooperation in this request by reminding him that he owes Paul a favor (19). In the final instruction (21–22) Paul expresses the hope that Philemon will honor this request and do even more. The closing (23) names some other co-workers of Paul who also send greetings.

Interpretation

So what is so revolutionary about Paul's letter? It does not attack the institution of slavery as such, as we might expect (or hope). In Paul's day, slavery was an accepted fact of society. Slaves were property. By rights, Philemon could have punished Onesimus severely or sold him to another owner. But Paul insists that

---

TITLE: The Letter of Paul to Philemon

AUTHOR: St. Paul

DATE: Ca. A.D. 60–63

STRUCTURE:

Vv. 1–3	Opening
Vv. 4–7	Thanksgiving
Vv. 8–20	Body
Vv. 21–22	Ethical instruction
Vv. 23–25	Closing

THEMES: Effects of Christian faith on community relationships

---

baptism into Christ changes relationships. By baptism Onesimus had become a "brother" to Philemon. He was now to be treated as one of the community.

If it is ever true that "big things come in little packages," I think this saying applies to Philemon. Deep down it provides testimony to how truly revolutionary Christianity can be when we recognize the implications of our faith.

Exercise

Read the entire letter to Philemon (it's short). Place yourself in the roles of Philemon, Onesimus, and then Paul. How does each role feel? Do you sense the revolutionary nature of the letter? What aspects of faith can you discern in it?

Hebrews

Hebrews is one of the most beautiful but controversial documents in the NT. It is called a letter, yet it exhibits almost no characteristics of this genre. Some ancient traditions assumed it came from Paul, but neither the author nor the intended audience are named. When read next to one of Paul's genuine letters, one sees that there is almost no similarity.

The contents seem very Jewish, which might point to its being written before the destruction of the Temple in A.D. 70. Yet its exalted image of Jesus Christ might point to a later first-century

TITLE: The Letter to the Hebrews

AUTHOR: Unknown, but at times attributed to St. Paul

DATE: Ca. A.D. 60

STRUCTURE:

1:1–4	Introduction
1:5–2:18	The Son's exalted position
3:1–10:39	Jesus Christ as High Priest
11:1–12:29	Examples of faith
13:1–19	Ethical instruction
13:20–25	Closing

THEMES: Jesus Christ the High Priest, superiority of Jesus, faith of the ancestors

date of origin. Scholars are divided on such issues, and its origins so far remain a mystery.

Structure and Content

If Hebrews is not a letter, what is it? It does not begin like a letter, but the conclusion slightly resembles a letter form. Probably the best description is found in Hebrews itself. The closing refers to "this message of encouragement" (13:22). It may have been a sermon or a treatise written to encourage a group of Christians in their faith. It is thus an example of hortatory literature. Despite this speculation, it is still appropriate to refer to it as a letter because that is its designation in the NT.

The introduction (1:1–4) is very broad and places the coming of Jesus Christ in the context of Jewish history. It leads immediately to a section that compares Jesus as God's Son to the angels (1:5–2:18). In every way Jesus is superior, a theme that reappears when he is compared to Moses and others throughout the letter. The bulk of the letter is devoted to a unique image found nowhere else in the NT, Jesus as the High Priest (3:1–10:39). This image evokes explicit Jewish background. The High Priest was an important cult figure in Jewish history. Only he had access to the innermost part of the Temple, the Holy of Holies, where God dwelt. Hebrews applies this image to Jesus as a christological assertion: Jesus is superior to any High Priest in history because he is God's Son. Despite his exalted position, he tenderly identifies with us because of his humanity. Paradoxically, he is both the High Priest who presides over worship and the sacrificial victim who is offered to God as a pure offering for the remission of sins.

The next section (11:1–12:29) praises the faith of the Jewish ancestors (Abel, Abraham, Moses, etc.). Despite this "great cloud of witnesses" (12:1) God's plan was for something better — salvation in Jesus Christ. The letter concludes with a series of exhortations that urges the readers to live upright lives (13:1–19) and a greeting (13:20–25) that sounds almost like the closing of a Pauline letter, especially with its mention of Timothy (13:23).

Interpretation

Hebrews is not easy to understand without knowing many figures from the OT and without understanding the nature of OT Jewish worship. If you read large sections of it, you will have to be patient perhaps by looking up the OT references found in your Bible. The entire letter has two purposes. First, it tries to explain in orderly fashion the significance of Jesus Christ in comparison to OT heroes. Hebrews thus presents its own "christology." Jesus now replaces OT worship that was centered on animal sacrifices at the Temple. Second, the letter provides strong ethical exhortations to its readers for the sake of encouragement. They are encouraged to reflect at length on their understanding of Jesus and how God has worked through him. The letter also urges them to live out their faith in such a way that they both continue and advance beyond the faithful examples known from OT history. Hebrews uses a complicated method of Jewish scriptural interpretation that can be hard for novices to follow. Don't get bogged down by this tendency. Instead, try to obtain the larger perspective of what is means to call Jesus Christ the High Priest.

Exercise

Read Heb 4:14–16. How does the image of Jesus Christ as the great High Priest relate to you? How do you understand the assertion that Jesus Christ is like us in everything but sin? Do you find this image comforting? How do you think the author of Hebrews understood this concept?

James

Although the NT calls James a letter, it is another example of a different literary genre disguised as a letter. Scholars generally agree that it was not actually written by James, the brother of the Lord (see Mark 6:3, Matt 13:55, and Gal 1:19). It is a pseudonymous work written in the late first century A.D. to a group of Jewish Christians. If it were written by James, the relative of Jesus, the absence of any mention of that relationship or any details of James' life would be most unusual.

Structure and Content

The greeting is very short and general (1:1). Scholars are uncertain who "the twelve tribes of the dispersion" are. The twelve tribes of Israel, of course, functioned symbolically in early Christianity as a prefigurement of the new Israel. The dispersion, or Diaspora, referred to Jews who had been scattered all over the world as a result of the Babylonian exile. In James could this expression refer to Christians scattered in the Roman empire? It may simply refer to Christians in general as the successors of Israel.

The first section (1:2–18) explains how trials and testing are a common ingredient in Christian life. The main section (1:19–5:12) is an extended series of moral exhortations and warnings. Much of the material resembles traditional Jewish wisdom literature. We might even call it common sense. It includes advice on sharing wealth, caring for the poor, showing no partiality, balancing words and deeds, not slandering others in speech, seeking true wisdom, and so on. Many times concrete images illustrate the main idea. These ideas lead to the final section (5:13–20) where James presents several examples of the importance of prayer. He advises prayer under all sorts of circumstances. He concludes with a hopeful example. If someone in the community strays, and someone else brings that person back, it is a blessed deed.

Interpretation

This book has been controversial in its interpretation. Martin Luther, in particular, rated it very low. He called it an "epistle of straw" and saw such little value in it that he placed it at the end

TITLE: The Letter of James

AUTHOR: Unknown, but attributed to James, the brother of Jesus

DATE: Ca. A.D. 90–100

STRUCTURE:

1:1	Greeting
1:2–18	Trials and testing
1:19–5:12	Exhortations and warnings
5:13–20	Exhortation to prayer

THEMES: Faith and good works, rich and poor, true wisdom, prayer

of the NT. Because it never mentions Christ nor emphasizes salvation, some have found it to be less "Christian" than Paul's letters or other letters in the NT. An even bigger obstacle for some is the supposed opposition to Paul's teachings that faith alone justifies (see 2:14–26).

Today, however, interpreters have recognized that this opposition between faith and good works is more apparent than real. Both Paul and James would be satisfied that there has to be a relationship between the faith you professes in words and how you lead your life. James's practical advice to Christians is not as a means to earn salvation (it is God's free gift), but a way of living out responsibly what we have come to know in faith. Words and deeds must go together.

Exercise

Read James 2:14–26. This is the classic NT statement about the interrelationship between faith and good works. Do you find it a helpful measure of your own faith? If so, why? If not, why not?

1 Peter

Scholars are divided on whether this letter is pseudonymous, written in Peter's name late in the first century, or genuinely comes from the apostle much earlier (ca. A.D. 60). It reads like a genuine letter, yet it sounds at times like a sermon or instruction on the nature of Christian baptism. Another concern is persecution

---

TITLE: The First Letter of Peter

AUTHOR: Unknown, but attributed to St. Peter

DATE: Late first century A.D.

STRUCTURE:

1:1-2	Greeting
1:3 - 4:11	Body
5:1-11	Ethical instruction
5:12-14	Closing

THEMES: Baptism, Christians in the world, perseverance under persecution

---

against the Christians. Since such persecutions did not arise until the late first century, this could justify a late dating of the letter. The presumed church structure (as in the mention of presbyters, 5:1) could also reflect a late period when church structure had become more defined.

Structure and Content

The greeting (1:1–2) identifies the recipients of the letter as Christian communities in various parts of Asia Minor. The body of the letter (1:3–4:11) launches into an understanding of Christian baptism as "new birth." The result of this new existence includes various responsibilities as well as the privilege of receiving God's abundant blessings. A large section is devoted to instruction on how Christians should live in the midst of a hostile world (2:11–3:12). It contains advice seen elsewhere in the NT directed to the household of God (e.g., the Pastoral Epistles). The exhortational character of the letter means that ethical advice is scattered throughout. But there is also an ethical section (5:1–11) that gives specific advice to Christian leaders (called presbyters) and to the rest of the community.

One lasting image is that of the devil prowling around like a hungry animal waiting to gobble up inattentive Christians (5:8–11). The advice to "resist him, steadfast in faith," resounds in Christian ears in every era. The closing (5:12–14) mentions mysteriously "the chosen one at Babylon" (5:13). For Christians late in the first century, Babylon became a familiar code term for the Roman empire, the enemy that persecuted them mercilessly.

Interpretation

The most productive way to understand this letter may be to see it as an instruction on the meaning of Christian baptism. What is accomplished in the life of a Christian by baptism? It brings one into the Christian community. It takes away one's innate tendency to sin. It transforms the meaning of suffering into participation in the suffering, death, and resurrection of Jesus Christ. It brings salvation. And it brings with it responsibility to live a morally sound life, respectful of proper authority and one another. First Peter also warns Christians about the danger of living in the world (2:11–12). It is not easy to give witness to Christian virtue. Many also find difficulty in avoiding the temptations of worldly desires. Our own times are no less dangerous. Indeed, maybe the temptations of modern life are greater than those faced by the author of 1 Peter. The advice contained in this letter is, then, no less applicable to us today than it was to the original audience centuries ago.

Exercise

Read 1 Pet 1:3–9. What is meant by gold tested by fire? Have you ever found yourself in such a situation of suffering? How do you understand v. 8? Can you relate "not seeing" and faith in your own life?

2 Peter

The Second Letter of Peter is the latest book in the NT. Despite its attribution to Peter, most scholars agree it is a pseudonymous letter that reflects a situation in the early second century A.D. One section on the false teachers (2:1–18) closely resembles the Letter to Jude from which it was copied. It has the nominal form of a letter, but it sounds more like an extended exhortation loosely dressed up in letter format. Already from the earliest days of Christianity some questioned whether this document could have been from the apostle Peter. Consequently, it had trouble being accepted in the NT canon.

TITLE: The Second Letter of Peter

AUTHOR: Unknown, but attributed to St. Peter

DATE: Early second century A.D.

STRUCTURE:

1:1–2	Greeting
1:3–3:16	Body
3:17–18	Closing

THEMES: Delay of parousia, danger of false teachers

Structure and Content

Since the letter format is probably artificial, the greeting (1:1–2) sounds a general note "to those who have received a faith equal to ours...." The body of the letter (1:3–3:16) treats several topics. First it contains an exhortation to Christian virtues (1:3–21). Then it proceeds to warnings about false teachers who can easily mislead believers and disrupt community life (2:1–22).

Finally, it discusses the question of when Jesus will return in glory (3:1–16). This expectation is known as the *parousia,* a Greek term that means "coming." The early Christians used this expression to talk of Jesus' eventual return in glory for the final judgment. As time went on and Jesus' "second coming" did not occur, great anxiety arose. This letter reminds the readers that time, in God's eyes, is deceptive. We cannot use our understanding of time to control God's mysterious plan of salvation and judgment. The readers are urged to be patient and faithful, for the parousia will arrive unexpectedly in God's good time. The closing (3:17–18) is a final exhortation to stay alert and to remain stable in faith.

Interpretation

Second Peter may not be the most interesting of NT books, but it contains sound advice typical of later NT works. Many different realities can challenge one's Christian faith. Some are internal, like not understanding fully how Jesus' teaching about his second coming should be interpreted. Others are external, like those who scoff at believers or try to twist Christian doctrine so that believers will become shaky in their faith. This letter essentially gives encouragement to anyone who faces such realities. Don't lose hope, don't give up. Instead, remain firm in your faith and do your best to seek understanding from those who teach the faith. Above all, do not try to interpret too narrowly some of the NT teachings, such as the parousia (ch. 3). Be patient, and God's intentions will be revealed at the appropriate time.

Exercise

Read 2 Pet 3:15–16. This passage speaks of the difficulty of understanding some things in Paul's letters. Those who are so inclined could twist them and misinterpret them. Have you ever felt that way about any of the scriptures? Do you find the Bible difficult to understand at times? What advice does the author of 2 Peter give for this situation?

1 John

You will notice by the proposed structure for 1 John (see box) that this letter or epistle is not really either. Identifying the type of literature of 1 John is difficult. It might be more properly called an instruction or a treatise, despite its title.

The author may be the same as the author of the Gospel of John but more likely is someone else from the Johannine community writing sometime after the composition of the Gospel. The purpose is to correct certain false impressions about Jesus Christ that some in the community have developed. Many of the themes treated are found in the Gospel.

Structure and Content

The prologue (1:1–4) provides a poetic introduction to the letter with the theme of testimony. The author explains "what we have heard, what we have seen with our eyes" (1:1) concerning the "word of life" (Jesus Christ). The first main part of the letter (1:5–3:10) discusses the notion that God is light and what it means to see ourselves as the children of that light. You cannot claim to be of the light if your life remains in darkness (2:9). True children of the light live lives that reflect that truth. The letter also explains that some have gone out of the community (2:19).

TITLE: The First Letter of John

AUTHOR: Unknown, but probably someone in the Johannine community

DATE: Ca. A.D. 100

STRUCTURE:

1:1–4	Prologue
1:5–3:10	God is light; we are children of light
3:11–5:12	God is love; we must love one another
5:13–21	Epilogue

THEMES: Love, light, truth

This action makes them outcasts, for they have denied Jesus as the Christ.

The second main part of the letter (3:11–5:12) shifts to the related theme of love. This was Jesus' most important commandment: love one another. Since God is love and we are God's children, our lives should reflect that love. One cannot claim to love in general terms while specifically hating a neighbor (4:20). The letter concludes with an epilogue (5:13–20) that exhorts the reader to pray for sinners who have gone astray. God's mercy will touch them through Jesus Christ.

Interpretation

As with the Gospel of John, the language of 1 John is simple yet has profound meaning. Basic themes like love, light, sin, truth are treated over and over again. One can feel the hurt that was caused by the departure of some members of the community. The need to exhort love for one another is all the more important in such circumstances. Betrayal often elicits nasty reactions from those who feel betrayed, but this letter insists that one must still love with the intensity that God loves. Sometimes the letter employs very strong language. "All who hate a brother or sister are murderers..." (3:15). The letter, like the Gospel, is a combination of the practical and the sublime. Love is not merely a pious platitude but a real invitation to "remain" in the tradition that has been handed down (2:24).

Exercise

Read 1 John 3:16–22. How realistic is this vision of love? What gives you confidence that you can live out this vision in your own life? Can you describe ways to assist you in this task?

2 John

Unlike 1 John, this document is truly a letter, albeit somewhat mysterious. Who is the "elect lady and her children" to whom the letter is addressed (v. 1; *note*: no chapters, only verses)? And who are "the children of your elect sister" from whom greetings are sent (13)? These designations refer to different Christian communities that share the Johannine tradition.

The author is also a mystery, identifying himself only as "the elder" (Greek *presbyteros*). Scholars suspect that 2 and 3 John were written by a member of the Johannine community but not the same person as the author of the Gospel or 1 John. He is often called John the Presbyter. Yet the letters clearly belong to the Johannine tradition, and they are of similar length and tone.

Structure and Content

In typical fashion the opening (1–3) and closing (12–13) frame the body of the letter (4–11), which is concerned with "deceivers who have gone out into the world." They have denied that Jesus was truly human (7), an early heresy that appears now and again in Christian tradition. The tone is one of exhortation, warning to remain true to the commandment of love that is so familiar to the community. The author urges the community to be on guard against those who do not adhere to the truth as they have been taught it.

Interpretation

Many Christians fear that the biggest danger to faith is the denial that Jesus is divine, the Son of God. This denial is indeed a danger among those who are skeptical. Yet an equal danger comes from the other side — a denial that Jesus was truly human. The Johannine community faced both of these exaggerations. Christian faith, especially as expressed in the ecumenical creeds like

TITLE: The Second Letter of John

AUTHOR: Unknown, but probably someone in the Johannine community

DATE: Ca. A.D. 100

STRUCTURE:

Vv. 1–3	Opening
Vv. 4–11	Body
Vv. 12–13	Closing

THEMES: Truth and love

the Apostles' Creed or the Nicene Creed, requires a balance. Jesus is both human and divine. The one aspect cannot swallow up the other. This is an essential Christian doctrine. Ultimately it remains a mystery, but 2 John testifies to its importance in order to remain attached to the Christian community.

Exercise

Read 2 John 4–6. What does it mean to "walk in truth"? The elder also mentions another familiar commandment. What is it? How do you apply it to your own life?

3 John

Like 2 John, this is also a letter of typical size for the Hellenistic-Roman world. It is addressed to "beloved Gaius," who is otherwise unknown but is a wealthy member of the Christian community. The "elder" writes to commend Gaius for remaining faithful and to complain about a rival Christian leader who is unwilling to accept the elder's authority.

Structure and Content

This is the shortest book of the NT (based on the number of words, not verses). The very brief opening (1; *note:* no chapters, only verses) and standard closing (13–15) frame the body of the letter (2–12). The elder expresses joy over the information he has received that Gaius and his community are remaining faithful to

TITLE: The Third Letter of John

AUTHOR: Unknown, but probably someone in the Johannine
    community

DATE: Ca. A.D. 100

STRUCTURE:
    V. 1   Opening
    Vv. 2–12   Body
    Vv. 13–15   Closing

THEMES: Christian hospitality, respecting authority

the teaching they have been given. But a certain Diotrephes, the leader of another community, is causing trouble. He is spreading rumors about the elder and refuses to accept those who are sent to him to restore order. The letter exhorts Gaius and his followers to remain firm and "imitate what is good" rather than falling into evil. The author also commends a man named Demetrius, who probably carried the letter to its destination.

Interpretation

The Johannine community experienced various divisions and hardships over time. These are reflected primarily in the letters of John. In 3 John we have an example of a personal letter addressing a practical matter — rival authority. A sad byproduct of the Christian tradition has been disunity. Paul had to address this issue at Corinth, and the NT itself has many examples of disagreements that erupted among Christians over many details of the faith. This letter exhibits some of these characteristics. It also shows that every community inevitably establishes a line of authority that helps to keep the community together. Discerning who is right in the midst of conflict was (and is) not always easy. The elder's recommendation was to examine the evidence carefully. Truth testifies to itself. One must judge conformity to Jesus' commandment of love on the basis of one's actions, not merely words.

Exercise

Read the entire letter. Have you ever experienced rivalry over roles involving leadership or authority? How do you handle such situations? Do you agree or disagree with the elder's advice to Gaius? Why?

Jude

This little letter is one of the "General Epistles" written to an unknown community. The author, too, is unknown. Most scholars think that Jude is pseudonymous, written in the late first century A.D. Most likely, the Jude being referred to (v. 1; *note:* no chapters, only verses) is probably one of the relatives of Jesus rather than one of the twelve apostles (see Mark 6:3 and Matt 13:55). This letter resembles part of 2 Peter (especially 2 Pet 2:1–18) so that some scholars suggest a literary relationship between the two.

Structure and Content

Jude has the usual format of a NT letter. The opening (1–2) is followed by an explanation of the author's intention to write more at length about salvation. Instead, the author has heard of intruders in the community who are causing anxiety. The body of the letter is written to exhort the community to faithfulness and watchfulness (3–16). Certain OT images or personalities are called to mind as examples of how to deal with these troublemakers who are causing divisions. The ethical section (17–23) provides standard advice on remembering the apostolic teaching the community has received. It also exhorts them to have mercy on those who waver in their faith (22). The closing (24–25) is a prayerful wish for the readers that moves into a doxology, or song of praise to God.

Interpretation

The brevity of this letter can be misleading. Lots of OT imagery appears in short order that makes the letter somewhat difficult to follow without knowing the OT background. The biggest concern is that the community to whom the letter is addressed is undergoing dissension. Jude writes to give instruction, comfort, and

TITLE: The Letter of Jude

AUTHOR: Unknown, but attributed to Jude, the brother of James and relative of Jesus

DATE: Late first century A.D.

STRUCTURE:

Vv. 1–2	Opening
Vv. 3–16	Body
Vv. 17–23	Ethical instruction
Vv. 24–25	Closing

THEMES: Warning against false teachers

encouragement on how to handle such a situation. He finds some of the OT situations to be instructive. Ultimately, God's judgment comes upon those who do not adhere to God's instructions. The challenge is to remain faithful in the midst of these affronts to our faith (19–20).

Exercise

Read Jude 24–25. It is an excellent example of a Christian doxology, a hymn in praise of God's glory. Read it slowly and prayerfully. In your mind's eye conjure up loved ones for whom you might recite such a doxology. Are there times in your life when these words of praise could spontaneously be used to give honor to God?

Chapter 13

REVELATION

This book is perennially popular. At various times in history, including our own at the end of the twentieth century, it has been the focus of intense speculation. It is the last book of the NT and indeed the Bible, and it speaks appropriately of the last things, i.e., eschatology. It is thus an apocalyptic work related in style to the Book of Daniel in the OT (see the introduction to ch. 7 above, p. 102). Revelation is loaded with bizarre images that have made it the darling of science fiction writers and Hollywood epics of doom. Our fascination with Revelation is understandable. It is also, unfortunately, misdirected. It derives its name from the Greek term *apokalypsis,* which means "unveiling," whence its older title, the Apocalypse.

John of Patmos is otherwise unknown in the Bible. Some identify him with John, the author of the Fourth Gospel, or with John the Presbyter, author of the Letters of John. Most scholars deem these speculations unlikely, even though there are some affinities to the Johannine literature. Rather, John of Patmos was a Christian prophet who wrote the book near the end of the first century A.D., on the Greek island of Patmos in the Aegean Sea, to give hope and courage to a persecuted Christian community.

Structure and Content

Revelation is filled with symbolism. Numbers, in particular, are important symbolically. The number seven was the perfect number in biblical terms. One notices how frequently the number seven recurs in Revelation. It is likely, therefore, that the structure of the book is in seven parts.

The prologue (1:1–3) introduces the author and the circumstances of his writing. He calls his work a "revelation" (notice the singular, not plural, as in "revelations") about things to happen "soon." As with other apocalyptic literature, Revelation was written for the immediate future of the author's own time rather

TITLE: The Book of Revelation (sometimes known as the Apocalypse)

AUTHOR: John of Patmos

DATE: Ca. A.D. 90–100

STRUCTURE:

1:1–3	Prologue
1:4–3:22	Letters to the seven churches
4:1–5:14	The Lamb
6:1–16:21	The seven seals, trumpets, and bowls
17:1–20:15	Babylon punished
21:1–22:5	New creation
22:6–21	Epilogue

THEMES: Christ the Lamb, God's victory over evil, the new Jerusalem

than for two thousand years hence. Its preservation in the canon, however, assures that it still can have meaning today.

The first major section (1:4–3:22) consists of letters to seven churches in Asia Minor. The message is unique to each church based upon its own individual circumstances. Next comes a section devoted to the image of Christ as the Lamb (4:1–5:14). Although the Lamb was a sacrificial victim, he was nonetheless victorious. He thus deserves all the glory that God has bestowed on him. This image is followed by the lengthy unveiling of various symbolic images that foretell God's ultimate victory over evil, symbolized by beasts (6:1–16:21; 17:1–20:15). Revelation describes a cosmic battle in which evil's demise is assured. After the battle Revelation paints a picture of God creating a new heaven and earth (21:1–22:5). With the old having proved unworthy and submitted to evil, a whole new heaven and earth are needed. The city of Jerusalem is the centerpiece of this new creation. But it will be a city without a Temple, for God will be the only Temple needed. Nor will the city need lamps, for the Lamb himself will provide all the light that is needed (21:23). The conclusion of Revelation gives testimony to the authenticity of John's words and offers a word that simultaneously is a prayer and a hope: "Come, Lord Jesus" (22:20; Aramaic *maranatha*).

Interpretation

As I indicated above, this book has a troubled history of interpretation. All too often the imagery of the book has led people down a smooth path of literalist interpretation that is inappropriate to the apocalyptic genre. In the first place, the book is not a series of revelations (plural) but one grandiose revelation (singular) that God will ultimately be victorious over evil. To a church suffering severe persecution, as happened under the Roman Emperor Domitian around the time of this book's origin, these words must have been soothing balm. Despite appearances in history, John of Patmos says, God is still at work behind the scenes.

Using code language and symbolism that was intended to mislead any outsiders who might stumble on the book, Revelation offered the struggling Christian community hope in a time of suffering. Babylon was the symbol of the evil empire, Rome. The beast with seven heads represented the various Roman emperors who succeeded Domitian. The number 666 symbolically represented the worst of evil. (It can never be the perfect number seven and, in Jewish fashion to express superlative degree, is tripled.) All of this indicates the true nature of this book: Christian apocalyptic prophecy that imparts courage and perseverance to those under persecution. A modern analogy might be the Star Wars trilogy, which chronicles the battle of good and evil in a space age setting. The meaning is profound yet simple, embedded in symbolic details. Revelation can function just as effectively today as it did originally, provided we keep it in perspective and in context. It sounds an appropriate final note to conclude an introduction to the entire Bible.

Exercise

Read Rev 21:1–4. This passage describes the new heaven and new earth that God will establish one day. Have you ever longed for this vision to become a reality? How would you apply this passage to yourself in the midst of difficult personal circumstances? How would you understand and describe this passage as the literature of hope?

Appendix A

COMPARISON OF THE CANONS
OF THE BIBLE

People sometimes can be confused that the content of their Bible, that is, their canon is different from that of friends of different denominations. The reasons for these differences are complex, but they need not be a source of anxiety. All Christian denominations accept the same twenty-seven books of the NT in the order in which they are given in your Bible. The canon of the OT, however, is where considerable differences occur. Both the content and the arrangement of the books can be different. The following chart lists the various canons so that these differences can easily be seen.

OLD TESTAMENT CANON

Hebrew Bible	Catholic	Protestant	Orthodox
Gen	Gen	Gen	Gen
Exod	Exod	Exod	Exod
Lev	Lev	Lev	Lev
Num	Num	Num	Num
Deut	Deut	Deut	Deut
Josh	Josh	Josh	Josh
Judg	Judg	Judg	Judg
1 and 2 Sam	Ruth	Ruth	Ruth
1 and 2 Kgs	1 and 2 Sam	1 and 2 Sam	1 and 2 Sam
Isa	1 and 2 Kgs	1 and 2 Kgs	1 and 2 Kgs
Jer	1 and 2 Chron	1 and 2 Chron	1 and 2 Chron
Ezek	Ezra	Ezra	Ezra
Hos	Neh	Neh	Neh
Joel	Tobit	Esther	Tobit
Amos	Judith	Job	Judith
Obad	Esther	Pss	Esther
Jonah	1 and 2 Macc	Prov	1 and 2 Macc
Mic	Job	Eccl	Job
Nahum	Pss	Song	Pss
Hab	Prov	Isa	Prov
Zeph	Eccl	Jer	Eccl
Hag	Song	Lam	Song
Zech	Wis	Ezek	Wis

Hebrew Bible	Catholic	Protestant	Orthodox
Mal	Sir	Dan	Sir
Pss	Isa	Hos	Isa
Job	Jer	Joel	Jer
Prov	Lam	Amos	Lam
Ruth	Baruch	Obad	Baruch
Song	Ezek	Jonah	Ezek
Eccl	Dan	Mic	Dan
Lam	Hos	Nahum	Hos
Esth	Joel	Hab	Joel
Dan	Amos	Zeph	Amos
Ezra	Obad	Hagg	Obad
Neh	Jonah	Zech	Jonah
1 and 2 Chron	Mic	Mal	Mic
	Nahum		Nahum
	Hab		Hab
	Zeph		Zeph
	Hag		Hag
	Zech		Zech
	Mal		Mal

Note: The Orthodox OT canon is somewhat fluid. There are different Orthodox churches, as well as Oriental traditions. No universal norm for their canon exists. It appears that Orthodox Christianity basically accepts the deuterocanonical works as scripture. They sometimes are labeled "the readable books" rather than apocryphal or deuterocanonical. Occasionally they add to these works 3 Maccabees and the Book of Esdras and sometimes 4 Maccabees.

NEW TESTAMENT CANON

All Christian versions contain the same twenty-seven books in the following order: Gospels, Acts, Letters of Paul, General Letters, and Revelation.

Matt	1 and 2 Thess
Mark	1 and 2 Tim
Luke	Tit
John	Phlm
Acts	Heb
Rom	James
1 and 2 Cor	1 and 2 Pet
Gal	1, 2, and 3 John
Eph	Jude
Phil	Rev
Col	

Appendix B

NAMES OF OT BOOKS IN OLDER EDITIONS OF THE BIBLE

Older Catholic editions of the Bible, such as the Douay-Rheims, used names for some OT books that are no longer used. This chart lists alphabetically the name changes that have taken place. Although I recommend using a newer edition of the Bible, this chart is for the convenience of those who may have access only to the Douay version.

Common Name	*Douay Name*
1 and 2 Chronicles	1 and 2 Paralipomenon
Ezekiel	Ezechiel
Ezra	1 Esdras
Habakkuk	Habacuc
Haggai	Aggeus
Hosea	Osee
Isaiah	Isaias
Jeremiah	Jeremias
Jonah	Jonas
Joshua	Josue
1 and 2 Kings	3 and 4 Kings
1 and 2 Maccabees	1 and 2 Machabees
Malachi	Malachias
Micah	Micheas
Nehemiah	2 Esdras
Obadiah	Abdias
Revelation	Apocalypse
1 and 2 Samuel	1 and 2 Kings
Sirach (Ecclesiasticus)	Ecclesiasticus
Song of Solomon (Song of Songs)	Canticle of Canticles
Tobit	Tobias
Zechariah	Zacharias
Zephaniah	Sophonias

Appendix C

ABBREVIATIONS FOR THE BOOKS OF THE BIBLE

Different schemes exist for abbreviating the books of the Bible. Unfortunately, there is no real consistency in these various formats. Each Bible edition should have near its Table of Contents a Table of Abbreviations used in that particular edition. Two prominent systems exist, however, which you may likely encounter in reading about the Bible. One system uses the briefest possible abbreviation for each book, often only two letters. The other system uses three- or four-letter abbreviations to help avoid confusion. The table below gives you these two systems, which sometimes use the same abbreviation. Note that there are also differences between the use of Arabic numerals and Roman numerals for books that have multiple volumes.

Books of the Bible	*Short Abbreviation*	*Standard Abbreviation*
Genesis	Gn	Gen
Exodus	Ex	Exod
Leviticus	Lv	Lev
Numbers	Nm	Num
Deuteronomy	Dt	Deut
Joshua	Jos	Josh
Judges	Jgs	Judg
1 and 2 Samuel (I and II Samuel)	1 and 2 Sm	1 and 2 Sam
1 and 2 Kings (I and II Kings)	1 and 2 Kgs	1 and 2 Kgs
1 and 2 Chronicles (I and II Chronicles)	1 and 2 Chr	1 and 2 Chr
Ezra	Ezr	Ezra
Nehemiah	Neh	Neh
Tobit	Tb	Tob
Judith	Jdt	Jdt
Esther	Est	Esth
1 and 2 Maccabees (I and II Maccabees)	1 and 2 Mc	1 and 2 Macc
Job	Jb	Job
Psalms	Ps (plural: Pss)	Ps (plural: Pss)
Proverbs	Prv	Prov
Ecclesiastes (Qoheleth)	Eccl (Qoh)	Eccl (Qoh)
Song of Solomon (Song of Songs or Canticle of Canticles)	Sg (or Ct)	Cant (or Song)

Books of the Bible	Short Abbreviation	Standard Abbreviation
Wisdom of Solomon	Wis	Wis
Wisdom of Ben Sirach	Sir	Sir
Isaiah	Is	Isa
Jeremiah	Jer	Jer
Lamentations	Lam	Lam
Baruch	Bar	Bar
Ezekiel	Ez	Ezek
Daniel	Dn	Dan
Hosea	Hos	Hos
Joel	Jl	Joel
Amos	Am	Amos
Obadiah	Ob	Obad
Jonah	Jon	Jonah
Micah	Mi	Mic
Nahum	Na	Nah
Habakkuk	Hb	Hab
Zephaniah	Zep	Zeph
Haggai	Hg	Hag
Zechariah	Zec	Zech
Malachi	Mal	Mal
Matthew	Mt	Matt
Mark	Mk	Mark
Luke	Lk	Luke
John	Jn	John
Acts	Ac	Acts
Romans	Rm	Rom
1 and 2 Corinthians (I and II)	1 and 2 Cor	1 and 2 Cor
Galatians	Gal	Gal
Ephesians	Eph	Eph
Philippians	Ph	Phil
Colossians	Cl	Col
1 and 2 Thessalonians (I and II)	1 and 2 Th	1 and 2 Thess
1 and 2 Timothy (I and II)	1 and 2 Tm	1 and 2 Tim
Titus	Ti	Titus
Philemon	Phl	Phlm
Hebrews	Hb	Heb
James	Jas	Jas
1 and 2 Peter (I and II)	1 and 2 Pt	1 and 2 Pet
1, 2, and 3 John (I, II, and III)	1, 2, and 3 Jn	1, 2, and 3 John
Jude	Jd	Jude
Revelation	Rv	Rev

Appendix D

JEWISH FEASTS
IN THE BIBLE

Frequently the Bible mentions Jewish feasts and celebrations that figured prominently in both Jewish and early Christian life. These can be confusing to someone new to the Bible. The following chart explains these major feasts and points out where the Bible makes reference to them. Three of the feasts (Passover, Pentecost, and Tabernacles) constituted the most important pilgrimage feasts. Jewish males were required to travel to the Temple in Jerusalem for the celebrations (Exod 23:14–17; Deut 16:16; cf. Luke 2:41; John 2:13; 11:55). The NT describes Jesus and his followers observing some of these rituals. They have provided a rich background for the development of several Christian liturgical rites.

Feast	Alternative Name(s)	Explanation	Bible References
Sabbath	Shabbat	The basic weekly "feast" for the Bible based upon six days of work and one day of rest. For Jews Saturday was the sabbath, but Christians eventually adapted it to Sunday to commemorate Jesus' resurrection.	Gen 2:1–3; Exod 20:8–11; 31:12–17; Lev 23:3; Deut 5:12–15; Matt 12:1–8; Luke 6:1–11; John 5:1–10
Sabbatical year		The practice of allowing land to go fallow every seventh year; giving the land a "rest." Some fruits were left on the trees for the poor and for animals.	Exod 23:10–11; Lev 25:1–7; Deut 15:1–11
Jubilee year		The practice every fiftieth year (after seven cycles of sabbath years) of releasing slaves and returning land to original owners. It may have been a way to equalize society's great disparities between rich and poor.	Lev 25:8–17

238

Feast	Alternative Name(s)	Explanation	Bible References
Passover	Unleavened Bread (Pesach)	The preeminent Jewish festival commemorating the angel of death "passing over" the Israelites during their Egyptian captivity and their subsequent passing to freedom in the exodus event; celebrated in the spring (March–April); Christians associate Passover with the death of Jesus	Exod 12:1–13:10; Num 9:1–14; 2 Kgs 23:21–23; 2 Chron 35:18–19; Ezra 6:19–22; Mark 14:12–16; Matt 26:17–19; Luke 22:1, 7–13; John 2:23; 13:1; 18:28, 39
Pentecost	Weeks (Shavuot)	Celebrated seven weeks (fifty days, from Greek *pentēkostē*) after Passover (May–June), it originated as an agricultural feast but eventually became a commemoration of God's giving Moses the Torah on Mt. Sinai; Christians transformed it into a celebration of the coming of the Holy Spirit	Exod 34:22; Lev 23:15–22; Num 28:26–31; Deut 16:9–10; Tob 2:1; 2 Macc 12:32; 1 Cor 16:8; cf. Acts 2:1–13
Trumpets	Rosh Hashanah (New Year)	Celebrated in the harvest time (September–October) to begin a new year of blessing by "blowing the trumpets"	Lev 23:23–25; Num 29:1–6
Day of Atonement	Yom Kippur	Celebrates reconciliation for sins of the past year; takes place ten days after the start of the new year (September–October); ritual of the "scapegoat" upon which the sins of the people were placed to be driven out into the wilderness	Lev 16:1–34; 23:26–32; Num 29:7–11; Heb 8–9 contains subtle references to this feast to explain Jesus Christ's role in atonement
Tabernacles	Booths (Succoth; Ingathering)	Commemorates God's protection of Israel during the wilderness period when they dwelt in tents or booths in the desert; celebrated for eight days in late September or early October during the autumn harvest	Lev 23:33–44; Num 29:12–40; Deut 16:13–15; Neh 8:13–18; John 7:2, 10–11
Hanukkah	Dedication (Lights)	Commemorates the cleansing and rededication of the Temple during the Maccabean revolt (167 B.C.); celebrated for eight days in November or December [based on a legend that a small vial of holy oil burned for eight days until supplies could be replenished]	1 Macc 4:36–61; 2 Macc 10:1–9; John 10:22

Feast	Alternative Name(s)	Explanation	Bible
Purim	Lots	A minor feast commemorating the deliverance of the Jewish people by Queen Esther and Mordecai from a Persian plot to destroy the Jews on a day chosen by the drawing of lots	Book of Esther (esp. 9:18–32)
Ninth of Ab		A minor feast that commemorates the two-time destruction of Jerusalem and the Temple, once by the Babylonians in August 587 B.C. and once by the Romans in A.D. 70	Book of Lamentations

GLOSSARY

acrostic poem: a poetic device using the letters of the alphabet to begin each verse or section (A, B, C, D, E, etc.). The psalms and wisdom literature sometimes exhibit this literary form using the Hebrew alphabet.

amanuensis: a scribe, one who could read and write and who acted as a personal secretary for letter writing.

anawim: the Hebrew word for the "remnant" that would remain after the destruction of God's people in order that the people would rise again. Many of the prophets predicted that only a remnant would survive to remain faithful to God.

apocalyptic: literally from Greek, unveiling or revelatory. The term now designates a worldview and a type of biblical literature that arose periodically in times of suffering and persecution, such as the Books of Daniel and Revelation.

apocrypha: from the Greek, meaning "hidden." This term applies to those books in the OT considered by Protestants to be noncanonical, that is, not inspired scripture. Catholics call these works deuterocanonical. The term also applies to Christian writings that never were accepted into the NT because they were not thought to be inspired scripture, such as the apocryphal gospels.

apodictic: a type of law which declares boundaries of behavior in terms of categorical dos and don'ts, as compared with casuistic law, which defines legal behavior according to cases and circumstances. The Bible contains primarily apodictic laws.

Aramaic: a Semitic language closely related to biblical Hebrew; it was the primary spoken language of Jesus and his disciples. Occasional glimpses of Aramaic are found in the NT, such as the liturgical expression *maranatha* ("Our Lord, come!"; 1 Cor 16:22; Rev 20:20) or the term *mammon* ("wealth"; Matt 6:24).

241

Asherah: the name of a Canaanite goddess, wife of the god Baal (or El). In the OT the name is associated with the Israelites' periodic temptation to revert to the worship of pagan idols.

Baal: the name of a Canaanite god, from a word meaning "lord" or "husband." In the OT the name often occurs in the plural (Baals) and symbolizes idolatry. It also appears in many compound names (Baal-hazor; Baal-peor). Some of the prophets preached strongly against this idolatry.

canon: from Greek, meaning "rule" or "norm." This label applies to the biblical books accepted as inspired literature from God. Different religious groups and churches have had different canons or lists of sacred books during history.

Christology: the study of Christ. This term refers to the various faith statements about Jesus of Nazareth that developed in the course of Christian history. All the NT documents contain christological ideas but they are not uniform.

cosmology: the understanding of the universe that one has. Ancient cosmology differs greatly from modern cosmology, for example, in the belief that the earth is flat and the idea that the universe contains three layers, an upper layer (the heavens), a middle level (earth), and a lower level (the underworld, Sheol).

covenant: a sacred agreement between at least two parties that binds them to one another. Different types of covenants developed in the course of history, but they always involved obligations and sanctions for violating them.

Dead Sea Scrolls: Jewish documents dating from around the second century B.C. found in caves at Qumran near the Dead Sea in 1947. These included excerpts from biblical books (such as Isaiah) as well as sectarian documents from an obscure group of Jews generally identified as the Essenes.

Diaspora: also known as the "dispersion." This label applies to the scattering of the Jews to different parts of the world after the first destruction of Jerusalem by the Babylonians in 587 B.C. Eventually, Jews in the Diaspora stopped speaking their native Hebrew language when they adopted local languages and developed other translations of their sacred texts, the most important being the Greek Septuagint.

deuterocanonical: from Greek meaning "second canon." This is the Catholic designation of what Protestants call the OT apocrypha.

doxology: from the Greek *doxa* (glory), this term refers to a type of prayer, a liturgical expression of praise to God. The Bible contains many doxologies that give glory to God.

eschatology/eschatological: from Greek (*eschaton,* end) pertaining to the end times. As part of an apocalyptic worldview, late Jewish and early Christian beliefs developed elaborate ideas about what God planned to happen at the end of human history. Many biblical books contain eschatological notions, but they are not meant to be understood literally in every detail.

gnosticism/gnostic: from Greek *gnōsis,* "knowledge"; a form of Greek philosophy in the Hellenistic-Roman world that emphasized secret knowledge as the key to salvation. Some scholars think this complex set of ideas influenced many later NT works, but others believe that the influence was in the other direction. The discovery of the Nag Hammadi documents helped to flesh out the development of various gnostic teachings in early Christianity.

gospel: literally from an Old English expression (godspell) meaning "good news." Now this term can designate either the message of Jesus Christ (as in St. Paul's letters) or the four canonical stories of Jesus in the NT that Christians call Gospels (capitalized). Christians invented the type of literature called Gospel.

Hellenistic-Roman: refers to the society and empire that existed from approximately 333 B.C. to A.D. 250. It began with Alexander the Great's vision that Greek (Hellenistic) culture should dominate the world. When the Roman empire came into existence it adopted and adapted many aspects of Greek culture but also had its own unique interests that impacted the world of the NT. Later OT books and all the NT books show some Hellenistic-Roman world influence.

heresy/heretical: beliefs rejected by the church because they are inconsistent with the approved doctrines of the church. Some of the NT (e.g., Johannine literature) was at least partially formed in the context of controversies over what was or was not heretical.

hortatory literature: writings that encourage and exhort people to act in certain ways. Hebrews is an example of such literature, and many of the NT letters contain sections of ethical exhortation.

inerrancy: belief that the Bible contains no errors of any type because it is inspired by God. All Christian denominations accept the notion of biblical inerrancy as it pertains to doctrinal teaching, but only some denominations apply biblical inerrancy to all matters, including scientific and historical data.

inspiration: belief that God rather than human beings is the authority behind the Bible. There are many different theories of inspiration, none of which successfully explains in a universally accepted manner *how* inspiration takes place.

lament/lamentation: a type of psalm or ancient hymn that expresses confidence in God despite the harsh realities of suffering encountered in human existence.

lectio divina: ancient Christian practice of the slow, meditative reading of scripture for the purpose of prayer and inspiration.

manuscript: a text written or copied by hand by professional scribes. No original manuscripts of the Bible have survived either in Hebrew or in Greek. Rather, the manuscripts that now exist are copies of copies made in the course of history.

monotheism: belief in one God as contrasted to polytheism, belief in multiple gods.

myth/mythology: in a religious sense refers to casting sublime truths (love, birth, creation, death, etc.) in the form of stories or tales. In everyday use "myth" often connotes contrast to "the truth" or "the facts," but that is not its theological use.

Nag Hammadi documents: some three hundred ancient Coptic Christian documents, including various noncanonical gospels, found at Nag Hammadi in Egypt in 1945, which illustrate the influence of gnostic thought on some Christian concepts.

oracle: an oral utterance. Prophets spoke oracles of many types but primarily of judgment and salvation. These oracles later were preserved in writing for posterity.

patriarch: from the Greek for "father." This title is used of the ancient ancestors of the Jews, beginning with Abraham and his descendants, Isaac and Jacob. The time of the patriarchs is generally described in Gen 12–50.

Pentateuch: from the Greek word for "five." It is the Septuagint's title for the first five books of the Bible (Genesis through Deuteronomy), which the Hebrew Bible designates as "the Law," or Torah.

polytheism: belief in many gods rather than one God. This belief was common in the ancient world until monotheism, belief in one God, eventually dominated religious convictions.

pseudepigrapha: literally, "false writings." This is the term for noncanonical OT works often written in someone else's name. The total collection of OT pseudepigrapha is some sixty-five texts written over the span of around five hundred years.

pseudonymous: from Greek meaning "false name." This word designates biblical writings written by unknown authors in the name of well-known heroes or authors. Many of the letters of St. Paul are considered of this type, such as 1 and 2 Timothy and Titus. This practice was common in the ancient world and was not considered improper.

rib: a Hebrew word meaning "lawsuit." It represents a style of writing familiar to the prophetic literature in which God brings a "lawsuit" (metaphorically) against the chosen people for their sinfulness.

sage: also known as "wise man." The sages collected, edited, and composed Israel's wisdom literature over the course of many centuries. Primarily a male-dominated group, these professionals founded schools to educate upper-class boys in the ways of wisdom.

scribe: a professional who could read and write. In later Jewish history scribes became a separate powerful group of political leaders, but scribes generally wrote and copied sacred texts or were hired to write letters for illiterate people.

scripture: literally, writing. Scripture eventually came to designate sacred writings such as the Bible, which is sometimes called sacred scripture.

scroll: Prior to the invention of books, scrolls were rolls of writing material made of animal skins or papyrus. Many animal skins could be sewn together to produce a large scroll. The Jews kept their sacred writings in elegant scrolls carefully preserved and used for liturgical ceremonies.

Septuagint: From the Greek word for seventy (abbreviated with the Roman numeral LXX), it is the name of the Greek translation of the Hebrew Bible composed for Jews in the Diaspora in Alexandria, Egypt, around 250 B.C. With its collection of OT books larger than the Hebrew Bible, it became the basis for the Roman Catholic canon of the OT. Tradition held that seventy-two different scribes (six from each tribe) produced the translation in a seventy-two-day period. Some form of the Septuagint greatly influenced many writers of the NT.

Sheol: The Hebrew name for the underworld. It is the place of shadows, where the dead go to dwell. This image frequently appears in the Psalms.

shephalah: the hill country of Israel that lies between the plain by the Mediterranean sea and the mountains. This area was always important in Israel's history for purposes of defense and for agriculture.

Slavonic Bible: a translation of the Bible in the Slavic languages of Eastern Europe. It dates from at least the ninth century A.D., the time of St. Cyril and St. Methodius, who evangelized that region.

theodicy: the study of why evil exists in the world and the attempt to explain innocent suffering. Some biblical books, such as Job, explore this mystery in detail.

theology: literally from Greek, the study of God. This modern word means many things in different contexts. Regarding the Bible, it can mean the Bible's teaching about God or it can mean the religious (or theological) perspective that emerges from specific texts.

typology: a theory about how the OT relates with the NT. The OT is thought to contain "types" or "prototypes" of later NT figures. Thus, Adam was a type of Christ as new human being, Moses a type of Christ as the giver of a law, Melchizedek a type of Christ as the High Priest, and so on.

Vulgate: St. Jerome's Latin translation of the Bible, dating from the fourth century A.D., taken from the original Hebrew and Greek languages and supplemented by the extra books found in the Septuagint. A revised form of the Vulgate (from the Latin word for "vulgar," meaning "common") remains an authoritative translation of the Bible for Roman Catholics.

Yahweh: the revealed name of God according to the Hebrew Bible (Exod 3:14). It actually appears as an ineffable word with four Hebrew letters (YHWH) called the tetragrammaton. Jews regularly substituted the designation "Lord" (*adonai*) or simply "the name" (*ha shēm*) to avoid the blasphemy of saying God's name.

RESOURCES FOR FURTHER STUDY

This book is merely a beginning. If you want to deepen your knowledge of the Bible, you will want to use other resources. The following list contains some resources that would provide good follow-up to this introductory book. Choose resources appropriate to your level of knowledge and interest. Don't buy a big, technical work unless you are really sure you can use it effectively. It is better to progress in stages than to "bite off more than you can chew." I have selected only a few items; bookstores contain many, many more. I include a few remarks on each resource to provide some hints about what may or may not suit your individual needs. References marked with an asterisk (*) are well suited as nontechnical and accessible "next steps" in your Bible education.

General

Achtemeier, Paul J., gen. ed. *The HarperCollins Bible Dictionary.* 2d ed. New York: HarperCollins, 1996. This is a basic reference dictionary filled with entries from scholars of diverse denominational backgrounds; one of the best available one-volume Bible dictionaries.

Bergant, Dianne, et al.*The Collegeville Bible Commentary.* Collegeville, Minn.: Liturgical Press, 1989. This nontechnical commentary is available in either a one-volume hardback or a two-volume paperback edition. Each book of the Bible is covered in short commentary fashion; based upon the NAB translation.

*Brown, Raymond E. *Responses to 101 Questions about the Bible.* New York: Paulist Press, 1990. This internationally known scholar has a knack for summarizing difficult biblical concepts easily for the average lay person. This small book covers a wide range of important topics about how to read the Bible.

*Brown, Raymond E., et al. *The New Jerome Bible Handbook.* Collegeville, Minn.: Liturgical Press, 1992. This is a nontechnical, condensed version of the famous Catholic one-volume commentary, *The New Jerome Biblical Commentary* (Prentice-Hall, 1991).

*Harris, Stephen L. *Understanding the Bible.* 4th ed. Mountain View, Calif.: Mayfield Publishing Co., 1997. Designed as a college textbook, this book contains all sorts of information introducing each book of the Bible.

Kee, Howard C., et al. *The Cambridge Companion to the Bible.* New York: Cambridge University Press, 1997). An extensive resource book of contemporary information about the Bible, it functions somewhat like a Bible dictionary for nonspecialists.

Mays, James L., gen. ed. *Harper's Bible Commentary*. San Francisco: Harper & Row, 1988. Intended as a companion volume to *The HarperCollins Bible Dictionary,* it offers thorough commentary in one volume on each book of the Bible.

Sheeley, Steven M., and Robert M. Nash, Jr. *The Bible in English Translation: An Essential Guide*. Nashville: Abingdon, 1997. Contains further information on the canon and the formation of the Bible. It also provides an evaluation of the major English translations of the Bible and a listing of electronic versions.

Walker, William O., gen. ed. *The HarperCollins Bible Pronunciation Guide*. HarperSanFrancisco, 1994. Many of the words in the Bible are unfamiliar and difficult to know how to pronounce. Although some Bible editions have built-in pronunciation guides, this one is thorough and easy to use.

Old Testament

*Boadt, Lawrence. *Reading the Old Testament*. New York: Paulist, 1984. Although this book is somewhat dated, it is still an excellent next step for OT issues. It is filled with charts, maps, and other helpful hints, and it is written in nontechnical language.

*Murphy, Roland E. *Responses to 101 Questions about the Psalms and Other Writings*. New York/Mahwah: Paulist Press, 1994. The question/response format permits this well-known biblical scholar to address many issues about the Psalms and Writings of the OT in forthright, nontechnical language.

*———. *Responses to 101 Questions about the Torah*. New York/Mahwah: Paulist Press, 1996. With its particular format this book will provide much more detail on issues in the study of the Pentateuch. The responses are well formed by this master teacher.

New Testament

Brown, Raymond E. *Introduction to the New Testament*. New York: Doubleday, 1997. The best current introduction to NT studies available, this book would provide an excellent overview of each book of the NT as well as general issues in NT studies. It also includes helpful bibliography.

*Perkins, Pheme. *Reading the New Testament*. 2d ed. New York: Paulist, 1988. A nontechnical introduction to the NT, this work explains the background influences on its development and introduces each book of the NT. It includes study questions and helpful exercises at the end of each chapter.

Of related interest

John E. Thiel
GOD, EVIL, AND INNOCENT SUFFERING
A Theological Reflection

In this timely book, John Thiel allows for the reality of innocent suffering while affirming God's opposition to evil, suffering, and death. Faithful to the tradition, Thiel challenges classical, modern, and postmodern accounts of God's relation to evil. In doing so, he offers the outlines of a systematic theology based on God's promise to destroy sin and death.

0-8245-1928-0, $19.95 paperback

Richard Rohr
THE GOOD NEWS ACCORDING TO LUKE
Spiritual Reflections

Now in paperback!

"Rohr not only offers a wealth of insight on Luke, but also proclaims a clarion call for us to follow Jesus today."
— *Spiritual Book News*

0-8245-1966-3, $16.95 paperback

crossroad